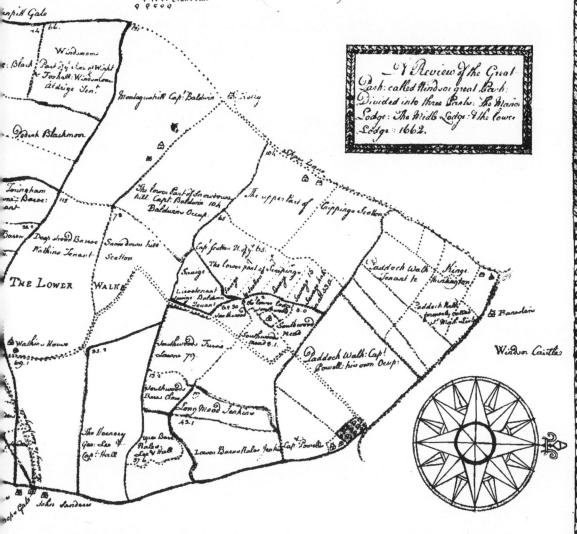

Windsor Great Park in 1662.

CUMBERLAND LODGE

—◆—

A House through History

Her Majesty Queen Elizabeth The Queen Mother, Patron of The King George VI and Queen Elizabeth Foundation of St Catharine's, Cumberland Lodge, on the occasion of the 40th anniversary of St Catharine's in 1987.

CUMBERLAND LODGE

A House Through History

Helen Hudson

The signature is Andrew Motion who is the Poet Laureate

For Doug
with best wishes
Andrew Motion

Phillimore

1997

Published by
PHILLIMORE & CO. LTD.,
Shopwyke Manor Barn, Chichester, West Sussex

First edition, 1989

© Helen Hudson, 1997

ISBN 1 86077 053 3

Printed and bound in Great Britain by
BUTLER AND TANNER LTD.
London and Frome

To Her Majesty,
Queen Elizabeth The Queen Mother
gracious Patron
of The King George VI and Queen Elizabeth Foundation
of St Catharine's, Cumberland Lodge
whose vision and generosity
gave new life and purpose to this historic house.

◆

Contents

List of Illustrations

Frontispiece: Her Majesty Queen Elizabeth The Queen Mother

Colour Plates

Illustration Acknowledgements

Grateful acknowledgement is made to the following, who supplied illustrations: Aerofilms Ltd., 29, Plate XI; The Earl Bathurst, Plate II; the late Dame Joyce Bishop, 117; Countess de Brauwere-Bentinck and the Stichting Iconographisch Bureau, The Hague, 22; British Library, 36, 54, 67, 70, Plate VI; © British Museum, 21, 46; Charterhouse, 133; College of Heralds, 108; Mrs. Peggy Cottrell, 109; *Country Life*, 107; Mrs. Eleanor Davis, 118; Deputy Ranger of the Great Park, back endpaper; Dr. Williams's Library, 3; Messrs. Edgington Spink & Hyne, 123; Getty Images, 61; Her Majesty Queen Elizabeth The Queen Mother, 111; Walter James, 123; Sir John Johnston, 106; His Grace the Duke of Marlborough, Plate III; Lord Montagu of Beaulieu, photograph Courtauld Institute of Art, 33; The Director, The National Army Museum, Chelsea, 5; The National Portrait Gallery, London, 1, 7, 8, 19, 23-26, 32, 34, 39, 42, 64, 68, 105, 112; His Grace The Duke of Norfolk, Plate IX; His Grace The Duke of Northumberland, 4, 6; University of Nottingham Library, 27; The late Mr. G.D.R. Palmer, 82, 86, 87; Petworth House, the Egremont Collection (National Trust), photograph Courtauld Institute of Art, 30; Public Record Office (Crown Copyright and reproduced with the permission of the Controller of Her Majesty's Stationery Office), 16, 38; Trustees of the Queen Alexandra's Royal Army Nursing Corps Museum, 85; Roger Mann Collection, 134; Royal Archives © 1997 Her Majesty The Queen, 72, 73, 75-79, 81, 83, 88-92, 95-99; Royal Collection © 1997 Her Majesty The Queen, 2, 11-14, 37, 47-50, 52, 53, 55, 56, 58-60, 63, 65, 69, 94, Plates V, VIII, IX; Sotheby's, 43, 45, 57, 103; Robert Szewczyk, 128; The Board of Trustees of The Victoria and Albert Museum, 15; The Hon. Mrs. Ward, 104, 113; Mrs. Jane Whaley, 62; Miss Kathleen Whelan, 84; Dr. Geoffrey Williams, 67; the late Hon. Maud Wilson, 44 and tailpieces to chapters 2 and 6.

Photographs were taken by: Dr. John Cook, 102, 129, Plate VII; Kingsley-Jones, 93, 132, Plate X; Gary Laverick, 9, 28, 41, 51, 71, 122; Veryan, 74, 84, 101, 108, Plates I, II, IX; Peter Warner, frontispiece, 130; Dr. Geoffrey Williams, 66, 100, 110, 120; Douglas Wilson, 124, 125, 131.

St Catharine's is particularly grateful to those organisations and individuals who have waived reproduction fees.

Acknowledgements

I am deeply grateful to Her Majesty The Queen for her gracious permission to reproduce pictures from the Royal Collection, prints from the Royal Library, photographs from the Photograph Collection and excerpts from Queen Victoria's Journal and other material in the Royal Archives; and for the privilege of consulting documents and maps in the Royal Archives and the Royal Library. To Her Majesty Queen Elizabeth The Queen Mother I am much indebted for her gracious acceptance of the dedication of this book, and for allowing me to use a personal photograph of the Hon. Elizabeth Elphinstone.

In my researches I have received generous help and encouragement from the Hon. Jane Roberts, Curator of the Print Room of the Royal Library, and Frances Harris of the Department of Manuscripts of the British Library. Elizabeth Cuthbert, Registrar of the Royal Archives, and Frances Dimond, Curator of the Photograph Collection, gave valuable help and advice, as did members of the staff of the Public Record Office, Linda Shaw of the Manuscripts Department of Nottingham University Library, Sara Rodger, Assistant Librarian at Arundel Castle, Kathleen Whelan, Matron of HRH Princess Christian's Hospital, and the Principal and Librarian of the Royal School of Needlework. Lord Charteris of Amisfield (former Chairman of the Trustees of St Catharine's) gave me practical help as well as much encouragement. Dame Joyce Bishop, David Harris, Walter James, Nada Jennett, Roger Lockyer, Christopher Mann, the Hon. Margaret Rhodes, Jacqui Rose, Nicola Smith and Kathleen Symonds were among those who advised me on particular points, and Harry Judge's notes on his research when he was Director of Studies at Cumberland Lodge pointed the way for my own research.

Many people in and around the Great Park have helped and contributed, sometimes unknown to themselves. I am grateful to the Hon. Maud Wilson for contributing not only her line drawings, but also much enthusiasm for the project; to Andrew Jackson, who organised tours of exploration in the Park, W.R. Grout, editor of *Windsor Estate News*, whose local knowledge is unrivalled, Mr. and Mrs. Ron Brown with their vivid memories, and Raymond South whose books about Windsor set me a high standard of scholarship; many others by listening with interest to the story of the house on their visits to the Lodge have given me the impetus to carry out this task, as well as contributing by their comments and observations. I hope they will all feel they have a share in the history of Cumberland Lodge and in this book— though the latter's shortcomings are entirely my own.

I owe a debt of gratitude to the late Lord Vaizey, who first suggested that I should write the history of Cumberland Lodge; to the Trustees of the King George VI and Queen Elizabeth Foundation of St Catharine's and the Francis C. Scott Charitable Trust who have sponsored the enterprise, undertaken in connection with the 40th anniversary of the Royal grant of the Lodge to the Foundation; to Kodak Ltd. for generous assistance towards the cost of photographs; to my former colleagues at Cumberland Lodge for their continual help and support—Peggy Cottrell and Jane Whaley and their teams, Iain Lynch, George Molan, Tim Slack, Elizabeth Squire, Douglas Wilson, and Diana Wood; to Ruth Norton who has processed my script, and Geoffrey Williams who has seen it through publication; and finally to my family and friends who have put up with three years' neglect.

Acknowledgements to this Edition

In the eight years since the first edition appeared, new material has come to light about the history of Cumberland Lodge, through continued research and through suggestions from people interested in this historic house. The jubilee of St Catharine's in 1997 seemed to the Trustees an appropriate moment for the production of a second edition, and I am grateful to the Principal, Dr. John Cook, for his support of the project.

My thanks to all those mentioned previously are warmly renewed. I have again benefited from the generosity of Frances Harris, Jane Roberts and Kathleen Whelan in sharing their knowledge of Sarah Churchill, Windsor Great Park, and Princess Christian respectively. Alathea Ward has generously contributed material of the greatest interest for the FitzAlan period; Andrea Cameron of Hounslow Library and Kenneth Cooper of the Isleworth Society have shed light on the Byfield era.

I am much indebted to Peter Turtle who has cheerfully processed several versions of the text and given valuable advice, to Christine Hanson of Phillimore & Co. for heroically seeing the book through all its stages, and to John Hudson for his continued help and support. Finally, I owe special thanks to Geoffrey Williams, who has co-operated in the whole venture, contributing new ideas as well as dealing with the illustrations; without his help and encouragement this edition would not have seen the light of day.

Preface

Cumberland Lodge has been the home of a sequence of remarkable people over the centuries. Its republican origins are unexpected in a royal preserve such as Windsor Great Park, and since Charles II made it the Ranger's official residence, it has always been a coveted place, in the very special gift of the sovereign. The perspective given by the unfolding of its history makes all the more impressive the faith and vision shown by King George VI and Queen Elizabeth when they granted the house in 1947 to the newly-formed foundation of St Catharine's, which has used it ever since for the benefit of students. Over these 50 years the house has received tens of thousands of students, scholars and young professionals from all over the world, who come together to discuss ethical issues and matters of current concern. Arriving at such an imposing mansion, they are curious to know about its origins and the people who have lived in it; it was out of this curiosity and interest that the book came to be written.

At first sight the façade of the house appears flat and stark. Go round it and you find a completely different face on its garden side: King George III, enamoured of the Gothic style, did not have the same architectural notions as a plain puritan soldier. The house is a patchwork of various styles, part of the effect it has had on every occupant being the wish to improve it. Even as early as 1724 Defoe remarked that the rangers of the Great and Little Parks at Windsor 'thought nothing too much to lay out to beautify their apartments, in a place, which it was so much to their honour, as well as conveniency, to reside'. They were not inhibited by the thought of an ancestral heritage to be left to their children, since the house was not their own; but they wanted to make it serve their purpose, and leave their mark upon it. So the house offers a gloss on the history of architectural fashion over several centuries.

Apart from the fascination of its history, the Lodge exerts a powerful influence on those who visit it. The sometimes arduous journey to find it—perhaps involving getting lost at Staines, like Pepys—is forgotten in the pleasure of arrival. People of opposing views, often stridently expressed elsewhere, are led to put the search for truth before the repetition of their own opinions. For the duration of their stay, they find themselves willingly captive in a charmed environment.

For some the whole area is full of reverberations. Lord Denning, a former Visitor of St Catharine's, would frequently remind law students of the nearness of Runnymede where Magna Carta was signed; Windsor Castle represents a seat of power going back to the earlier Saxon palace of the kings at Old Windsor; the Long Walk is thought by some to take us back even further, to the old straight track and ley lines with their mysterious resonances; the Forest itself, hunting-ground of kings and queens since early times, is also the domain of Herne the Hunter with his horns and rattling chains.

If the house has ghosts, and some claim to have seen them, these are benign. Though a sceptic in such matters, I have not been able to explain away the sound of a merry throng of people, clapping and chattering, heard in the hall of the empty house. An Indian visitor, arriving late one cold wet night after a series of misfortunes, exclaimed on stepping inside, 'The spirits are good!'. Princess Marie Louise said of her birthplace, 'For all of us, Cumberland Lodge was more than a home; it was buried in history and romance'.

So the task of discovering its history and writing about it was enthralling, although arduous for one untrained in historical research. I was as yet a stranger to the dark corridors of the Public Record Office, where I was to discover that a Patent Roll really was a roll, yards of it, which has to be unwound to reveal (in Latin of course) the grant of the rangership to the Marlboroughs. John Byfield at least left a beautifully clear will, but of the litigious John Barry's will no trace is to be found; hence we are left in frustrating ignorance about the fate of Anne Barry and the five children (hers, his and theirs) she and John had between them. He was too canny a lawyer to leave even his signature to posterity. It was not easy to coax Bab May out from the shadow of his royal master; but with Bentinck and the Marlboroughs the mists cleared as one moved into an era of great letter-writers.

Sarah Churchill left little about her life unrecorded, and the record was always gripping, as when, absorbed in reading one of her more tempestuous letters to Queen Anne in the hush of the North Library at the British Museum, I all but called out, 'Sarah, don't send it!'. The deficiencies of the two Dukes of Cumberland as letter-writers are compensated for from other sources, notably their Twickenham neighbour Horace Walpole, whose stories never lose anything in the telling. In George III's time evidence again becomes sketchy, as much of the correspondence of his middle years has been lost.

As the 19th century proceeds, information about the house becomes more plentiful, even if much of it is contained in discussions between officials about such matters as water supply and drains. There is a dearth again at the turn of this century, because in 1906 when fire broke out early one morning at the Crown Estate Office a mile away from the Lodge, the coachman refused to harness horses to take the fire engine to the rescue, so valuable records were destroyed.

With the arrival of St Catharine's at Cumberland Lodge we step into another world (though one in which drains and fire prevention still play a part); its archives are still in the making, and it is hard to realise that what we decide and do, now, is also history; but the Foundation itself came into being in response to the dire history of the times, and the hope, after the Second World War, of building a better future.

Helen Hudson

Chapter One

Republican Origins
1650-1660

Cumberland Lodge, set in the heart of Windsor Great Park, has been a royal house for over three centuries; but, paradoxically, it was built by a republican soldier, one of Cromwell's Ironsides, fresh from battle against the King.

The Civil War had been divisive and disturbing in a way we can barely imagine; and the killing of the King sent a shock through the nation. The memory of these grim events gave people an anxiety about the monarchy and the succession which persisted for at least 100 years. Settling down after a period of such turbulence was difficult, to put it mildly, and the war had been immensely costly. A special problem was that the victorious parliamentary army, composed of volunteer forces, had not been paid for years; the last thing the new rulers wanted was to have bands of disgruntled soldiers marauding the land in search of food.

They found a solution when they realised that having disposed of the monarchy they could now dispose of crown property; so early in 1649 Parliament passed a bill authorising the sale of the King's houses, goods and lands for the purpose of settling the soldiers' arrears. A few places such as Windsor Castle were reserved for the use of the state, and Oliver Cromwell was granted Hampton Court as his personal residence. A committee was set up to take care of the administration, and it commissioned detailed surveys of the royal lands, including one produced in February 1650 of 'the parke called the great parke lyeing and being in the parishes of New Windsor Old Windsor Egham and Sunninghill in the counties of Berkshire and Surrey late parcell of the possessions of Charles Stuart late King of England'.[1]

1   Oliver Cromwell, a miniature by S. Cooper, 1656. in the National Portrait Gallery. Prince Rupert nicknamed him 'Old Ironside', and this became a term of pride for Cromwell's army.

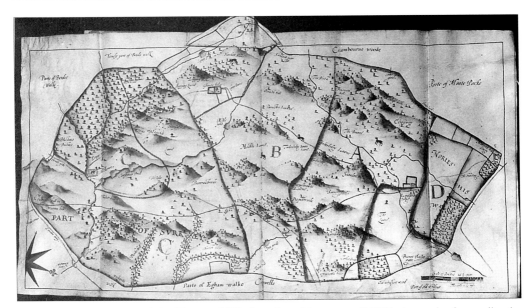

2   Norden's Description of the Honor of Windsor, from his survey of 1607, shows the four walks, A, B, C, D; in the Middle Walk (B) the Cow Pond is marked near the lower edge of the map; Byfield built his house on the hilly ground above this, near the road leading to Bishopsgate.

The Park had changed little since John Norden made a survey for James I in 1607. It was divided into four deerwalks, named on his map after their keepers, but in the parliamentary survey called Manor walk (at the Blacknest Gate end), Middle Walk, Lower Walk and Paddock Walk (nearest to Windsor). Each walk had a keeper's lodge, and in Manor Walk there was also a larger house called Manor Lodge, which had been built by Henry III as a royal residence and hunting-lodge; it was situated where Moat Island now is, on the side of Virginia Water. Manor Walk was separated from Middle Walk by the 'olde banke and ditche', an earthwork stretching from east to west which can still be traced beyond Cumberland Gate near the Wilderness; Middle Walk, in which Cumberland Lodge now stands, was to the north of this.

In 1648 Parliament appointed the Earl of Pembroke Constable of Windsor Castle and Keeper of Windsor Forest. Windsor had fallen early to the parliamentary forces, and since 1642 the Castle had been their headquarters. Cromwell therefore knew the area well. The surveyors reported to the Commissioners of the Great Seal that two men found measuring ground in Windsor Forest had produced a 'kind of warrant' from Lieutenant General Cromwell; the Commissioners, unimpressed, declared that 'it were to be wished that such men as Lieutenant General Cromwell would not so irregularly meddle with such matters'. This story is told by one of the Commissioners, Bulstrode Whitelocke (a former Treasurer of Middle Temple), who had a special interest in the Park as he had obtained the office of keeper of Manor Walk, together with the use of Manor Lodge, and had been made the Earl of Pembroke's Lieutenant.[2] He was not at all in favour of the carving up of the Park into lots for soldiers to farm.

Arrangements for the sale of crown lands for the benefit of the army went ahead. Instead of being paid, the soldiers had been given debentures ('debenters', from the Latin *debentur*, 'there are owing') for the money owing to them, rather like post-war credits, and these could now be exchanged for land. The transaction was complicated, and the regiments appointed 'attorneys' from among their officers to carry out the administrative arrangements. The soldiers were as sceptical about these debentures as their 20th-century descendants were about post-war credits; they wanted cash to take home to their families, rather than a little plot of land possibly far away. The officers, on the other hand, welcomed the possibility of acquiring land and improving their status in society, and they were well placed to know of men willing to sell their debentures. Some bought up the arrears of their entire troop at a fraction of the face value of the certificates: 12s. in the pound was considered a fair offer; some offered as little as 1s. This abuse was widespread, with men desperate for money, and officers seizing the chance to set themselves up as country gentlemen in the new republic.

The official transactions were all recorded in the Register of Debentures, where the actual bills were presented in payment for a specific piece of royal land; for example, on 6 February 1650 the following is listed:

> Lieut. John Byfield the Assignee of Edm^d Dyson a Dragooner under Maio^r
> Charles Burkett two bills each 7^l 1^s 11^{od}————14.03.11

This is one of a set of 18 such transactions with individual soldiers, producing £614 19s. 11d., to be used to pay for 'a parcell of Meadow ground commonly called Kinges Meade in the countie of Berks' on behalf of Nathaniel Byfield—the lieutenant's uncle, who, being a cleric and not a soldier, could not buy debentures himself. What we do not know is how much Lieutenant Byfeild (as he signed himself) actually paid to Dragooner Dyson.[3]

By this means John Byfield 'of the Cittie of Westminster Esquire' was able to purchase plots of land at Bray and Burnham as well as King's Mead, but his most significant purchase was of land in Windsor Great Park, where he became by far the greatest landowner in this prestigious area. Here the procedure was different. What happened was that a man called Captain Edward Scotton, acting as attorney for Colonel John Desborough's regiment, bought up the whole of Windsor Great Park through the debenture system, the contract dated 3 April 1650 being one of the earliest to be signed after the sale of crown lands began (see Appendix One). Once purchased the land was shared out among the officers, who had bought up many of their soldiers' debentures. The cost was determined by the survey of February 1650, which valued the Park at £1,371 per annum; purchases were for 14 years; Captain Byfield paid £4,000 for his land, which was mainly in the Middle Walk.[4]

It need surprise no one to learn that 'Grim Gyant Desborough', as he was called, whose regiment got such preferential treatment, was Cromwell's brother-in-law, as well as being an influential member of the Council of State; hence the presence of Cromwell's men measuring ground in the area. On the Earl of Pembroke's death in 1650, Bulstrode Whitelocke succeeded him as Constable of Windsor Castle. Though he longed to be made Provost of Eton, 'where he hoped he might spend the remnant of his days in learned calm', Cromwell refused his request and instead sent him to Sweden as ambassador.[5] When Whitelocke vacated Manor Lodge it was taken over by Desborough. The Park was full of parliamentary officers, settling down uneasily with a few resentful keepers who had been allowed to stay on. There were some 30 different owners of 'parcells' of ground and many of these had tenants. Captain Scotton built himself a house in Lower Walk, and in a later petition mentioned 'about one hundred parcels of land now enclosed with hedges and ditches ... and converted into farms'.[6] As can be seen from the 1662 map (see front endpaper) the Park underwent a complete transformation from parkland to farmland and must have been barely recognisable as the royal hunting-ground of earlier days.

∗∗

Who was this John Byfield who was thus able to establish himself among the ranks of a new landed gentry? He came from a line of puritan divines, his father Nicholas Byfield having been vicar of Isleworth from 1615 to 1622, and his grandfather Richard Byfield vicar of Stratford-on-Avon from 1596 to 1606. Isleworth parish was a 'peculiar', exempt from the jurisdiction of the diocesan bishop, and its patrons were the Dean and Chapter of Windsor. Clergy of some erudition were appointed to it, and in Nicholas Byfield's time a theology lectureship was established. Nicholas was described as

> a divine of a profound judgement, a strong memory, quick invention, and unwearied industry, which brought the stone upon him which sent him to his grave, in the forty-fifth year of his age ... Mr. Byfield was a Calvinist, a non-conformist to the ceremonies and a strict observer of the sabbath.[7]

He achieved celebrity as a preacher and writer, and was a nine-days' wonder after his death because of the enormous stone removed from his bladder, weighing 33 oz., measuring 13 in. across, and solid like flint. His books, scriptural commentaries and religious works with titles like *The Patterne of Wholsome Words*, *The Marrow of the Oracles of God*, and *The Spirituall Touchstone*, continued to be published until the end of the century. He is said to have been a friend of Shakespeare, who once visited him at Isleworth: perhaps they had known each other at Stratford-on-Avon.[8] Byfield Road near All Saints' Church, Isleworth, is named after him.

3 Nicholas Byfield, an engraving from a portrait in Dr. Williams's Library in London. His scholarly distinction was eclipsed by the fame of his stone, which is shown beside him.

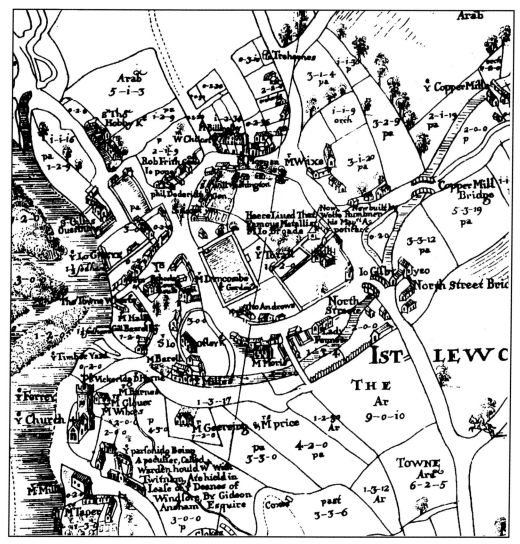

4 Detail from a map of Isleworth at Syon House, drawn in 1635 by Moses Glover, Surveyor to the Earl of Northumberland. Nicholas Byfield's church and vicarage were close to the river and ferry; Dr. Horne was Byfield's successor. Thomas Willis's school is just off the map, top left by the river. Sir Thomas Hobby befriended Adoniram Byfield after his father's death. The orientation of this map is unusual with north at the bottom.

Nicholas married twice and there were two sons and three daughters of each marriage. John, born in 1619 or 1620, was the younger son of the second marriage; he was orphaned at an early age as Nicholas died in 1622 and his wife Elizabeth in 1623. She was a woman of property and was able to leave some provision for her children. To her elder son Benjamin she left her 'great brick house in Isleworth'; to John she left property in Isleworth and in Brainford (Brentford). No hint is given in her will of how the young orphaned family was to be looked after; but there is a clue in the dedication of a book of Nicholas's sermons published by Elizabeth in 1623.[9] She dedicated it

To the Honourable Knight, Sir Horatio Vere, Generall of the English forces in the Low countries; and to his most worthy Lady, the Lady Mary Vere; all happiness that a poor widow may, in their

5 *Far left.* Robert Devere[ux] Earl of Essex, from an engrav[ing] at the National Army Muse[um]. He led a parliamentary ar[my] successfully against the King [at] the Battle of Edgehill (16[42]) where Adoniram Byfield ser[ved] as chaplian. He died in 1646 a[fter] hunting the stag in Wind[sor] Forest.

6 *Left.* Algernon Percy, [10th] Earl of Northumberland (16[02–] 1668), a portrait at Syon Ho[use]. His father, the 9th Earl, w[as] patron of Nicholas Byfi[eld]. After Charles I's capture [and] imprisonment at Hamp[ton] Court, the younger royal chil[dren] were looked after by the [10th] Earl at Syon House.

7 *Below left.* Horace Vere Lord Tilbury, d. 1635; a portait by Miereveldt dated 1629, in the National Portrait Gallery. He [and] his elder brother were known as 'the fighting Veres'. He was a patron and friend of the Byfield family at Isleworth.

8 *Below right.* Sir Thomas Fairfax, Captain-General of the New Model Army; an engraving by William Marshall, after Edw[ard] Bower, in the National Portrait Gallery. He served under Sir Horace Vere in the Low Countries. As romantic a figure as [any] cavalier, he rode a white horse and was nicknamed 'Black Tom' because of his dark good looks and long black hair.

behalfe, pray for at the Throne of Grace ... It pleased you to take into your Family a childe of his body: be further pleased (I pray you) to take into your Patronage this childe of his *Soule*; which as an *Orphane*, yea, as a *Posthumus*, in all humility is presented unto you ... Accept, I beseech you, this poor acknowledgement of thanks.

Your humble Oratrix
Elizabeth Byfield

No doubt their bounty would have continued after Elizabeth's own death that same year, and this generous couple would have had an influence on John's upbringing, particularly as one of the children was adopted by them. At some stage Nicholas's father, who left the living of Stratford-on-Avon in 1606, had come to live in Isleworth, where he died in 1633. There was therefore a family network around Nicholas's orphan children. His sons could conveniently have attended a school a short distance along the river from the church, run by Thomas Willis, Gentleman, another Warwickshire man, a writer of Latin grammar books and schoolmaster at Isleworth for 50 years. The Earl of Northumberland sent his younger son, Henry Percy, to his school.[10] The Byfield sons all went up to university—the oldest, Adoniram, to Emmanuel College, Cambridge, a noted puritan stronghold, in 1620, and the other three to Oxford as their father had done. John matriculated at Lincoln College in 1640 when he was twenty.

Because of all the traffic going up the Thames to Windsor, Isleworth was a place of some importance. The church was close to the river and close also to Syon House, home of the Earl of Northumberland. The Earl was generous to Nicholas Byfield, giving him a pension of £80. The Countess of Northumberland was the daughter of the Earl of Essex, to whom Sir Horace Vere was also related. Sir Horace's daughter Anne married Sir Thomas Fairfax, who was to become Captain-General of the New Model Army in the Civil War. The Earls of Northumberland and of Essex were opposition peers supporting the parliamentary cause, and Essex became Commander-in-Chief of the parliamentary forces. John may well have known all of these people.

Coming from a puritan family and with such examples before him, John Byfield could hardly not have been a parliamentary supporter. While he was a student at Oxford the city became the King's headquarters and the colleges supported the royalist cause. Anthony à Wood wrote that in November 1642 'Oxford was garrisoned for the King. The scholars were put out of their colleges: and those that remained bore arms for the king in the garrison'.[11] Those who refused to do so were constrained to leave. In the Oxford lists there is no record of John Byfield's graduation, though he was created M.A. in 1648, when the fighting was over, and for full measure incorporated at Cambridge in 1650. Other members of his family were already deeply involved in the struggle. Adoniram, 'a most zealous and forward brother for the cause', had become chaplain to a regiment in the Earl of Essex's army and was present at the battle of Edgehill in 1642; soon afterwards he was appointed one of the two scribes of the Westminster Assembly of Divines, of which his uncle Richard Byfield was a member. The pressures on John to join in the struggle must have been irresistible, and he left Oxford just at the moment when Cromwell was launching a recruiting drive.

The battle of Edgehill made Cromwell realise the need to recruit and train a disciplined professional force, especially cavalry. John Byfield was typical of the kind of men he wanted as officers: 'Be careful what captains of horse ye choose, what men be mounted; a few honest men are better than numbers ... If you choose godly honest men to be captains of horse, honest men will follow them'.[12] John Byfield became a lieutenant in Cromwell's regiment of horse, under Fairfax's overall command. After the decisive battle of Naseby in 1645 and the fall of Oxford

9 The Cow Pond was one of the amenities of Byfield's chosen site. Approached by the Lime-Tree Avenue, it is barely ten minutes walk from the Lodge.

in 1646, fighting ceased for a time, only to break out again two years later and to end with the capture of the King, followed by his trial and execution in January 1649. Much of the army was then disbanded, hence the urgency of paying off their arrears, and officers like John Byfield, now a captain, were making plans for civilian life; in his case to buy land and take on the rôle of a country gentleman.

As the army headquarters were at Windsor, Byfield was well placed to spy out the land and choose his 700 acres; his holding was by far the largest of any in the Great Park. There was no house on his land so he chose a site on rising ground, Holmes Hill on Norden's map, where there were some fine oak and chestnut trees; near to a stream, dammed to form the Cow Pond, which provided water; and close to the roads leading from Bishopsgate south to Blacknest Gate and west to Sandpit Gate. Here he built 'a very fine new house with orchard, garden, and good accommodation of stables, and outhouses, which cost £4,000 the building'. This was a very large sum, and a petition of 1662 goes even further, saying that £5,000 was expended on building, besides the purchase of the land which cost £4,000.[13] Even allowing for exaggeration to further the petition, it is clear that a huge amount was spent. At that time the average annual income per household was £7 2s. A cavalry officer's pay was quite high at 10s. a day. A loaf of bread cost between °d. and 2°d. Pepys, who was comfortably off, thought that the £7 a month he spent on housekeeping was 'a great deal'.[14] Byfield spent a small fortune on the house, building no doubt for his children's children. The debenture system made it possible for him to do this, and he had property elsewhere which he might have sold to finance his new venture.

***

What was this costly house like? A document of 1660 says that,

> he did erect one very faire dwelling-house with stables barns and outhouses answerable thereto planted orchards and enclosed ye same and garden plotts with brick walls and built other farme houses for tenants.[15]

It was indeed a 'very faire dwelling-house', for the elegant mansion we see on a later engraving was in essence the house built by John Byfield; and its ghost can still be traced in the present house. For the next 100 years there seems to have been no pulling down and rebuilding, though alterations were made and buildings added according to the inclination of the occupants. As the 1662 map emphatically shows, it was by far the most prominent building in the Park (see front endpaper).

Byfield was a very modern man. Having helped to turn the country upside-down and create a republic he could only look forward, not back; so he built a modern house in the classical style introduced by Inigo Jones, and followed by John Webb and Roger Pratt among others, which in its sobriety was more suited to the period after the Civil War than earlier more elaborate styles. Royalist Pratt and Roundhead Byfield were contemporaries at Oxford and both may have known Newington House near Oxford, built about 1630, which was remarkably similar in style to the central portion of Byfield's house. Architects were as yet rare, and someone like John Byfield might have employed a knowledgeable bricklayer-contractor to build the kind of place he wanted.

The basic plan of Byfield's house was a compact central section seven windows across, the form set by Inigo Jones himself with the Banqueting House in Whitehall in 1622 (see Figure 21). Roger Pratt must have been building Coleshill in Berkshire at about the same time as Byfield's house was being built, but he enlarged its width by two extra windows. What is unusual about Byfield's house is its enlargement by the addition of a gabled pavilion at each end, a feature that did not appear at Newington or other similar houses.[16] One might be tempted to think this was a later addition, made to accommodate royal use in the early 1670s, were it not for the hearth records, where the 25 hearths listed for 1663 are consistent with the larger size.[17]

10 Newington House, Oxfordshire, *c.*1630: a drawing by Michael Pickwoad (from *The English House* by James Chambers) representing the original house before later alterations. It follows a style favoured by Inigo Jones, and bears a close resemblance to the central portion of Byfield House. Its builder, Walter Dunch, had connections with Roger Pratt.

Perhaps the pavilions, along with the two flourishes expressed by the circles of trees at either side of the house, tell us something about the style of John Byfield's aspirations as he established himself in his brave new world.

Thomas Sandby's print (see Figure 18) shows an elegant building with a hipped roof sloping steeply up to a balustraded platform on top, surmounted by a weathervane as centrepiece. The dormer windows and chimneys form part of the design, the only decoration on the classical front being a series of small pediments over the ground-floor windows, alternately pointed and rounded; this feature is also to be seen on the front of the Banqueting House, and is repeated in other houses of the period.

The drawings made by Flitcroft for the Duke of Cumberland show a plan of the interior which, since it was still essentially the same house, gives some idea of the 17th-century lay-out. The front door led into a hall going from front to back of the house where a door opened on to the garden. On either side of the hall were four main rooms, which would be parlours, withdrawing-rooms and chambers. The staircase leading from the garden side of the hall went up to a great chamber, perhaps used as a grand dining-room, dignified with a window larger than the others; on either side were four more chambers. On this floor there was a passage going from end to end, giving access to all the rooms—a more convenient arrangement for bedrooms, and the plan favoured by Pratt on both main floors in his houses. When visitors came, such as John's brother Benjamin from Northamptonshire with his large family, or Adoniram from Wiltshire, the long journey would merit a long stay and all the rooms would be in use. Above the chamber floor were attics and garrets where servants would sleep, though some also would be in the cellars in rooms beside the 'offices', the servants' hall being under the central hall.

The description of Manor Lodge given in the parliamentary survey of 1650 gives an idea of what would be included in such an establishment:

> a kitchen, a hall a parlour a wash house a brew house a sellar a paintry, a milke house, a dairy a venison house a colehouse two chambers, three butteries and a long entry, with other convenient rooms below the stairs. A dining roome, ten chambers, three closetts, a corne loft a gallery and other necessary roomes above staires.[18]

Byfield House was more imposing than Manor Lodge: perhaps the young captain was tempting fate in building a house which so outshone that of his colonel.

Beyond the main house, to the north, was a small but charming house which is sketched in on the 1662 map, and which as 'Groom's House' still remains to give us a notion of the appearance of the main house. It has four rooms on each floor, an attic storey with dormer windows, and a hipped roof; it would probably be occupied by the steward or farm manager whom Byfield would employ, as his own background does not suggest much knowledge of farming, and he had a large acreage to look after. Next to this house, though not adjoining it as now, was a stable block. The gardens, situated on the sunny south-west side of the house, were two large rectangular plots, one divided in two, enclosed within brick walls and looking more like formal orchards than gardens. In front of the house, to left and right of the entrance and forming a notable and enduring feature, were two large circles of trees with a courtyard between them, from which a drive led out to join the road leading to Bishopsgate; from there a track led on to the Cow Pond stream. An intriguing feature on the 1662 map is 'the Banquiting House', situated a short distance to the west of Byfield House, perhaps crowning the raised ground where Chaplain's Lodge now stands, and offering a magnificent view of the park.[19] Its purpose was probably similar to that of the Belvedere erected by the Duke of Cumberland a century later.

11 The House that Jack Built. In Flitcroft's drawing of the house a century later, the central part resembles other 17th-century houses such as Newington, and Chevening in Kent. The originals of Flitcroft's drawings are in the Royal Library.

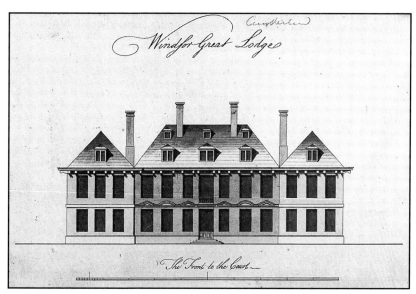

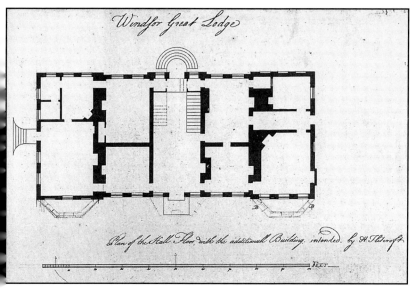

12 & 13 Flitcroft's Plan of Windsor Great Lodge: (*above*) Hall floor, (*right*) Chamber floor.

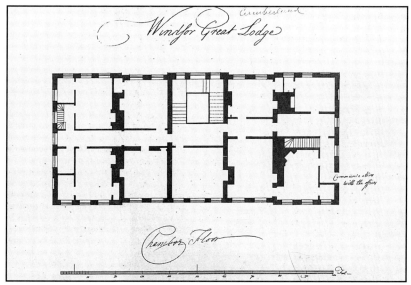

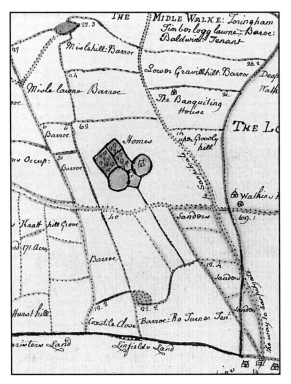

14 Detail of the 1662 map of Windsor Great Park, which was part of the survey made after the Revolution. The map, which is in the Royal Library, emphasises the dominant position of Byfield House; in comparison Manor Lodge (shown to the south on the front endpaper) is insignificant. The circles of trees at either side of the house were to remain an enduring feature.

Byfield by now was married with one child, a daughter called Anne after her mother. He ranked as Esquire, which put him just below knighthood in the social hierarchy. He was considered sound in official circles, as in June 1657 he was appointed one of the government's Commissioners for Berkshire, along with his neighbour Ted Scotton. He was now well settled in his fine house, farming his acres and looking forward to a return on the investment of money and labour he had made in the barren land of the Park. Only 38 years old, he must have believed that the Commonwealth would last for ever, and that he himself had many years before him to enjoy his property. But in September 1657, something prompted him to make his will; and by November he was dead.

It is only in his will that we can hear John Byfield's own voice, and it is here, paradoxically, that he comes most alive. The will is couched in the pious terms usual at that time, and his longing for a son comes through like a refrain: 'If it please the Lord to send me Issue male ... if it please God to send me a Sonne and Heir ... for want of such Issue male then my will is that my daughter Anne Byfeild be my sole heir'. How it must have pained him to list as contingent heirs the five sons of his brother Benjamin and after them his half-brother Adoniram's two. His daughter is to inherit 'when she shall attaine to ye years of Eighteen or be lawfullie married', but she is not to marry without her mother's written consent—a precaution against fortune-hunters. If she does she is not to benefit from the estate 'without her mother's grace' until after her mother's death. His wife is provided for even if she should remarry, and she may continue to have the use of my 'mansion house, barnes, stables, yeards, orchard and gardens ... until my issue comes of age'.[20]

Anne Byfield did remarry, her new husband being a barrister called John Barry; they were living in the 'faire brick house' when the whole scene changed dramatically with the restoration of the monarchy in 1660.

Chapter Two

The King Returns
1660-1671

John Barry, the man who stepped into Captain Byfield's shoes, had a similar background. He too was the son of an Anglican clergyman, John Barry senior, who was rector of Cottesmore in Rutland from 1617 until his death in 1660. There were three sons who like their father went to Cambridge, where they were all students at about the same time. John went up to St Catharine's in 1629, and was admitted to the Inner Temple in 1631, being eventually called to the Bar in 1639; like his counterparts today he probably started keeping term at the Inn while still an undergraduate.[1] The Byfield and Barry families shared the same religious and political outlook, though John Barry as a lawyer might well have avoided involvement in politics.

Barry, a widower with young children, must have known the Byfields, as he had come into the Windsor area when he purchased Bagshot Park from a soldier cousin who had acquired it through the debenture scheme. There was trouble over the transaction as Barry refused to pay up, and the quarrel even went as far as a petition to the Council of State. Whether or not John Barry was 'out for what he could get' as G.M. Hughes suggests,[2] he must have thought that marrying a widow with possession of a splendid house and its surrounding acres in Windsor Great Park was going to solve all his problems; but nothing was further from the truth. To begin with, Byfield seems (not surprisingly) to have built an establishment beyond his means and left his estate burdened with debts; trouble enough, but with the return of the monarchy everything they had built up was threatened with collapse.

On reclaiming his throne, Charles II had given an undertaking to accept the situation as he found it in his kingdom. Apart from the regicides, he gave a free pardon to all, and agreed to leave people where they were in their various positions. The transactions by which soldiers had gained land were specifically mentioned in the Declaration of Breda which preceded his arrival in England:

> And because, in the continued distractions of so many years and so many and great revolutions, many grants and purchases of estates have been made to and by many officers, soldiers and others, who are now possessed of the same and who may be liable to actions at law upon several titles, we are willing that all such differences, and all things relating to such grants, sales and purchases, shall be determined in Parliament which can best provide for the just satisfaction of all men who are concerned.[3]

This statement adroitly shifted responsibility from King to Parliament, and it might at first have reassured the new owners of former crown lands; but soon there were signs that a particular interest was being shown in the Great Park. The King had loved Windsor as a boy and he was passionately fond of hunting; it was natural that he should want to know what the

situation was in his favourite hunting-ground, and hope eventually to get it back. No time was lost: he arrived in England in May 1660 and that same month an 'account of the Great Park of Windsor' was produced, naming those in possession of each of the lodges and walks, and, with regard to the Middle Walk, making the earliest mention of the house that was to become Cumberland Lodge.

> *a very fine new house, with orchard, garden, and good accommodation of stables, and out houses; which cost 4000 the building, built on part of the same walke by one Cap: Byfild, now in the possession of Mr Barrow a lawyer that married Byfills widow.*

16   A 'very fine new house, with orchard, garden and good accommodation of stables, and outhouses, which cost £4000 the building, built on part of the same walke by one Captain Byfeild, now in the possession of Mr. Barrow a lawyer that married Byfeild's widow'.[4]

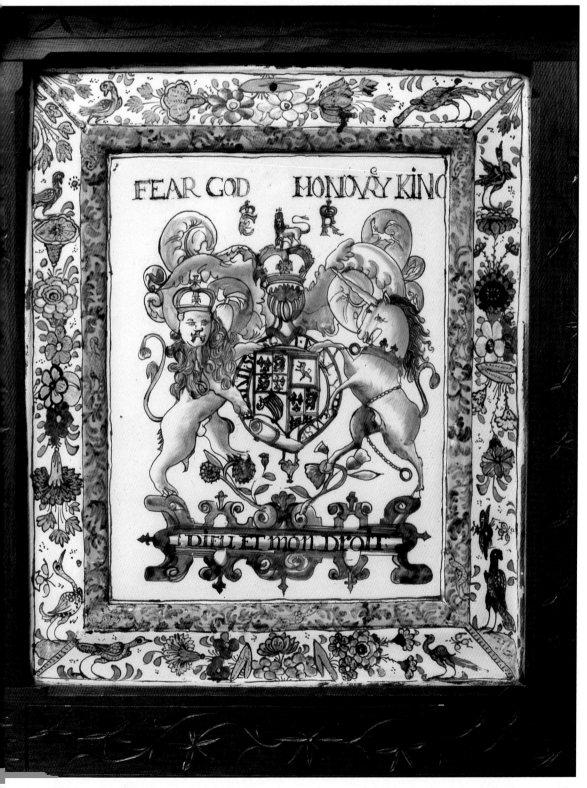

A curious old tile at Cumberland Lodge, showing the royal coat of arms encircled by the Garter symbol and motto. The
ide the C indicates Charles II, and the lion may be a cartoon of the King, whose long curling hair astonished his puritan
cts when he returned to England in 1660.

II Baptist May, by Lely, at Cirencester Park. Compared with the picture of the Earl of Essex (Figure 5) his elaborate attire, like his master's, shows the revolutionary change of fashion which occurred at the Restoration.

Even before setting foot in his kingdom Charles was deluged with petitions. Those relating to the Great Park came equally from people who had lived there as keepers before the Civil War and been displaced, and those who had displaced them and wanted to hold on to their new property. The officer residents who had fought against the King felt particularly insecure despite the assurances given. Although the purchase contract signed in 1650 was only for 14 years, they must have hoped to be established for life, particularly if like Byfield and Scotton they had built rather grand houses on their land. The King's return threatened the future they had marked out for themselves as a new landed gentry.

Their enemies tried to blacken their characters in order to get them out, and rumours of plots abounded. In June 1660 Thomas Symonds, anxious to reclaim the keepership of the Park granted him by Charles I, wrote to the Secretary of State, Sir Edward Nicholas, implicating Desborough, Scotton and others, 'all men whose fingers hath been deeply dipt in innocent blood', in a supposed plot to kill the King; if he is restored to his former post he promises to 'clear the park of a great many bloodsucking vermins'.[5] Though Symonds did not include Barry's name in the list of 'vermins', he can have had no love for him as he also claimed the custody of Bagshot Park.

The next move in the King's recovery of the Park was the presentation to Parliament in September 1660 of a Bill of Sales for the redemption of the crown lands. This caused immediate alarm. John Barry, not for nothing a lawyer, was one of the first to take action. He promptly lodged a petition against the possible loss of his land—and he had much to lose, since Bagshot Park, like Windsor Great Park, was Crown land. He puts the somewhat dubious circumstances of his purchase of Bagshot Park in the best light possible, and gives an account of Byfield's acquisition of land in Windsor Great Park, and the burden caused by his debts and by the barrenness of the land in both parks

> which are but now coming into their improvement ... And Mr. Barry's and his wife's condition is such, that they have great debts to pay and no other estate ... whereby to make payment or to provide for themselves and five small children they have between them. And if they shall neither enjoy the said lands nor have recompense and satisfaction for such disbursements they must expect the rigour of the law from their creditors and thereby the ruin of themselves and theirs will necessarily follow.[6]

In November Edward Scotton petitioned on behalf of himself and other officers with property in the Park, begging to be accepted as tenants at a reasonable rent, and describing the work of 'grubbing, ploughing and husbandry' they have put into their land over many years, only to have their crops claimed by the King. Suspecting that the King wants to take over the Park for hunting, they point out that since the pale has been taken away it is 'utterly unserviceable for the keeping of deer'.[7] With the passing of the Bill of Sales their status automatically changed from owners to tenants, and the best they could hope for was to be allowed to stay on as leaseholders.

Other petitioners crowded round the King asking for their keeperships to be restored, claiming that these were granted by the late King whom they or their fathers served at court. A powerful petitioner was Sir Edward Nicholas, who had been Secretary of State to Charles I and resumed this office under Charles II. He had been appointed Ranger of Windsor Great Park in 1644, but the civil troubles prevented him from taking up the position and he was superseded by the parliamentary nominee. In August 1661 he renewed his claim, asking for a lease of 'all the grounds known by the name of the Great Park of Windsor'. The claim was allowed, but with the proviso that 'Whensoever His Majesty shall think fit to store the same again with deer that our petitioner shall resign such lease and have only the custody and herbage thereof: as it was granted to the petitioner by his late Majesty'.[8]

The King comments that the Park 'is fitter to be kept in way of a farm' than as a park, but in granting a lease of 31 years (a usual term in those days) he leaves open the possibility of turning it into a park again before the 31 years are up; and already in 1661 red and fallow deer were being transported from Germany to restock Windsor Forest.

Nicholas's request resulted in the carrying out of a complete survey of the Park with all its separate lots, together with recommendations as to how the existing tenants should be treated. This invaluable document and the map relating to it list everyone holding land in the Park at that time, with details of the size and value of their property (see front endpaper). At the end of the list comes a particular mention of a 'faire brick house built by Mr. Byfield with new stables and other outhouses and about 310 acres of Ground now held by Mrs. Barrow or her under-tenants worth £70 per annum'. The map, however, shows 'Mr. Barrow's' holding as much larger than this. The advice given by the surveyors was that the ex-officers should be allowed to keep their property, on payment of rent, for three years until 1664, and 'thenceforth until further order', a term coinciding with the 14 years of purchase dating from April 1650.

A condition of tenancy was that the lessees were to repair the houses and farms and to plant

> yearly twenty or more young thriving saplings of Oake, Ash, or Elme upon some parte thereof and to preserve the same from spoyle and harme, that they may grow up and become Timber trees for his Majesties future benefit and to returne such parte of the premises as conveniently may be into pasture ground without destroying the trees or bushes thereon growing whereby it may become serviceable and fit for deere, in case his Majesty shall be minded to restore it to a park.[9]

Barry protested angrily against this take-over by defiantly ploughing up the pasture ground. It was a punishable offence to plough up royal land, and on 29 January 1662 the Surveyor-General instructed two law officers in Windsor to go at once to the new house in the Park and restrain Barry who

> hath presumed to plow up part of the meadow-ground within his Majesty's Greate Parke of Windsor contrary to law and without any warrant or authority soe to doe he having no interest at all therein, being only permitted to enjoy the Herbage thereof untill the Annunciation next; and that he hath layd open the Orchards Gardens and other inclosed Grounds belonging to the new house erected within the said Greate Parke and suffers the said House, Gardens, Orchards and Inclosures to be wasted and spoiled contrary to all justice and good conscience.

The law officers were instructed to go to the house and forbid further ploughing of the meadows, and to see that the gardens, orchards and 'inclosures' were sufficiently fenced and that cattle were not allowed within them (because they would damage the trees); and any person ploughing up the meadows was to be arrested and brought before a Justice of the Peace, and reported to the Lord High Treasurer of England.[10] It was Barry's misfortune that the 'faire brick house' had attracted special interest in the highest quarters. Apparently he did not co-operate with the law-officers, for the next we hear is that he is in prison: a sharp punishment which shows the firm control now being exercised over what went on in the Park.

In March 1662 a King's warrant affirmed Sir Edward Nicholas's lease of the Park 'and of the ground and soyle thereof and of the Lodges houses buildings and other things now standing upon the same', for a rental of £200 a year.[11] All the residents now became Nicholas's sub-tenants, even in houses they had built for themselves; and Nicholas was a tenant of the King. Barry continued his protest even from prison. In April he and Anne sent a petition to the Lord Chancellor repeating the story of Byfield house and the tale of their debts; their plight was even more desperate now as 'John for want of his liberty is deprived of the benefit of his calling'. They refer to their earlier petition:

> His most Excellent Majestie ... was gratiously pleased out of commisseration of your petitioners condition to refer it to his Lordshipp the Lord Treasurer to doo therein according to equity but his Lordshipp was pleased not to doo anything therein for your petitioners releife and in ye meantime Sir Edward Nicholas hath prepared a pattent thereof to himself which is ready for ye great Seale and which lyeth before your Lordship to be sealed.

They beg him to stay the sealing of the patent, and the Chancellor orders this to be deferred—for a week. 'In the meane time lett the Petitioner prosecute the getting of my Lord Treasurer's Report, otherwise I shall not be able to stopp it longer'.[12] They seem to have been allowed to continue living in the Park, though from the hearth tax returns it looks as if they refused to pay their taxes: 'The mannor house in the great parke wch they that live in it say they will pay nothing it being the King's house'. Indeed, the hearth tax return of January 1663 notes

17 Groom's House survives from the 17th century; at first it stood on its own, but later was joined up to the Duke of Cumberland's new stables.

that the manor house is 'voyde', and that no tax has been paid on its 25 hearths. Yet John Barry Esq. is listed as having paid for five hearths, so it is possible that the family had moved into Groom's House, thus hoping to get away with paying its modest tax only.[13]

In the year 1665 to 1666 Elias Ashmole, the Windsor Herald, carried out a visitation of Berkshire, the main object of which was to register the arms of those who claimed the right to bear them. His list for the parish of Old Windsor, which includes most of the Great Park, contains the name of 'John Barry Esq.', together with those of three of the army captains who had managed to stay on in the Park.[14] The last we hear of John Barry is in the *Calendar of Inner Temple Records*, where it is noted that John Barry of the Inner Temple, Esq., was buried in the Rounde Walke, 25 May 1668, this probably being the external area about the 'Rounde' of the Temple Church in London. After this Byfield and Barry disappear from the scene.

In August 1670 the King ordered that the Park should be 're-assumed': it was to become once more a royal preserve for hunting, for the keeping of deer and the growing of trees. The remaining tenants were told to plant acorns and to make their land level and fit for riding, and the Park was again stocked with deer. Orders were given for it to be fenced, and in December £6,000 was paid to one Simon Smith for carrying out this work. Sir Edward Nicholas had died in 1669, and his son Sir John Nicholas was asked to surrender his father's interest in the Park, which had passed to him, for payment of £4,500 in compensation. Others with interests in the Park were also compensated, though in the case of the various tenants it was simple enough to terminate their leases. In January 1672 the order was given for no more rents or taxes to be collected in the Great Park as it had been enclosed.[15]

Step by step over ten years the King had recovered his beloved hunting-ground; now he was free to enjoy it and leave his mark upon it.

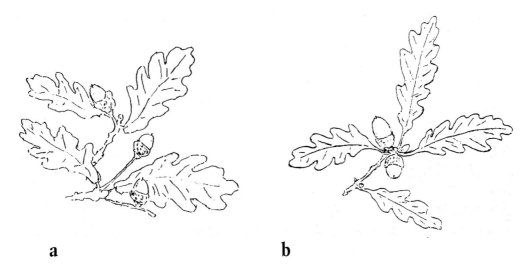

a   b

Two types of oak grow in the park: (a) pedunculate (b) sessile (drawn by the Hon. Maud Wilson).

Chapter Three

The Ranger's Lodge
1671-1697

The diarist John Evelyn, visiting Windsor in 1670, said that 'the King passed most of his time in hunting the stag and walking in the park, which he was now planting with rows of trees'.[1] We can picture the tall figure of Charles II striding out into the Park, his spaniels at his heels, his less energetic courtiers panting along behind him. The old track from the Castle to the Great Park led him to the vantage point of Snow Hill, from which he had a magnificent view of the Castle. Going a little further he would come to Byfield House, attractive, available and in just the right place to provide a secluded retreat from Windsor. It had long been fashionable for owners of great houses to have a lodge a little distance away from their main dwelling where they could entertain friends privately, or a place on the edge of a deer-park where they could rest while out hunting. Royal personages felt even more the need to escape from the formality and publicity of court and live as private persons; the Palace of Versailles had its origin in just such a lodge, a few miles from the French court at St Germain. Byfield House seemed ideally situated for this purpose.

Anne Barry and her family had presumably either moved away after her husband's death, or been compensated for the loss of her property which in any case reverted to the Crown. It was easy therefore for the King to possess himself of the house, and it now received special attention. It is most unlikely that Anne and John Barry had done much in the way of repairs and maintenance once they knew the King was taking over. The house must have needed refurbishment to make it fit for royal use, but priority seems to have been given to security measures, mainly to control the deer. In September 1671 Simon Smith was instructed to add to his contract the 'empaling' of ground around the various lodges, 'as likewise such grounds about the new erected building called Byfeild house as were lately empaled'. He was told to 'impale a paddock and the plantation and garden at New Lodge in the Great Park with an extraordinary pale and controll and toppe and convenient gates', and he also put 'long pales' about the garden to protect it from the deer with which the Park had recently been restocked. His contract included 'making great gates and providing locks and keys with stiles and bridges for our passage into the said park'.[2]

Though built 20 years earlier the house was thought of as new, and new it was in comparison with the old keepers' lodges such as Manor Lodge which had been there since the 13th century. For a time it was called New Lodge, a confusing title as there had for many years been a New Lodge a few miles to the west in Windsor Forest. By the end of the century it was known as Ranger's Lodge, or Windsor Lodge, or the Great Lodge. By the next generation, when this second great upheaval in the Park had long been completed and the memory of the

18 'A View of the Lodge in Windsor Great Park'. This is a simplified variant of a drawing by Thomas Sandby dated 1754 (see Plate V). The house Baptist May knew is little changed in this picture.

short period when it was occupied by republican soldiers was fading, people thought the house had been built by Charles II. The Windsor Herald Elias Ashmole, who died in 1692, says in his *History & Antiquities of Berkshire* that King Charles II built a lodge 'for the use of the keeper, and for his own diversion'. G.M. Hughes says that the house may have been converted into a place suitable for the King's *fêtes champêtres*, and this is probably how the King planned to use it.[3]

Naturally the King wanted this special house to be in the hands of someone congenial, and the person he chose was a companion and servant of long standing, Baptist May, whom he had already made Keeper of St James's Park. During the first decade of his reign Charles had been easing out the old counsellors such as the Secretary of State, Sir Edward Nicholas, and the Chancellor, Lord Clarendon, who had served his father and indeed himself in exile, and replacing them with advisers who were less prone to offer him good advice. Closer to him than those appointed to great offices of state were the people he kept around him in his private life: his mistresses and members of his household who pandered to his vices, according to his critics: 'those wicked creatures', wrote Evelyn, 'who took him off from all application becoming so great a king'.[4] Sir John Nicholas, hustled to give up his own claim to the keepership, had as Clerk to the Privy Council to record the granting of it to the King's boon companion, Baptist (or Bab) May, certainly one of the 'creatures' Evelyn had in mind.

> June 1671: His Majesty is pleased to reimparke ye Great Parke of Windsor from ye first day of October next, And to grant the Office of Keeper of all ye said parke (excepting the Paddock Walke) with ye herbage and pannage thereof unto Baptist May Esq. Keeper of his Majesty's Privy Purse

to hold ye said office with all fees etc from ye first of October next during his Majesty's pleasure. Subscribed by Mr. Attorney Generall by Warrant under his Majesty's Signe Manuall procured by ye Lord Arlington. John Nicholas.[5]

For this May received £1,500 a year, as well as the perquisites of the office—the house, and a generous allowance of wood and venison.

Baptist May, born in 1628 and so only two years older than the King, was the sixth son of Sir Humphrey May, a Norfolk squire who was Chancellor of the Duchy of Lancaster. Sir Humphrey's younger brother Hugh was Groom of the Privy Chamber to James I and Charles I, and acquired Mote Park, Old Windsor, thus giving the family a link with Windsor. Bab's older brother Algernon was to become an M.P. for Windsor, and his cousin Hugh became Comptroller of the King's Works and architect of the extensive alterations to Windsor Castle begun in 1671. The family was thus well established in the royal entourage. Bab May probably went to court in boyhood as a page; by 1648, when he was 20, he was page of honour to the Duke of York (the future King James II), and was one of those detailed to attend the Duke in November of that year when he left England for Holland; he remained with him in exile. On his return as King, Charles II distributed rewards to his faithful followers; May was granted, jointly with the Earl of St. Albans, the lucrative office of Registrar in the Court of Chancery which he kept for life. In 1662 he was made Groom of the Bedchamber to the King, and in 1665 Keeper of the Privy Purse, posts he retained until the King's death in 1685. These two offices, often held together, kept May in a position of great personal influence close to the King. Bishop Burnet, who knew May, wrote of him:

> Mr. May of the privy purse ... had the greatest and longest share in the king's secret confidence of any man in that time; for it was never broke off, though often shaken, he being in his notions against everything that the king was for, both France, popery, and arbitrary government, but a particular sympathy of temper, and his serving the king in his vices, created a confidence much envied, and often attempted to be broke, but never with any success beyond a certain coldness.

He was sought out if the King was in a difficult mood, or needed to be persuaded into a particular course of action:

> He was called upon to come and manage the king's temper, which no man understood better than he did; for he had been bred about the king ever since he was a child: and by his post he was in the secret of all his amours ... He was so true to the king in that lewd confidence in which he employed him, that the king charged him never to press him in any thing so as to provoke him. By this means he kept all this while much at a distance; for he would not enter into any discourse with the king on matters of state, till the king began with him.[6]

At court May had many uses. He was 'of singular service' to the King in his 'private pleasures', and has been called 'one of the potentates of the back stairs'.[7] As Groom of the Bedchamber he could exercise control over who came to see the King, so there was plenty of opportunity for bribery. He was on good terms with Charles's powerful mistress Barbara Villiers, who became Lady Castlemaine and later Duchess of Cleveland. Lord Clarendon states that she used her influence with the King to get May the place of Keeper of the Privy Purse; in return she made lavish demands on the funds he controlled. Speaking of 'Bab May, my Lady Castlemaine, and that wicked crew', Pepys tells how she chose what plate she liked from a goldsmith saying 'make a note for this and for that to the Privy purse for the money'.[8] No wonder the King was perennially short of funds.

19 Barbara Villiers, Duchess of Cleveland, by J.M. Wright. Famous for her beauty and influential at court, she was mistress of Charles II, and briefly of John Churchill. (National Portrait Gallery)

When Charles married Catharine of Braganza in 1662 he foisted Lady Castlemaine, pregnant with his child, upon his bride as Lady of the Bedchamber. This post entitled her to apartments at court, and here night after night she used to entertain the King and their intimate circle to wild parties. Clarendon says 'his majesty spent most of his time in her company, or in the conversation of those, whose greatest talent consisted in being able to raise a laugh at the expense of everything serious and sacred'.[9] He wrote with feeling as he himself was often the butt of their wit, and they plotted to get him sacked. When in 1667 the King at last dismissed him, Pepys tells us 'Bab May fell upon his knees and ketched the king about the legs and joyed him, and said that this was the first time that ever he could call him King of England, being freed this great man—which was a most ridiculous saying'. May's lodge must also have been the scene of wild parties, like the one Pepys reported at Cranbourne Lodge, when the King and all the company were 'in such a maudlin pickle as never people were'.[10]

Puritan England, and even people far from straightlaced such as Pepys, were shocked by the licentiousness of the court. When Bab May presented himself at Winchelsea in 1666 to be chosen as their Member of Parliament, bringing letters of recommendation from the Duke of York, the people cried out 'they would have no Court pimp to be their Burgesse'.[11] It was well known that to become a lady-in-waiting to the Duchess of York was to meet a fate worse than death. Arabella Churchill became maid of honour in 1665 at the age of 17, and by 1673 had had four children by the Duke. Her younger brother John began his career by following her into the Duke's household as a page, thus founding the fortunes of the brilliant Churchill dynasty. The tale was told of how, when Lady Castlemaine's favour was waning, the King surprised her in her bedroom with another lover who escaped by jumping out of the window: it was the young Jack Churchill. The reputed result of this liaison was a daughter, Barbara. Another result was a gift of £5,000 from his lover to Jack, who prudently bought an annuity with it.

***

As the years went by it became clear that the Queen was not going to produce an heir to the throne. Bab May was a prime mover in an attempt to engineer a divorce, thinking this would please the King. The problem was that there was no culpability on the Queen's side: she was a dutiful as well as a long-suffering wife, who had tried her best to fit in with the ways of the frivolous court. Various ideas were mooted, such as spiriting her away to America, never to be heard of again, or persuading her to enter a convent; the King recoiled from these schemes, so May pursued the more orthodox plan of putting a special bill through Parliament. In January 1670 he had succeeded in becoming a Member of Parliament in a by-election at Midhurst, and he plotted to get the bill through. Since he was no orator himself, he arranged for others to present the motion; but three days before this was to happen, as May told Bishop Burnet, 'the King called for him, and told him, that matter must be let alone, for it would not do. This disturbed him much, for he had engaged himself far in laying the thing, and in managing those who were to undertake the debate'.[12] It was shortly after this that the King made May Ranger of the Great Park, perhaps to show his appreciation of his efforts.

The divorce question was still in the wind several years later. 'They think I have a mind to a new wife; but, for all that, I will not see an innocent woman abused.'[13] Charles (who had abused her himself all their married life) uttered these words during the scandal of the Popish Plot, a monstrous fiction concocted by an unsavoury individual called Titus Oates, who whipped the nation up into a frenzy. One person after another was implicated and sent to the scaffold, and Oates dared to go so far as to cast suspicion upon the Queen, who was vulnerable, being both foreign and Catholic. The King had seen through Oates from the start, though he felt powerless in face of the strength of public feeling; but with this attack Oates had gone too far, and May, realising this, played a part in discrediting him and his accomplice Israel Tonge. An investigative journalist of the day persuaded Tonge's son Simpson to make a statement saying that his father and Oates had made up the whole story. May's lodge provided a convenient place where people could be taken to wait in the wings until the right moment came for them to be presented to the King at Windsor; so Simpson Tonge was brought by a certain Captain Ely to 'a place in the Great Park, two miles from the town, which belonged to Mr. May, the Keeper of the Privy Purse, where they were both entertained by a Mr. Nunn, Mr. May's gentleman'.[14] Unfortunately Tonge, who between cajolement and threats, money and drink, did not really know what was happening, was frightened into withdrawing his statement, and it was still some time before the national frenzy subsided and Oates was denounced as a fraud; but the Queen's honour was saved.

From the time the Park was restored to its former state and May was installed as Ranger, the King visited Windsor more and more. There he had the company of his old comrade-in-arms, his cousin Prince Rupert, whom he had made Constable of the Castle and Keeper of Windsor Forest. The court frequently moved out of London to escape the plague, and by 1671 Hugh May was renovating the Castle to make it more habitable. Charles liked to spend the late spring and summer months at Windsor, and found recreation in walking, riding and hunting, hawking, fishing and picnics in the Park.

Charles was Louis XIV's cousin and during his exile he had spent some time at the brilliant French court where his mother Queen Henrietta Maria, aunt of the French King, had taken refuge, and this became a model for his own court, though he never had enough money to equal it in magnificence. French influence was particularly marked in the gardens Charles created around his palaces. Louis's gardener Le Nôtre himself advised him on the lay-out at Greenwich, and splendid French gardens were designed for Hampton Court by Le Nôtre's pupil John Rose who became the royal gardener. The vogue was for grand avenues giving distant vistas, radiating out from the house like the rays of the sun, emphasising the importance of the person at the centre. Louis XIV's plan for Versailles included a grand avenue leading out into the park, flanked by a double row of trees. Similarly, Charles II planned a royal way leading into the Park from Windsor Castle to the high point of Snow Hill, so that from each end there was a fine vista. A more modest way led on from Snow Hill to Byfield House.

The Long Walk, as it came to be called, was begun in 1680 when the privately owned fields separating the Little Park from the Great Park were purchased for the Crown, thus effectively joining the two, though each has continued to retain its own identity. The Walk was 240 ft. wide, its double row of elms giving it majestic proportions—Swift called it 'the finest avenue I ever saw'. However, the planting was barely complete when Charles died in 1685. The elms lasted, with replantings, until 1940, when they were felled and replaced by rows of horse chestnuts and London planes. A favourite walk from Cumberland Lodge is to follow the track leading northwards to the statue of the Man on the Copper Horse which now dominates Snow Hill, there to be rewarded with one of the great views of Europe. Here one can meditate on Henry VIII who, according to Harrison Ainsworth, stationed himself on its summit to await the gunfire from the Castle announcing Anne Boleyn's execution at the Tower; or on Charles II, dreaming of an avenue to rival those of Louis XIV; or George IV, worst of sons, commissioning a statue to 'the best of fathers'; or Queen Elizabeth II, celebrating her Silver Jubilee with a great bonfire among her own people.

The Lodge itself was not neglected in this creation of avenues. About 1675, according to William Menzies, a Victorian surveyor of the Great Park, a double avenue of oaks was planted from Bishopsgate to the Lodge.[15] This avenue continued on the other side of the house in a straight line west to Sandpit Gate, and another avenue led south across what is now Smith's Lawn. To the north towards Ox Pond Hill oaks and beeches were planted in a grove, and many of these remain. Menzies gives a date of 1695 for the 'wilderness' still to be seen to the south of Cumberland Lodge, planted as a pleasure-ground with trees of different types, and woodland walks; if this date is correct, it must have been one of May's last innovations as Ranger.

The Park had been impoverished during the Civil War and Commonwealth, and wood was needed in huge quantities to supply the Navy. During the first years of Charles's reign the Park was reverting from a mixture of woodland and cultivated land to woodland pasture and, when the King resumed control of the Park and appointed a Ranger, tree-planting received a great impetus. The plantations or 'rows of trees' were concentrated in the area of the Park nearest to Windsor, and were mainly of oaks, with some beeches. These were in particular demand for shipbuilding, and the soil, though poor for cultivation as John Barry had found, was good for oaks.

The visitor to the Lodge can easily get into the way of spotting these old trees, not only by coming across the occasional dated plaque, but by looking at the 60-year-old oaks in the 1937 Coronation Grove to the east of the Lodge, alongside the road to Bishopsgate, and then at the century-old oak commemorating the coming of age in 1888 of Prince Christian Victor of Schleswig-Holstein, just off the Lime-Tree Avenue. It is then not too difficult to identify oaks three times that age, planted during Baptist May's Rangership. If May organised the planting of trees in the neighbourhood of the Ranger's Lodge and extended John Byfield's gardens, he had advice near home since his cousin Hugh was working at Windsor, and was almost certainly involved in the creation of the Long Walk.[16]

Bab May lived well; he kept a fine stud of horses, loved racing, and was according to Pepys 'one of the best players at tennis in the nation'.[17] He shared with his master an appreciation of the arts, and encouraged the King to employ a little-known carver called Grinling Gibbons to

20   The Long Walk looking north towards Windsor Castle: an engraving of *c.*1840. The avenue was created in Charles II's reign, and leads due south into the Park from the Castle.

21   The Banqueting House was designed by Inigo Jones and completed in 1622. It survived the fire of 1698 which destroyed Whitehall Palace, where monarchs from Henry VIII to William III had held court. On the right is the 'Holbein' Gate, which was taken down in 1759; an unsuccessful attempt was made to re-erect it in the Great Park at the end of the Long Walk. This engraving is in the Crace Collection in the British Museum.

work at Windsor Castle under Hugh May's supervision. He was a friend of Lely, who painted his portrait, and he owned a portrait of Charles II by him and one of Moll Davis the actress, a mistress of the King. A bachelor (though he had an illegitimate son called, naturally, Charles), he was a convivial person, dining out frequently with his friends in town or entertaining them at home. Pepys gives us a glimpse of his affable nature when he tells how one day he had waited hours at Whitehall for an audience with the Duke of York, 'and there meeting Mr. May, he took me down about four a'clock to Mr. Chevin's lodgings, and all alone did get me a dish of cold chicken and good wine, and I dined like a prince, being before very hungry and empty'.[18] A man of property, May had an estate at Pleshey in Essex, and acquired land in Pall Mall where he built a square of fine houses; his busy presence in St James's is still recorded in the name of Babmaes Street, off Jermyn Street.

These were halcyon days for May. He was devoted to the King and made himself indispensable to him; wherever the King was, he was. He enjoyed intrigue and being at the hub of affairs, though he did not seek the limelight and is a somewhat shady figure in contemporary accounts; but everyone knew him. Unlike his brother Algernon he never received a knighthood, despite his long service with the King; perhaps this was a reflection of the King's estimate of his character. All this bustling life came to an abrupt end with the unexpected death of King Charles in 1685. With the accession of James II, May's appointments as Keeper of the Privy Purse and Groom of the Bedchamber ended, though he kept the Rangership. There might well have been a change of Rangership with the accession of William and Mary, but May had given William his support, and in return he was allowed to continue as Ranger for life.

Being now retired from court, May spent his time between his town house in Jermyn Street and the Lodge in the Great Park, where he was near to his favourite brother Algernon. The Lodge was managed for him by his 'gentleman' Robert Nunn, who was rewarded by being given a keeper's house (probably Manor Lodge) to live in—the brothers Robert and Baptist Nunn who were still active in the Park in the next century were probably his sons. May had time to tie up a few legal matters connected with the Rangership, such as the question of the payment of taxes for the Park. In 1690 he stood for parliament at Windsor along with Sir Christopher Wren, and they were both returned by the Mayor and Corporation; but the towns-people disputed this, returning two people of their own choice, and petitioned Parliament successfully in favour of them. This rebuff must have reminded May of the incident at Winchelsea in 1666, though this time it was an electoral rights issue rather than a personal one. In 1693 Wren (as Comptroller of the Works) authorised payment of £328 16s. 5½d. for repairs done for May at the Lodge two years earlier. May's service to the court was not forgotten, for in 1695 he received a royal bounty of £1,000.[19]

Baptist May died in Berkshire—probably at the Lodge—on 2 March 1697, and was buried in St George's Chapel, Windsor. It was perhaps the most religious act of his whole life.[20]

22 This unusual picture of William III Prince of Orange and Hans Willem Bentinck, with its baroque surround, was pai
by W. Souven to commemorate their recovery from smallpox in 1676. It hangs in the Kasteel Amerongen in Holland, a
reproduced by courtesy of the Countess de Brauwere-Bentinck.

Chapter Four

The King's Friend
1697-1702

The story of the Lodge under the next Ranger is the story of a great friendship.

> March 9, 1697. This day the King went to Windsor, and returned on Friday; the Lord Portland, accompanied him to take possession of the lodge and place of ranger of Windsor park, worth 1500 l. per annum, which Mr. May enjoyed during his life.[1]

So wrote Narcissus Luttrell, an onlooker whose diary is a valuable source-book of contemporary observations. Baptist May had not been dead a week when King William granted the Rangership to his beloved friend William Bentinck, Earl of Portland. It must have irked the King that May had hung on so long to a post usually granted to a favourite of the sovereign, but, as it happened, the timing was opportune for at that moment the King was particularly anxious to please his friend.

To understand the close relationship between the King and Lord Portland we have to go back to their boyhood. William Prince of Orange was the only child of Charles II's sister Mary and William II of Orange, Stadhouder, or governor, of the Dutch States. His father had died before he was born, his mother when he was 11, and he was placed in the care of his grand-mother as 'a child of the State'. He was barely 14 when in 1664 Hans Willem Bentinck, a year older, joined his household at The Hague as page of honour and companion.

Bentinck was the youngest son of a nobleman of Gelderland, whose family had for generations defended the Dutch States against the encroachments of powerful neighbours. The older sons were to inherit family estates, but Hans Willem had to seek his fortune elsewhere. His father had served as deputy to the States General at The Hague, and so was aware of the orphan Prince's situation. What better arrangement could there be than that he should have a companion of his own age, and that Hans Willem should fulfil this rôle and be given a placement with such promise for the future? This promise was to be amply fulfilled; but at the time few could have foreseen that he was to establish a dynasty which was to serve Europe for generations; and that the frail youth he had come to serve was to rule over both the Dutch States and England, save them from the domination of France, and redress the balance of power in Europe.

The young prince's life was bleak and lonely; his health was poor, his guardians were always at odds, his political position insecure and his country constantly under threat. The advent of the tall handsome young nobleman into his entourage, with his charm and gentle manners, must have been a godsend. Strong ties of affection were formed between them— perhaps with an element of hero-worship on the younger boy's part and of protectiveness on Bentinck's. For the next 30 years they were seldom apart.

They underwent military training together, and in 1670 Hans Willem was part of the Prince's entourage when he visited England, no doubt with the hope of strengthening ties with his uncle Charles II. They were well received by Parliament, but neither they nor Parliament knew that the King had recently signed a secret treaty with Louis XIV, promising support in a fresh attack upon Holland in return for a subsidy. When the attack happened in 1672, the Dutch people threw off their old rulers, acclaimed William as Stadhouder, and opened the sluice-gates to flood the country in order to stave off the French advance. King Charles was forced by Parliament to withdraw from a conflict it had never sanctioned, and the country was saved. For the rest of his life the cardinal point of William's foreign policy was opposition to France.

There was trouble of a different kind ahead. When the Prince at 25 contracted smallpox, the dread disease which had carried off both his parents, Bentinck proved his devotion and probably saved his life. It was difficult to find people willing to nurse a smallpox victim, as it might mean a sentence of death; but Bentinck nursed the Prince night and day until he recovered. 'Whether he slept or not, the Prince could not tell, but in sixteen days and nights he never called once that he was not answered by Monsieur Bentinck as if he was awake.'[2] According to a family tradition, Bentinck even shared the Prince's bed, the belief being that a healthy person placed beside the patient would draw out the fever. Small wonder that Bentinck caught the disease himself, and on the Prince's recovery begged leave to go home, as he 'could hold up no longer'.[3]

Prince William was now in his mid-twenties and it was time to arrange an appropriate marriage. Royal marriages were part of political strategy. Bentinck, together with Sir William Temple, Ambassador at The Hague, was entrusted with the negotiations for a marriage between William and his cousin the Lady Mary, elder daughter of the Duke of York. An alliance with England would strengthen the Dutch States against the ever-present threat from France, and the marriage of the possible future queen with a Protestant prince could affirm the Protestant succession in England. Of course Mary herself, a 15-year-old girl, was not consulted. When the news was broken to her, she was aghast at being disposed of to a man she hardly knew, whom she considered a dwarf because he was so puny (she was very tall); and she was dismayed at the prospect of leaving home and country for the forbidding Dutch court. However, her wishes were irrelevant. They were married in November 1677 on the Prince's birthday, the Prince going to bed 'in a blew satin waistcoat which was the Dutch fashion', as Sarah Churchill recalled many years later.[4]

A fortnight later the bridal pair left for Holland. Mary at least had the comfort (or so she thought then) of taking with her as companions her two girlhood friends Elizabeth and Anne Villiers, daughters of her former governess (and, incidentally, cousins of Charles II's mistress Barbara Villiers). In the event Anne became Bentinck's wife and, to complete this strange set of relationships, Elizabeth became the Prince's mistress. Bentinck and Anne Villiers were married at The Hague in March 1678, and over the next 10 years until her death in 1688 she bore him seven children. Princess Mary, unlike her prolific sister Anne, had none after a miscarriage in 1678. In the unhappy early years of their marriage her husband paid her little attention, being preoccupied with affairs of state, and preferring the company of her maid of honour. Her sister in England was deeply offended by the reports she heard, and when Bentinck visited London in 1685 Princess Anne told him 'to check the insolence of Elizabeth Villiers to the Princess of Orange'.[5] Whether he carried the message to his sister-in-law history does not relate, but Anne always bore a grudge against him.

During all this time William remained in the wings as a possible claimant to the English throne, and Bentinck, the most trusted of all his advisers, was in touch with influential English noblemen, especially after King James's accession when discontent greatly increased. The birth of a son to the Queen in 1688 precipitated events, and William was invited to invade England: he insisted upon a written invitation, so careful was he not to be seen as a usurper. Bentinck set sail with him at the end of October, but with a heavy heart, as his wife Anne was seriously ill. 'Farewell,' he wrote to her before embarking, 'I beg you to believe that all my life I shall love you with the same passion.'[6] She died soon after his arrival in England, with Princess Mary at her bedside.

As William's forces advanced, even those closest to the King deserted him, his daughter Anne among them, smuggled out of Whitehall by the backstairs with the help of Lady Churchill. Lord Churchill, as Gentleman of the Bedchamber to the King, dined with him late on 23 November and deserted to William the following morning; this was the final blow for the King, and he fled before the Prince's advancing forces. William was installed at St James's in December, and the following spring the Prince and Princess of Orange were crowned joint sovereigns of England.

As soon as William was in power he showered his favourite with honours: Bentinck was at once made Groom of the Stole, First Gentleman of the Bed-chamber, and Privy Councillor, and a week later Keeper of the Privy Purse, thus following in May's footsteps—a person he could hardly have resembled less, except in devotion to his royal master. Titles were heaped upon him in the coronation honours: Baron Cirencester, Viscount Woodstock, Earl of Portland. His court offices brought with them spacious lodgings in Kensington Palace as well as a house in Whitehall Gardens; but he also acquired a country house, Bulstrode, near Gerrards Cross in Buckinghamshire, to provide a permanent home for his family.[7] He anglicised his name from Hans Willem to William but never mastered the English language, remaining too obstinately Dutch ever to win acceptance in England; the many rewards lavished on him by the King did nothing to help. The latter's reliance on Dutch advisers was always a major grievance.

23 An engraving by R. White of William III and Mary II, who reigned with the unique position of joint sovereigns until her early death in 1694; at the same time he ruled the Dutch States as Stadhouder. (National Portrait Gallery)

24 William Bentinck, 1st Earl of Portland, a studio copy of a portrait by Hyancinthe Rigaud, probably painted when Portland was ambassador to France in 1698. He is wearing the ribbon and George, the jewelled pendant of the Order of the Garter. (National Portrait Gallery)

There was much angling for position in the new court which was full of rivalries, fears, and resentments from the King and Queen downwards. Princess Anne, who had apartments in the Palace of Whitehall, was happily married to Prince George of Denmark, a Protestant marriage which strengthened her position as heir presumptive; he was made Duke of Cumberland after the coronation. Though William and Mary were joint sovereigns, William's claim to the throne, should Mary die childless before him, was weaker than Anne's, a fact which did not endear her to him; and across the water there was a king with a better claim than any of them, upheld by the King of France. The insecurity of the throne was a disturbing undercurrent throughout this period.

The households of the two royal sisters were never on good terms, and within them powerful figures occupied strategic positions like pieces on a chessboard. Bentinck, now Lord Portland, had an English counterpart in John Churchill, also created earl in the coronation honours and Gentleman of the Bedchamber to the King. His wife Sarah was Lady of the Bedchamber in the rival household of Princess Anne. Another influential pair were Betty Villiers, who resented Portland's close relationship with the King, and her elder sister Lady Fitzharding who belonged to Princess Anne's household. At first a close friend of Sarah Churchill, this lady became suspect after an anonymous letter warned the Princess, 'have a care of what you say before Lady Fitzharding, remember she's Lord Portland and Betty Villarsis sister. You may depend upon't that these two are not ignorant of what is said and done in your lodgings'. They must have known for instance that Princess Anne and Sarah in their gossipy letters referred to the King as 'Caliban', 'the Monster', and even 'the Dutch abortion'—knowledge unlikely to improve family relationships.[8]

One of the chessmen was temporarily kept in check when in 1692 Marlborough, accused of intriguing with King James II, was sent to the Tower for two months and remained in disgrace for the next six years. Sarah blamed Portland for this: 'he had ever a great prejudice to my Lord Marlborough'. Princess Anne, too, was found to have been corresponding secretly with her father, which gave William and Mary an excuse to downgrade her. She was turned out of her apartments in Whitehall and told to dismiss Sarah, an order she defied. This only served to strengthen Sarah's influence over the Princess.

It was a mere pawn who had the greatest effect upon Lord Portland and his friendship with the King. This was the King's handsome debonair page of honour, Arnoud Joost van Keppel, a young Dutchman who gradually drew to himself more and more of the King's favour. Aided and abetted by Betty Villiers, he was promoted to be Groom of the Bedchamber when he was 21, a move which aroused fierce jealousy in Portland as it meant Keppel was firmly installed in the King's intimate circle.

***

Much else was going on politically, but in December 1694 a totally unexpected domestic tragedy occurred. Shortly after Purcell had composed his gloriously joyful 'Come ye Sons of Art away' to celebrate her 32nd birthday, the Queen, so much younger, livelier and healthier than her ailing husband, caught smallpox and died in a few days. The King realised too late that he had lost a treasure, and was at first so distraught that people thought he was going out of his mind. One of his first resolutions, in response it was said to the Queen's deathbed wish, was to get rid of Betty Villiers. She was married off to an earl and given a golden handshake in the form of vast estates in Ireland. Thus two significant pieces were removed from the chessboard.

The dismissal of Betty Villiers, though seemingly virtuous, had disastrous consequences. The emotional gap caused by the removal of the two women closest to him drove the King into greater dependence on the cheerful young Keppel. John Macky, another commentator on the passing scene, writes that Keppel

being supported by my Lord Sunderland, and Mrs. Villiers, to pull down my Lord Portland, came to be chief favourite of that Prince ... He was King William's constant Companion in all his Diversions and Pleasures ... had a great influence over the King, is beautiful in his Person; open and free in his conversation; very expensive in his Manner of Living.[9]

Soon after the Queen's death the King promoted Keppel to the position of Master of the Robes, provoking a bystander, commiserating with a friend who had a swollen foot, to remark, 'Portland and some others are suffering in their feet from new shoes'.[10] Two years later, when he was barely 27 and with no record of public service to his adopted country, Keppel was created Baron Ashford, Viscount Bury and Earl of Albemarle, titles as imposing as those given to William Bentinck after his many years of loyal service. Along with Betty Villiers and Portland, he was given great estates in Ireland—an extravagant hand-out which

25 Arnoud Joost van Keppel, 1st Earl of Albemarle, painted by the fashionable portrait painter Sir Godfrey Kneller. (National Portrait Gallery)

26 William III (artist unknown) in typical pose as a military leader, with soldiers in battle array in the background. A portrait of King William on horseback by Sir James Thornhill hung in the anteroom of the Great Lodge in William Duke of Cumberland's day. (An engraving in the National Portrait Gallery.)

annoyed Parliament. People openly likened the King and Albemarle to Edward II and Piers Gaveston, but William as always seemed impervious to the effect of his conduct on those around him. What Portland found insufferable was the King's open blandishment of Keppel around the court, and Keppel's insolent behaviour to himself. Without this he might have been able to understand that the King, who had never known his father and never had a son, needed both the wise old friend of a lifetime and the cheerful affection of his young protégé; but as it was, the situation was publicly humiliating as well as privately wounding to Portland, and he began to find it intolerable. The King tried to placate him by giving him other offices and rewards: he was made Knight of the Garter in February 1697, and, May having conveniently died, Ranger of the Great Park in March.

Though he was pleased with this appointment, Portland was not easily placated. His jealousy and sense of outrage reached such a pitch that he decided the only solution was to remove himself from the scene. He retreated to Windsor Lodge and wrote to the King declaring his intention of resigning from all his offices. This struck the King like a thunderbolt. There followed a series of letters between them, written in French, the language always used by these two English Dutchmen for their correspondence. Bentinck never stepped beyond the bounds of the respect due from a subject to a king, but the King wrote in the most affectionate terms, 'How can you do this after all the friendship I have shown you, and knowing in your heart how much I love you', and at six o'clock in the morning after a conversation with Portland had given him a sleepless night: 'What you have said leaves me no rest, loving you so tenderly, as I have done all my life, though you refuse to believe it ... Do not think of doing something you will regret all your life'.[11] Finally the King turned to a mutual friend, the Prince of Vaudemont, asking him to intercede for him, saying, 'I know his positive character which makes me very afraid'.[12] Previously the King had spoken to Portland about going as ambassador to France to discuss the vexed question of the Spanish succession, and it was partly because he felt committed to this that Portland agreed not to resign. The King greeted this decision with joy, ending his letter to his friend, and all subsequent letters until the final break, with the words, 'it is impossible to love you more perfectly than I do'.[13]

Portland left for Paris at the end of December 1697 accompanied by his 16-year-old son Henry and a large retinue. He made the most of his time there, living in grand style. He was much admired by the French and honoured by Louis XIV, as he was at pains to point out to his master. Saint-Simon gives a picture of how he appeared to a Frenchman:

> His suite was numerous and superb, his expenditure on a most magnificent scale at table, in horses, liveries, equipage, furniture, dress, crockery, in everything; and he displayed besides exquisite taste and refinement. Portland himself was characterised by a personal distinction, a polish, an air of a man of the world and of a courtier, gallant and graceful manners which surprised everyone. With all that, he had much dignity, even haughtiness, exercised however with discernment and ready judgement, which risked nothing. The French who run after a novelty, good entertainment, good cheer and magnificence, were charmed with him. He won them over with discrimination, like a man acquainted with our Court, and who only desired good and distinguished company. Soon it became the fashion to see him, to have fêtes for him, and to receive banquets from him.[14]

In France he was able to pursue the passionate interest in gardens which he shared with William who, according to Defoe, 'was allowed to be the best judge of such things then living in the world'. In 1689 the King had appointed him Superintendent of the Royal Gardens, and they continued the work begun by Charles II in creating magnificent gardens in the French style at Hampton Court, at a cost of £45,000; now they had plans for gardens at Windsor Castle, and Portland seized the opportunity to gain ideas for this project.[15] He took with him to France his Deputy Superintendent, George London, and they visited the gardens at various châteaux: Portland found these disappointing—he thought they did better in Holland; indeed it would have been hard to match the standard of the gardens at his fine estate at Sorgvliet or those of the King at Het Loo. They met Louis XIV's gardener Le Nôtre, who drew up plans for the gardens at Windsor and followed this up by sending his nephew and pupil Claude Desgots to England, where the King received him lavishly.[16]

Throughout this time in France there was a frequent friendly interchange of letters between the King and Portland. The King gives him news of home—reassures him about his eldest daughter's illness, tells him of the progress of work on his house (the Lodge was being put in order for him), and mentions borrowing his dogs to hunt in the Great Park, which he is glad to report is clear of rabbits, thanks to the instructions given by the new Ranger to his keepers. He asks Portland to go shopping for him for furniture, brocades and damasks, which like any modern tourist Portland finds to be of poorer quality and dearer than at home. The King's letters always end with his customary expression of affection.

Portland returned in the summer of 1698 with his mission successfully accomplished, but his respite was short-lived. Though it had been a relief not to be at court, it was also dangerous to be away because of the movements taking place in the meantime. He found the situation even worse than before: from Albemarle the same impertinence publicly displayed, and his old rival Marlborough reinstated and riding high in the King's favour through Albemarle's influence. Marlborough had been given the very special post of governor to Princess Anne's son the Duke of Gloucester who, if he survived, would one day become king. 'My lord', said the King, 'make him what you are, and my nephew will be all I wish him.'[17] Thus Marlborough was able to prepare the way for his own place close to the throne in days to come, whereas Portland, disliked by Princess Anne, had no political future without William. Seeing the way the wind was blowing, the timeservers at court turned against him, and Portland was too proud, or too hurt, to defend himself. Sir William Temple's sister, writing to her niece

Jane Temple, later to become Portland's second wife, told her how Portland had been 'used as a dog', and reflected,

> people are but too apt to insult, when one is falling, and when nobody will help to right one. I believe one has seldom the heart to do anything towards it themselves, this they say, has extremely exalted another person and altogether is thought more than my Lord Portland can bear any longer.[18]

In December 1698 the King granted Portland the keepership of the Little Park at Windsor; but this small gesture did nothing to improve the unhappy state of affairs at court. A solitary widower, his beloved eldest daughter Mary having recently married the Earl of Essex, Portland, at the King's request, spent most of his time at the Lodge, occupied with the gardens there and at Windsor. He had the expert help of George London and his gifted associate Henry Wise, who had set up a great commercial nursery at Brompton to the west of London, making the supplying of plants easier. The fine lime-tree avenue from the Lodge to the Cow Pond was planted at this time and probably the shape of the Cow Pond formalised (see Wise's map, Figure 36), providing the *allée* and *pièce d'eau* which were desirable, almost obligatory, at this time when the Dutch and French influences were so great. Limes were much in vogue as ornamental trees

27   William III's joyful letter to Portland after their temporary reconciliation in June 1697 (from the original in the Portland Collection in Nottingham University Library):

> I cannot express well enough the joy I have in what the Prince of Vaudemont has told me, that at last you have decided to come back to my side, I hope that your health will allow you to do this very soon, and that you will never regret it; to this I will try to contribute all that I can. And you also from your side; and be assured that it is impossible to love you more perfectly than I do.

and the fashion received an impetus under Dutch influence, Holland being almost as renowned for lime-trees then as it is for bulbs today. Lord Melbourne told Queen Victoria that the limes at Cumberland Lodge were brought over by William III and planted by the Whigs: 'They say if you see many lime-trees in a place it shows it belonged to a Whig'.[19] Sir William Trumbull, a neighbour of Portland living at Easthampstead, wrote to him in 1697 saying, 'I have been twice to view your Lordship's garden in Windsor Park and had great satisfaction to see the very fine avenue to the Lodge so well ordered and in so good a forwardness'.[20]

London and Wise were adept at tree-planting, having learnt methods used at Versailles where oaks 100 years old

> were taken up with so much art, and by the strength of such engines, by which such a monsterous quantity of earth was raised with them, that the trees could not feel their remove, that is to say, their growth was not at all hindered.

28 The Lime-Tree Avenue, looking towards Cumberland Lodge; it was created by Lord Portland, following a French fashion for grand avenues, and a Dutch fashion for limes.

At Hampton Court limes had been removed 'by the dextrous hand of the head gardener after some of them had been almost thirty years planted in other places'.[21] They were transported (sometimes from Holland) in huge baskets which were buried in the earth with the trees. This is how the neighbourly Trumbull was able to admire the forwardness of the avenue at Windsor Lodge. Anyone walking down it today can look with awe at these tall trees, their gnarled trunks bearing the scabs and scars of generations of lopping and pruning. The avenue is a fine memorial to William Bentinck.

An aerial photograph taken in 1952 shows shadowy traces to the south and west of the house, hinting at the walkways and terraces, the parterres and fountains which formed part of Portland's garden. There were flowerbeds, which he was surprised not to see in France, lawns and clipped evergreens, box and holly and yew (typically Dutch), which gave colour in the winter. The orchards were replenished with new fruit-trees brought from France: there were many more varieties than there are today. Rhododendrons appeared in England in the later 17th century, and became a feature of the gardens at Bulstrode; the soil of the Great Park was right for them, so a tradition lasting to the present day may have begun at this time. To say Portland was an enthusiastic gardener does not mean that he ever lifted a spade. The gardens at Windsor Lodge were included in the remit of the Superintendent of the Royal Gardens, who was supported by a Deputy Superintendent, a Comptroller, a Paymaster, a Clerk of Works, and a whole army of gardeners. Portland's annual allowance for the royal gardens was £4,800 (working out at about £60 an acre), so it was not too difficult to keep them in trim.

29 Aerial view of Cumberland Lodge, 1952. Traces of the old formal gardens can be seen in the bottom left-hand corner. In the middle distance to the right is Royal Lodge, and the Long Walk can be seen in the background, stretching to Windsor from the equestrian statue of George III on Snow Hill.

John Macky, after visiting Portland's house at Bulstrode, said that he 'had a very good Taste in Architecture and Furniture. Nothing can be finer than the Terraces, by which they descend from the Apartments to the Gardens'. Something of the same effect may have been achieved at Windsor Lodge, using the lie of the land on the south side. Carpingly, Macky also says, 'He is supposed to be the richest subject in Europe, very profuse in Gardening, Birds, and Household Furniture, but mighty frugal and parsimonious in everything else', a statement which conflicts with Saint-Simon's observation of his way of life in France, and perhaps illustrates the contemporary prejudice against the King's Dutch friends.[22]

Portland was said to have greatly improved the Lodge, but apart from the gardens and interior furnishings, we know nothing positively about this. Either he or Sarah (the fashion coming rather too late for Baptist May) installed 'shash windows', as they were called in a painter's bill of 1726 (the word came from the French word *châssis* meaning frame).[23] Like lime-trees, the fashion came via Holland and the Dutch connection points to Portland. Dutch joiners had installed them at Ham House in 1673, and they were put into a room at Windsor Castle about 1686.[24] Indoors at the Lodge there was the comfort of damasks and brocades, good furniture, some certainly brought from Holland, and portraits of people he knew and admired. Writing from Windsor to his friend the diplomat Richard Hill, Portland speaks warmly of a duchess known to them both, an unidentified lady for whom he expresses 'respect and venera-tion', whose portrait by Kneller 'forms the great adornment of my chamber, and the pleasant centre of my solitude, along with that of the Prince and Duchess of Vaudemont'.[25] Kneller painted all the great personages of the day: the King and Portland both sat for him in 1697, and Portland's daughter Mary, Countess of Essex, was one of Kneller's Hampton Court Beauties. The fine portrait of Portland in the National Portrait Gallery, painted about 1698 in the studio of Hyacinthe Rigaud, shows a handsome middle-aged man with strong features and half-smiling expression, bearing no resemblance to the 'wooden fellow' Marlborough had disparagingly called him.[26] Facing this picture in the Gallery is Kneller's portrait of Albemarle as a young man in his early twenties, whose rather fleshy face looks out with all the bland assurance of youth and favour.

During 1699 the situation at court became the main subject of gossip, and the climax came at the end of April. Gossip noted that instead of accompanying the King to Newmarket, Portland had retired to Windsor Lodge, pleading a cold; he was nerving himself for the final break. On the King's return, he waited upon him and begged leave to resign all his offices. He then returned to the Lodge. The King sent messengers after him to talk him into changing his mind, but without success. On 1 May Portland sat down and wrote a carefully worded and dignified letter, finally taking leave of the King; the draft can be seen today in the Portland archives, the crossings-out and rewordings making it all the more poignant. The King, deeply chagrined, came out to Windsor on 10 May, dining with Portland at the Lodge. There were unfortunately no witnesses to tell how the conversation went, but though it was rumoured at court that 'Portland has accepted of the key again' (the symbolic key of the Groom of the Stole), he remained obdurate.[27] The King wrote a last reproachful and tender letter, ending with the old affectionate formula; after Portland's firm reply, this formula was never repeated in their correspondence. How deeply hurt he was can be judged by his ability to withstand such pressure from the King.

The agreement between them was that Portland would keep the Rangership of the Great and Little Parks and remain in residence at the Lodge; he would also continue as Superintendent of the Royal Gardens, and he would be at the King's disposition for diplomatic missions as before.

They remained on civil terms, though both suffered deeply from their estrangement. However, for Portland, a sardonic bystander observed, there were compensations: 'Twenty millions that he had amassed, having had less than 100 florins of his own, served to console him, and to make his retirement supportable to him'.[28] Perhaps because he was released from this relationship he was able to turn his mind elsewhere; a year later, on 4 May 1700, he married Jane Temple, niece of his friend the ambassador Sir William Temple. Twenty-eight years old, she was the widow of Lord Berkeley of Stratton, and was said by the gossips to be 'worth £20,000'. After spending summer in Holland, in September Portland brought his bride to the Lodge, which had been repaired in his absence. With her he had a second family of two sons and four daughters.

With this new family, and the interest of the marriages of his older children, Portland was surrounded by warmth and domestic comfort. Publicly, however, things were not so pleasant. He had always had enemies, particularly among the Tories, and these seized their opportunity now that he was no longer high in the King's favour. In 1701 there was an attempt by the Tory majority in the House of Commons to impeach him over his conduct of diplomatic negotiations with France, but the impeachment was voted out by the Whig majority in the Lords. At this time Luttrell wrote,

> I am not a friend of the Earl of Portland, but it provokes me almost to compassion that among so many persons, who once in the time of his favour and power, counted themselves happy to receive from him a smile or a slight nod, or to drink chocolate with his lackeys in his ante-room, here not a single one standing up for him.[29]

30 Jane Temple, Countess of Portland: portrait by Michael Dahl, at Petworth. A widow of 28 when she married the Earl of Portland, she outlived him by 42 years.

Meanwhile a great sadness had befallen Prince George and Princess Anne in that on 30 July 1700 the only survivor out of her 17 children, the 11-year-old Duke of Gloucester, who like the others was hydrocephalic, died of a fever. It was an unutterable sorrow to Princess Anne, and indeed also to William. Though despite everything she still courageously hoped to bear a healthy child, it never happened, and this meant that though Anne would succeed to the throne after her brother-in-law, the future succession would again be in doubt. When her father died in 1701, his son was hailed by Louis XIV as King James III. Stuart hopes were far from dead, neither were Louis' expansionist ambitions: he again invaded the Dutch borders. With great foresight William gave Marlborough command of the force sent to deal with this latest threat; thus he put in place his military successor, and ensured that his life's work of resistance to the French king's aggression would be continued.

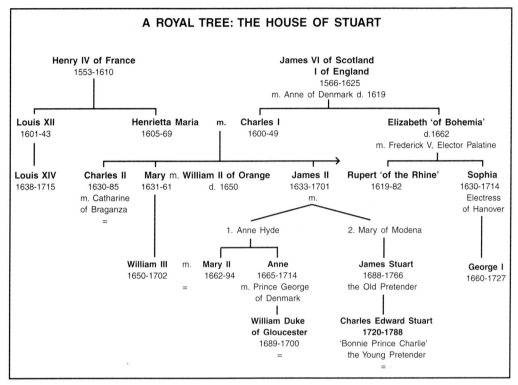

A ROYAL TREE: THE HOUSE OF STUART

Henry IV of France
1553-1610

James VI of Scotland
I of England
1566-1625
m. Anne of Denmark d. 1619

Louis XII
1601-43

Henrietta Maria
1605-69
m.
Charles I
1600-49

Elizabeth 'of Bohemia'
d.1662
m. Frederick V, Elector Palatine

Louis XIV
1638-1715

Charles II
1630-85
m. Catharine
of Braganza
=

Mary m. William II of Orange
1631-61   d. 1650

James II
1633-1701
m.

Rupert 'of the Rhine'
1619-82

Sophia
1630-1714
Electress
of Hanover

1. Anne Hyde

2. Mary of Modena

William III
1650-1702
m.

Mary II
1662-94
=

Anne
1665-1714
m. Prince George
of Denmark

James Stuart
1688-1766
the Old Pretender

George I
1660-1727

William Duke
of Gloucester
1689-1700
=

Charles Edward Stuart
1720-1788
'Bonnie Prince Charlie'
the Young Pretender
=

31 A royal tree showing the relationship between Louis XIV, Charles II and William III.

King William's health was deteriorating, though with heroic efforts, by ceaseless diplomacy and warfare, he strove to keep the balance of power in Europe and to protect the interests of his two states, England and the Netherlands; but his death when it came was unexpected. He was hunting the stag in Richmond Park in February 1702 when his horse stumbled on a molehill, causing him to be thrown off and break his collar-bone. He was expected to recover in a few days but his condition worsened dramatically; a fortnight later it was clear that he was mortally ill. Albemarle hurried over from Holland and was at the King's bedside before he lost consciousness; Portland, who was no further away than Bulstrode, arrived on 8 March in time only to hold the King's hand as he died. So the King was removed from the chessboard, to the secret delight of the Jacobites, who drank toasts 'to the little gentleman in black velvet'. Princess Anne became Queen, Portland retired to Bulstrode, Albemarle returned to Holland. The Marlboroughs were in the ascendant, ready for the start of another game.

32 Queen Anne with her son William Duke of Gloucester, on whose succession to the throne her heart was set; he
at the age of 11, the longest-lived of all her children. (Portrait from the studio of Kneller in the National Portrait Gal

Chapter Five

The Redoubtable Sarah
1702-1746

1: Sunshine Days, 1702-1714

Queen Anne was crowned on 23 April 1702, and with this event the story of the Lodge becomes the story of Sarah Churchill. It was Anne's 'sunshine day' (her own phrase), looked forward to through all the tribulations of her life during the previous régime. She was crowned, but Sarah managed the Queen, her husband commanded the armed forces, and their friend Sidney Godolphin was chief minister. Anne put all her trust in them: 'We four must never part, till death mowe us down with his impartial hand'. Long before, in her generous way, Anne had given them all nicknames, partly for fun and partly to avoid ceremony: she was Mrs. Morley, Sarah Mrs. Freeman 'because of my frank and open temper', Marlborough Mr. Freeman and Godolphin Mr. Montgomery.

Sarah's influence over the Queen went back to their childhood:

I came extreme young into the Court and had the luck to be liked by many in it but by none more particularly than the Queen who took such pleasure in my Company that as she had me much about her so upon her marriage she prevailed with her Father that I should be a Lady of her Bedchamber.[1]

In 1673, at the age of 13, Sarah followed her elder sister Frances Jennings, of legendary beauty, to court as one of the four maids of honour to Anne's stepmother, the 15-year-old Duchess of York. It says much for the strength of character of the two Jennings girls that they were able to avoid the pitfalls of this position, and make sound marriages. When Sarah was 15 she met Colonel John Churchill, who has already made his entry to our story by jumping out of Barbara Villiers's bedroom window. He was a member of the Duke's entourage, ten years her senior, handsome, gallant, ambitious. Both had come to court in the wake of an older sister and from similar backgrounds, their parents being country gentry. They saw each other at court receptions and 'drawing-rooms', at balls and festivities, and fell in love. It was a stormy court-ship—how could it have been otherwise with Sarah? John had Barbara Villiers to explain away, and his parents were intent on a match with a rich heiress; but these obstacles were removed: Barbara went to live in France, and the heiress became yet another mistress of the Duke of York, ending up as a countess. Unlike princes and princesses, John and Sarah were able to marry for love, and in 1678 or thereabouts (Sarah later said she had forgotten the date) they were married secretly in the presence of the Duchess of York. Secret marriages were quite usual, even rather chic, and it would have been in keeping with Sarah's character to avoid the fuss and expense of a grand wedding.

33 John and Sarah Churchill, Duke and Duchess of Marlborough. A portrait of the Duchess by Kneller (see Figure 39) has been put together with one of the Duke by Seeman to form this composite picture, now at Beaulieu.

At this time she was enchanting, a radiant beauty with masses of fair hair which she washed herself in honey water to preserve its colour. 'I fancy the best thing I had was the colour of my hair,' she wrote in old age to her grand-daughter.[2] Once in a fit of pique she cut it off to spite her husband. He studiously ignored the incident, refusing to be provoked; but after his death Sarah found the shorn tresses laid away among his greatest treasures, and dissolved into tears.

Their married life was unsettled as John was away so often on campaigns, but this prevented their love from becoming stale, and they were prodigious letter-writers. Sarah's petulance and vigorous opinions must have been an attraction in youth, but even when age and disappointments had hardened them into crabbedness and arrogance, John remained devoted to her, and after his death, though she was over 60, she attracted ardent suitors.

In 1683 Anne married Prince George of Denmark; when she set up a household of her own, Sarah was appointed First Lady of the Bedchamber with apartments near to her in Whitehall, and the close relationship between them developed. The Churchills' connivance with Anne during the 1688 revolution bound them together, as did the growing hostility between Anne and her brother-in-law, the new King. Anne's letters are full of expressions of affection for Sarah: 'Her fellow I do really believe is not to be found the world over, & I am sure I never can have any freind that will bee so deare to me as she is'; and 'As long as I live I must be Endeavouring to show that never any body had a Sincerer passion for another than I have for Dear Dear Mrs. Freeman'.[3]

Queen Anne lost no time in taking leave of her predecessor's household, and a new set of people moved into the palace of Whitehall. Like King William she showered her favourites with honours. The Earl of Marlborough was made Knight of the Garter, the highest royal honour the sovereign could bestow, as well as being appointed Captain-General of the army and Master of the Ordnance; before the year was out he had been made Duke. Sarah was given all the positions closest to the sovereign: Groom of the Stole, Mistress of the Robes and Keeper of the Privy Purse as well as First Lady of the Bedchamber, with emoluments amounting to £6,000 a year. The two older Churchill daughters, Henrietta and Anne, were among the ten Ladies of the Bedchamber; Sarah had already introduced a poor relation, her cousin Abigail

34 Sidney Godolphin, Lord High Treasurer under Queen Anne, by Kneller. He was the fourth member of the quartet ruling the country at this time, and was closely involved with the Marlboroughs: his son married their daughter Henrietta, and he was the godfather of their son John. He is shown holding the white wand of this office and wearing the garter and George of the Order of the Garter (St George being its patron saint).

Hill, as one of the four women of the bedchamber. Sidney Godolphin was appointed Lord High Treasurer. The Whigs were now in control, the Tories being tainted with Jacobite sympathies at this time.

It was Godolphin who gave the Queen a nudge about the Rangership, coveted by Sarah ever since, as a young woman, she used to ride in the Park with Anne and admire the Lodge, saying how much she would like to live there 'for the air'. Before she could have it, Portland would have to go. A week after Godolphin's appointment to the Treasury he wrote to Sarah,

> I have had no trouble about the Lodge but the troublesome visit I told you of [from Lord Portland], for which the Lodge was but a pretence, the reality being a debt of £10,000 which he says he layd out by the King's order, and [was] never repayed, which is not impossible, nor doe I think he will tell a lie in cold blood.

He was ready to push the matter of the Lodge ahead, for three days later he wrote again to Sarah,

> Being to attend her majesty tomorrow in the Treasury for the first time, I have asked her if I should bring a warrant with me to give you the Lodge, but she seemed rather inclined to deferr it till you came to town, being desirous, as I imagined, to settle that matter first with you.

The same day the Queen wrote to Sarah,

> Lord and Lady Portland took their leave of me this morning. She I thought looked a little grave, but he was in one of his gracious ways, and I fancy is fool enough to think his unreasonable demands will some time or other be complied with. But if they were never soe just, and that one has money to throw away, I think he should be one of the last to be considered. Mentioning this worthy person puts me in mind to ask dear Mrs. Freeman a question which I should have don some time ago, and that is if you would not have the Lodge for your life, because the warrant must be made accordingly, and anything that is of soe much satisfaction as this poor place seems to be to you, I would give my deare Mrs. Freeman for all her days, which I pray God may be many and as truly happy as this world can make you.[4]

With pointed spite Anne went out of her way to show generosity to Lord Albemarle. Portland wound up his affairs and retired to his country seat to redesign his splendid garden there, and leave court life behind him. He took an interest in local affairs, founding a school at Gerrards Cross. Still involved in diplomacy, in November 1709 he made his last crossing home from Holland in the company of the Duke of Marlborough, who was returning home from his last battle, Malplaquet. His constitution was no longer strong enough to resist the rigours of the North Sea, and he caught a chill. Two weeks later he died at Bulstrode.[5]

At the beginning of the new reign rumour was rife about who would be appointed to which office, not least the Rangership of the Great Park, since this appointment showed very particularly the sovereign's high favour. It was unusual for a woman to be made Ranger, and this perhaps explains why for the first time the grant was made out for the lives of three persons instead of one as in the past:

> Our Rt. Trusty and Wellbeloved Cousin and Counsellor John Earle of Marlborough and Sarah his wife and John Churchill Esqr. commonly called Lord Churchill son and heir apparent of the said John Earle of Marlborough and the life of the longest liver of them.[6]

Previous grants of the Rangership had been 'during pleasure' or at most for the life of the grantee, but with this grant the Marlboroughs were installed for two generations. It was the

i Daughter and Heiress
chard Iennings of Sandridge
e County of Hertford Esq.
of Iohn Churchill
uke of Marlborough

Sarah in mourning, by Kneller (in the Green Drawing Room at Blenheim Palace). This was probably painted after the
of her son John.

IV The Duke of Cumberland at the Battle of Dettingen, 1743, by Wootton & Hudson, on loan to Cumberland Lodge the Royal Collection. As in the portrait of Fairfax and William IV, the horse is used to suggest power; the baton symb command.

one position from which they could not be dislodged, come what may. The clerk drawing up the grant copied the text from earlier documents, using the same wording as for Baptist May and for Sir Edward Nicholas before him. Hence, though the 'Lodges commonly called Mannor Lodge, Hill Lodge, Middle Lodge and Lower Lodge' are included, there is no specific mention of the Great Lodge, except by a slip of the quill as the clerk writes 'and all that walk called the paddock walk within the said Great Lodge'. However, the Great Lodge is covered by the inclusion of 'all other houses edifices buildings stables barnes yards orchards gardens and curtilages within the said parke'—the all-embracing statement which had so upset John Barry. The Little Park (or Home Park) was included in the same royal warrant: Portland had eventually become Ranger of both parks, so the Churchills were given both from the start.

The grant was made out to Anthony Guydot and John Coggs as trustees. Anthony Guydot of Lincoln's Inn was legal adviser to the Churchills and was particularly fond of Sarah, to whom on his death in 1707 he left £5,000 (unnecessarily, one is bound to feel). John Coggs was their banker and also, conveniently, dealt with Sarah's accounts as Keeper of the Privy Purse and Mistress of the Robes. Marlborough saw to it that his brothers shared his good fortune. Charles was promoted to the rank of general in the army, and George became admiral of the fleet and also in 1704 Deputy Ranger of the Little Park at Windsor, where he amused himself by embellishing his lodge and creating fine gardens and a splendid aviary.

With their thriving family the Marlboroughs had the world at their feet. Sarah, now in middle age, was still dazzling both in looks and in vivacity. On public occasions she often occupied Prince George's place in the Queen's coach when he felt 'unable to endure the fatigue'.[7]

A grand lady indeed! John was said by a contemporary (who was no friend of his) to be 'one of the handsomest men ever seen'.[8] Three of their four daughters had already married into the high nobility, with extravagant dowries provided by the Queen, and the youngest, Mary, famed for her beauty, was engaged at 14 to the son of one of the richest noblemen in England. Their son John, 'a graceful person and a very promising youth' according to Bishop Burnet, was a 17-year-old student at King's College, Cambridge.[9] Though they had lost their first daughter in infancy, and a son Charles died in 1692 before he was two, compared with the Queen they were fortunate in rearing so many of their children. But early in 1703 they suffered a terrible loss: the young Lord Blandford caught small-pox after a visit to his godfather Lord Godolphin at Newmarket, and ten days later he was dead. Sarah, frantic with grief, repulsed the Queen's kind offers of help

35 Marlborough as Captain-General of the armed forces: an engraving by R. Cooper. In the background to the left a soldier looks on from outside a military tent.

and words of sympathy (though who could better understand what it meant to lose a cherished son and heir?), thus hurting and offending her and widening the rift that was beginning to form between them. For Marlborough, life now seemed pointless. He said to Lord Ailesbury at The Hague, 'I've lost what is so dear to me, it is fit for me to retire and not toil and labour for I know not who'.[10]

Duty called relentlessly, or perhaps mercifully, and Marlborough had to go abroad to prosecute the war against Louis XIV who was making a bid to dominate Europe, and whose support of the Stuart Pretender posed a constant threat to Anne's throne. He wrote lovingly to Sarah from The Hague:

> I received this morning two of your dear letters which I read with all the pleasure imaginable. They were soe very kind, that if it were possible, you are dearer to me ten thousand times than ever you were. I am so intierly yours, that if I might have all the world given to me, I could not be happy but in your love.[11]

Sarah told him to destroy all her letters, but one escaped and is quoted by Sir Winston Churchill in his biography of Marlborough:

> Wherever you are whilst I have life my soul shall follow you, my ever dear Lord Marl, and wherever I am I shall only kill the time, wish for night that I may sleep and hope the next day to hear from you.[12]

***

Marlborough was no doubt glad that while he was away on his endless campaigns Sarah had the new interest of arranging the Lodge to her liking. He was eager to hear about it, and in May 1703 he wrote, 'Since my last I have received none of yours, soe that I know not how you are satisfied with the Lodge'. Sarah was not satisfied. Changes had to be made, and Marlborough agreed with her: 'I find by what you write of the man that has a care of your Parke, that you should not lose time in parting from him'.[13] As for the house itself, Sarah embarked on important alterations and additions. If Portland did not install sash windows then Sarah certainly did. We know she liked them as she had them put into Marlborough House, and urged her grandson John Spencer to install them at Althorp. But her most important addition seems to have been the 'New Buildings' as they were called in an inventory at her death.[14] These included improved offices at the north end of the house, where a later plan shows small wing-like extensions, and where Sandby's engraving shows additional buildings. If this was the work referred to in an account at Blenheim relating to Windsor Lodge dated July 1704, it was considerable, costing over £2,500.[15] The account remains silent on what was done but lists by name the people concerned: mason, carpenter, bricklayer, glazier, plumber, painter, joiner and two smiths—all the people needed for a new building. They were all employees of the Office of Works, most of them in the Windsor Castle section. It was quite usual for outside work to be undertaken, and for Sarah at Windsor with her court connections this would be an obvious way of getting the work done. Nicholas Hawksmoor, Wren's assistant and also attached to the Office of Works, may have been involved, as Sarah certainly used his services. In 1715 she recommends him to a friend, referring to his unofficial work for her:

> I am so earnest with you to do him good, after the long experience which I have had of him, not only from what concerns hee had in the Building of Woodstock, but from what most people approved of my hous at Windsor, in which he assisted me under hands.[16]

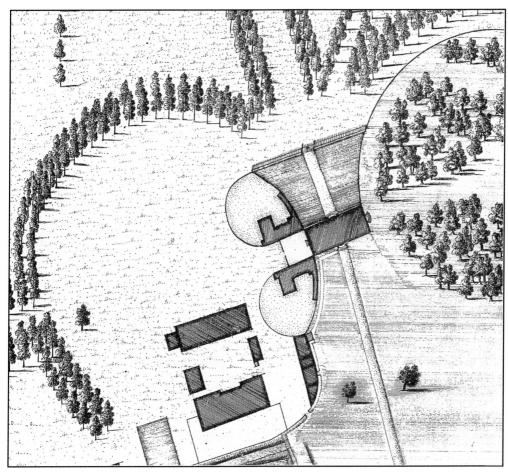

36 This detail of a plan dated 1747 shows the additions made to the north end of the Lodge, presumably by the Duchess of Marlborough. Byfield's circles of trees remain, and Portland's Lime-Tree Avenue can be seen at the top right of the drawing. It is in King George III's topographical collection in the British Library, much of which came from the Duke of Cumberland's library. (K Top VII 38 2a)

By April 1704 she had renovated the house enough to be almost ready to receive visitors: she wrote to her neighbour Sir William Trumbull (the same who admired Lord Portland's avenue), 'I shall be extreme glad to see you at the Lodge, which I hope will be in some order at your return'.[17] But further building operations had yet to be carried out in the outbuildings. Marlborough, interested in every detail, wrote from abroad while preparing his Blenheim campaign in June 1704,

> You have forgot to order Hodges to send me a draft of a stable, as I directed him for the Lodge; for it ought not to be made use of til the yeare after it is bilt, and as I see you have set your heart on that place I should be glad all conveniencys were set aboutt itt.

Charles Hodges, their steward at Windsor, quickly despatched a draft, but it was still not right: 'The draft of the stable that is sent mee, they have forgot to tell mee what breadth it is to have'. Flitcroft's plan (see Figure 50) shows 'the old stable' which he was later to incorporate into the new one he designed for the Duke of Cumberland, and this may have been the stable Hodges was concerned with. It can be seen today as the half of the Mews block nearer to the

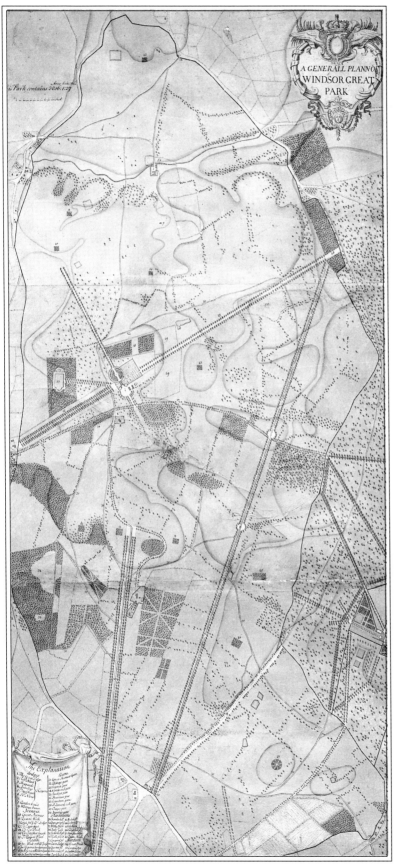

37 Plan of the Great Park by Henry Wise, who was in charge of the royal gardens after Portland's retirement. It shows the Park criss-crossed by Queen Anne's Chaize Ridings. Celia Fiennes must have ridden along Queen Anne's Ride (top right), turned right at Sandpit Gate in order to look at the Duchess of Marlborough's 'little house', then turned left to join the 'fine gravel way' (the Long Walk) to Windsor. The map also shows the Cow Pond given a formal shape, and the Lime-Tree Avenue leading to it. The original is in the Royal Library.

main house, between the present main entrance to the Mews and the link joining it to Groom's House, where in Marlborough's time there was a space. What is now the french window of the conference room was originally the main entrance. Outside can still be seen the fine herring-bone pattern of bricks, worn by countless carriage-wheels. Marlborough had a 'sett' of horses (probably a team of six) sent to Sarah from the Netherlands as a gift in 1703, but horses were not the passion for her that they were for Queen Anne. However, she made great use of coaches for visiting her various houses, and the block opposite Studio Cottage stands where the old coach-house stood.

In July 1704, when the major work on the Lodge was completed, Marlborough wrote to Sarah,

> I was soe happy yesterday as to receive yours of 22 and 23d of the last month, by which I find you are att the Lodge; and I doe not doubt much pleased with itt; for considering the whole, it is a very fine place; but as al fruit will not grow soe wel as at St. Albans, you should order Mr. Wise to plant noe fruit but such as is proper for that place.[18]

Sarah had little difficulty in looking after her ten acres of grounds as they were the responsibility of Henry Wise, the royal gardener. The same day that the Queen wrote to Sarah offering her the Lodge for life, she issued an order to Wise:

> It is Her Majesty's pleasure that you forthwith repair to the Lodge in Windsor Park, late the Earl of Portland's, and take into your care and charge the House and Gardens thereto belonging. And all persons concerned are to give obedience to her Majesty's pleasure.[19]

The Queen, thriftier than her predecessor, did not replace Portland as Superintendent of the Royal Gardens, and cut down the amount spent on them; Portland's allowance of £4,800 was reduced to £1,600, Wise's salary being £200 a year. For this he looked after the gardens at Hampton Court, Kensington, Newmarket and Windsor. What this involved was carefully set out. The grass had to be

> rowled, mowd and swept, the Gravele Rowld and wed the Border dungd dug hoed raked and wed the Hedge Lines Clipt, the severall hardy and other Plants Staked tyed up, pruin'd and clipt, the fruit Trees pruin'd and nail'd, and the severall collections of Housed Greens and Flower Rootes to be well managed and kept in good order.

As regards 'the House in the Great Park'

> The several gardens as now made and as now kept up at this time, to be looked after in all those works as before mentioned, finding and providing the several working tools and materials, dung only excepted, being always at the stable to the House; for it is impossible to have dung for the Gardens any other ways than from what is made at the stable.

The gardeners' working tools and materials included 'Tubbs and Potts for the Orange Trees and other Plants and Flowers, Trewolls, Sythes, Watering Potts, Edging Irons, and a sort of Ingine to sprinkle the Severall Trees and Shrubs'.[20]

Longing to be home from his exhausting campaign, Marlborough wrote after the victory of Blenheim, 'I can easily beleive that the Park is much changed for the better. I could wish with all my soul ... that I had the happiness of being there with you'.[21]

Visitors then as now admired the setting of the Lodge. In a letter to Stella, Swift told her he rode out from Windsor, 'to see Cranburn, a house of Lord Ranelagh's, and the duchess of

38 Marlborough's official despatch after the victory at Blenheim dated 14 August 1704, (from SP87/2) in the Public Record Office. The messenger delivered it to Sarah in London, and she sent it on to the Queen.

Marlborough's lodge, and the Park; the finest places they are, for nature and plantations, that ever I saw; and the finest riding upon artificial roads, made on purpose for the Queen'.[22]

Celia Fiennes also, in her chaotic way, describes riding from Cranbourne:

> in a mile you come to a broad open way to Windsor on the left hand, on the right to a little house of the Dutchess of Marlbroughs which is very exact gardens and fountaines cut hedges and groves pailed in, from this house is the fine gravell walk continued very broad between high rows of trees on one hand a fine grove of straite trees. This is three mile to Windsor all a clear visto to the Castle to that which is King Charle's Walke for shooting which you enter by a broad pallasadoe fences the whole breadth of the road.[23]

Queen Anne loved the Park and brought her own innovations to it. In 1710 she instructed Wren to have the Long Walk (then called King Charles's Walke or the King's Avenue) gravelled 'to the top of Snowdon Hill and from thence to pass the Gardeners House till it joins the road that leads from Bishops Gate to Sandpit Gate'.[24] The work was done by Henry Wise, at a cost of £900. Some time between 1704 and 1726 (when he retired) Wise drew a plan of the Park which shows the Queen's Chaize Ridings circling round the beloved Sarah's lodge to join Queen Anne's Ride which was being constructed in 1704. Mindful perhaps of her predecessor's fate, the Queen directed Wise 'to choose a person to catch the moles in both parks at Windsor'.[25] ... The moles have proved invincible.

The attention given to the Lodge in the early years of Queen Anne's reign was to be deflected after Marlborough's brilliant victory over the French at Blenheim in 1704. There was great jubilation in England over the news, dramatically brought to Sarah by an aide-de-camp on horseback who rode eight days to deliver Marlborough's message, which he had scribbled in pencil on the back of a bill. It was some time before Marlborough was able to return. Worn out by the strains of the campaign, he wrote longingly to Sarah in October:

> For thousands of reasons I wish myself with you. Besides, I think if I were with you quietly at the Lodge, I should have more health ... I hope that You may live many years after me, which both by my age and constitution you must do.[26]

Marlborough returned in December to tremendous public acclaim. Parliament awarded him a handsome pension, and the grateful Queen gave him the manor of Woodstock, where a palace worthy of his great achievement was to be built at her expense. This enterprise was destined to cause endless trouble. The Duke, away on further campaigns, left Sarah to supervise it, but the plan was altogether too grand for her taste, and she had no enthusiasm for it. 'By your saying nothing to me of your going to Woodstock, I find your heart is not set on that place as I could wish', he wrote plaintively in July 1706, after his victory at Ramillies.[27] When she did take an interest, the results were disastrous, as she constantly interfered with the work of the architect, Vanbrugh (who referred to her as 'that B.B.B.B. old B. the Duchess of Marlborough').[28] Her answer to Blenheim was to obtain from the Queen the grant of a site next to St James's Palace to build her own great house, which, unlike Blenheim, was to be plain and dignified. With Wren as architect, Marlborough House was begun in 1709 and completed in two years, whereas Blenheim ran into financial difficulties and was not ready for even partial occupation until 1719; by then Marlborough was too infirm to enjoy the tranquil retirement he had longed for.

In 1704 the Duke and Duchess had considered seeking the reassignment of the grant of the Rangership, because of their son's death. Sarah wrote asking Marlborough what name she might put in for 'the thord life in the Park'. He replied 'I desire you will please yourself in itt, and that is what I shall like best'. The new grant was not finally legalised until July 1709, the three lives now being Sarah, her oldest daughter Henrietta and her youngest daughter Mary. As it had always been understood that the Rangership was Sarah's rather than the Duke's, it was no slight to him to be left out. He did, however, make a special plea for his brother George, Deputy Ranger of the Little Park, 'that you would do his for life', adding, because Sarah had fallen out with him, 'When you see him pray say two kind words to him, as being brother to him that loves you with all his heart'.[29] The trustees for the renewed grant were James Craggs (Marlborough's man of business), Samuel Edwards and Charles Hodges, both of whom had keeperships in the Park. Mention was made of the office of Ranger of the Little Park at Windsor and of the new Lodge there now occupied by George Churchill. He died in 1710 and a few years later Sarah gave the Deputy Rangership of the Little Park to her daughter Henrietta, who had married Godolphin's son Francis.

***

During all this time the relationship between the Queen and Sarah had been steadily deteriorating. From the beginning of her reign, Anne had been subjected by Sarah to long political arguments aimed at converting her to Sarah's Whig policies and away from the Tory outlook which was natural to her. The Queen found this boring and out of place; it was one thing to have essential political discussions with her ministers, quite another to have to endure them from her Lady of the Bedchamber when she wanted to gossip and play cards and generally be entertained. Sarah was bored by the ritual of attendance on the Queen—handing her the fan which had been passed to her by the woman of the bedchamber who had been given it by the page. She found court life trivial and false, and absented herself more and more, using Windsor Lodge as her retreat; but this did not stop her from writing long political harangues to the Queen. Godolphin and other friends saw the way the wind was blowing and how dangerous it would be politically to lose their close contact with the Queen, but Sarah was deaf and blind to hints, and vaunted her own sincerity and frankness where a little finesse would have served her cause better.

Gradually and with sadness the Queen turned away from Sarah, and because of her absences from court it was some time before Sarah discovered what everybody else knew, that she had been replaced in the Queen's affections by 'a mere bedchamber woman', who was none other than Abigail Hill, now Mrs. Masham, the poor relation whom she had brought into the royal household herself. Bishop Burnet, a shrewd commentator, wrote of Abigail in words reminiscent of his remarks about Baptist May: 'She learned the arts of a court, and observed the Queen's temper with so much application, that she got far into her heart'.[30] This had a profound effect upon the affairs of the realm, as Abigail was able to help her cousin Harley, a Tory politician, to gain influence over the Queen and eventually cause Marlborough's downfall.

Among those who sympathised with Sarah was Lady Portland, with whom she carried on an amicable correspondence, exchanging occasional visits, as Bulstrode was not far from Windsor Lodge; Lady Portland obliged her by getting tea from Holland and cups and saucers from Japan, through the Dutch trade with the Far East. 'Ye uncertainty of all things in this world,' she wrote, 'and particularly what relates to a court is so well known by experience to me.' And again, 'Yr Grace indeed made me remember what I have seen done to my Lord, in peoples so great earnestness to enquire after ye new favourite'.[31]

Sarah, however, reacted quite differently from the restrained Earl of Portland. She stormed and raged at the Queen, and even went so far as to accuse her of lesbianism: '... nor can I think the having noe inclination for any but one's own sex is enough to maintain such a character as I wish may still be yours'.[32] A strange imputation to make about a woman who had borne 17 children! Hearing of this letter, Marlborough wrote with sublime understatement: 'You say Mrs. Morley has taken no notice of your letter. I think that is a trew sign she is angry'.[33] Even though Sarah hurried from Windsor Lodge by coach at night in October 1708 to be at the Queen's side when her husband was dying, this was more to forestall Mrs. Masham than out of sympathy, and the old friendship was never mended. There was almost a streak of madness in Sarah's relentless pursuit of the Queen. She picked quarrels with her over trifles, and it was reported that she could be heard shouting at the Queen

> in so loud and shrill a voice, that the footmen at the bottom of the back stairs could hear her ... As soon as she had done raging, she flounced out of the room, and said, she did not care if she never saw her more: to which the Queen replied very calmly, that she thought the seldomer the better.

Marlborough was unable to restrain her: 'a man must bear with a good deal, to be quiet at home', he said ruefully to Lord Dartmouth. But quiet at home was not what he got from Sarah. Lord Dartmouth gives us a picture of how Sarah was at this time:

> Lord Cowper told me, he went at this time to the Duke of Marlborough, and found him in bed with a great deal of company in the chamber, and the duchess sitting at the bed-side, ranting in a most extravagant manner against the queen, and said she had always hated and despised her but that fool, her daughter Henrietta (who stood by), had always loved her, and did so still, which she could never forgive her. That surprised him very much, though he had heard more of her temper than he believed: but the duke told him, he must not mind what she said, for she was used to talk at that rate when she was in a passion, which was a thing she was very apt to fall into, and there was no way to help it.

Marlborough hoped to delay the inevitable by persuading Sarah to write a letter of apology to the Queen, but to no avail. In January 1711 the Queen demanded Sarah's resignation: the golden key of the Groom of the Stole's office was to be handed to her within three days. When

Sarah Churchill, after Kneller, showing her proudly wearing the golden key of the Groom of the Stole, which symbolised right of entry to the sovereign's apartments. (National Portrait Gallery)

Marlborough conveyed this news to Sarah, 'she took it from her side and threw it into the middle of the room, and bid him take it up, and carry it to whom he pleased'.[34] The Queen gave the post of Keeper of the Privy Purse to Mrs. Masham, and those of Groom of the Stole and Mistress of the Robes to another new favourite, the Duchess of Somerset. Sarah retired to Windsor Lodge, just as Lord Portland had done. Writing to the Duchess to console her on her dismissal, the Duke's chaplain Dr. Hare shrewdly drew a parallel between her fate and that of Lord Portland:

> I believe your Grace will allow that nothing can come nearer the friendship you had with the Queen than that between Lord Portland and the King, and yet the early and faithful services of the most intimate friend were undermined by, and given up to the secret workings and insinuations of the new favourite ... The greatest difference between his lordship's case and yours is that he was dropt with more decency than your Grace has been, and there remained a civility when his friendship was in a manner gone.[35]

The golden key flung down by Sarah was key to more than her own office. With her influence gone from the centre, everything else began to unravel. Despite further victories at Oudenarde in 1708 and Malplaquet in 1709, the tide had turned against Marlborough, against the endless war with France, and against the Whig administration led by Godolphin. Marlborough returned from his campaigns, not to be acclaimed for his victories, but to face charges of misappropriation of funds. Though the charges were dropped, the Queen found it expedient to dismiss him. Louis XIV could hardly believe his luck on hearing that the invincible 'Malbrouk' had been sacked. Marlborough's experience on the withdrawal of the sovereign's favour followed the pattern of Lord Portland's: threatened with impeachment, avoided by former friends, and cold-shouldered at court. Even Swift, no flatterer, was shocked: 'I question whether ever any wise state laid aside a general who had been successful nine years together whom the enemy so much dread; and his own soldiers cannot but believe must always conquer'.[36]

A further gratuitous affliction was that their lifelong friend Godolphin died in September 1712, devotedly nursed by Sarah herself at her old family home, Holywell House in St Albans. No wonder that a few months later the Marlboroughs went into voluntary exile abroad. They were not to return until the Queen's death in 1714.

2: Out of Favour, 1714-1744

Though the Marlboroughs were much fêted during their travels abroad, in their hearts they longed for home. Sarah wrote to her friend Robert Jennens in 1713, 'I would not have you think that I don't want earnestly to see my friends, and to be in a clean sweet Hous and Garden, though ever so small, for here is nothing of that kind'. And again

> If I could bee now in a Court as pleasing as the present is disagreeable, I would never quit my dear Hous as I have don, but I should be glad to enjoy any of my Hous's with my children and a few friends. That was allways the life that would have been my own Choice, and is now the Height of my ambition: but I have learnt to be contented with any condition that I can't reasonably endeavour to change.

She generously offered the use of the Lodge to her friends, writing again to them in 1714:

> If you should have a mind to take the air when you happen to be in spleen, and cant bear any Company, I beg of you to goe and see my Lodge in Windsor Great Parke, where you will find a clean Place, and every thing that is convenient, and Nobody but a Hous Maid, the Gardener, and the Keepers, that will ride to fetch you anything you want at Windsor; and when the Court is not there, it is, of all the Places

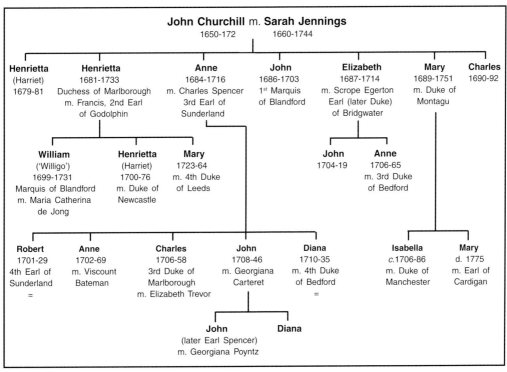

40 Family tree of the 1st Duke and Duchess of Marlborough.

that ever I was in, the most agreeable to me; though there is no Businesse, pray go and see it, for I love to hear that you have been in any place that is mine; and I am confident it will do you good, and if you send to Mr. Hodges, who I have given the best Lodge in the Parke, he will ride about with you, and entertain you with shewing you a great many very pretty Places thereabouts.

In March 1714 their much-loved daughter Elizabeth, Countess of Bridgwater, died of smallpox at the age of 27. 'The Loss of my poor dear Child is indeed very terrible to me,' wrote Sarah to Mr. Jennens.[37] Deeply grieved, and tired of their wanderings (which however Marlborough had put to good use in private diplomacy with both the Elector of Hanover and the Old Pretender), they decided to return home, and set off in July 1714. The Queen, who had been a semi-invalid for years with gout and dropsy, was desperately ill, and as it happened they landed at Dover the day after her death on 1 August. Fears of a French invasion to put the Pretender on the throne proved groundless, and there was no hesitation in proclaiming Anne's distant cousin the Elector of Hanover as her successor. When George I arrived from Hanover a month later he restored Marlborough to the post of Captain-General, saying 'My Lord Duke, I hope your troubles are now all over'.[38]

They were, however, far from over. There was the muddle of Blenheim to cope with: the building had remained becalmed during their absence, and this was a constant source of irritation to Sarah. Marlborough's health was giving cause for concern: he had suffered from headaches since his youth and these were getting worse. The immense physical and mental burdens of his long campaigns were taking their toll. In April 1716 they were again bereaved when their second daughter, Anne, Countess of Sunderland, died of tuberculosis. Anne and

Elizabeth were the daughters dearest to them, Sarah having fallen out with both Henrietta and Mary. The Marlboroughs took over the upbringing of their grand-daughters, sending them to Holywell House where they were looked after in the manner of children of the nobility at that time, by a little 'family' of servants. Sarah visited them as often as she could, but was much tied by her concern for the Duke's health, and rightly so, for a month after Anne Sunderland's death he suffered a stroke which affected his speech and movement. Later the same year Sarah had a final row with Vanbrugh over Blenheim, and shortly afterwards Marlborough had a second stroke, which left his speech impaired and weakened his limbs so that he got about with difficulty. Thinking he was dying, Henrietta and Mary hurried to his bedside, but refused to speak to their mother.

As the building of Blenheim proceeded, Sarah began to plan the interior decoration and furnishings, including 'a vast number of Feather Beds and Quilts ... all such things as will be wanted in that wild unmercifull Hous ... all good and sweet Feathers, even for the Servants'.[39] In the summer of 1719 they were at last able to move into a completed wing. For the Duke it was the beginning of the realisation of a magnificent dream and, surrounded by his grand-children, it was a happy time for him, apart from the undercurrent of bickering between Sarah and their surviving daughters. He tried to patch things up, always standing by Sarah: 'I am not well enough to write so long a letter with my own hand', he wrote to Mary in 1721, 'and I believe I am the worse, to see my children live so ill with a mother, for whom I must have the greatest Tenderness and Regard'.[40] But he wrote in vain; the rift had become permanent.

In 1716, depressed by the sadness of that time, and irritated by the difficulties over her grant as Ranger, Sarah had considered giving up the Lodge, 'which is never like I find to give me anything but trouble'; but by 1720 she was buoyant again, improving the house by adding 'a new eating-room', and improving the grounds by creating a nine-pin alley, where the Duke could take some gentle exercise.[41] Though Blenheim was now habitable, they continued to enjoy Windsor Lodge. In 1720 Sarah wrote to her son-in-law Lord Sunderland whose two younger sons were going to Eton: 'If they are at Eton I shall have opertunities of seeing them oftener then at any school, for as I have altered Windsor lodge tis a thousand times more agreeable than Blenheim & I shall pass the greatest part of my life there'.[42]

She particularly liked it in the summer months, when the grandchildren could come to stay, and she enjoyed having visitors. In May 1717 she wrote to Robert Jennens urging him to

make this Place your Home when the Weather is warmer and they all come to settle here; you may go as often as you please to London, and I am sure this Air will do you good, and no place can be more agreeable than this in the three warm months ... and though the Hous is not large, I am confydent you are all so good as to be contented with what there is.

Sometimes they stayed on into the winter. In 1718 they were still there in October and Sarah wrote to Mr. Jennens:

Notwithstanding the Winter is come, hee has sett no Time for leaving this Place, but says hee will continue here as long as hee can, and as long as hee likes it, and finds any good by going out to take the Air. I shall be better pleasd with being here then in London, but at this Time of Year wee cant stay long, and the Duke of Marlborough's humour allways was to remove of a sudden without giving much warning.[43]

Warning, however was important, as the house they were going to had to be prepared (Sarah was very insistent about beds being properly aired), and the one they were leaving made secure and left in the care of a few servants, the others moving with the family. It was the butler's task to see that the silver was stored in cupboards, chests and trunks and carefully listed. Sarah liked lists and several survive among her papers: 'All this plate was left at the Lodge the 14 November 1717'— but a note at the foot of the page in Sarah's hand reads 'There is more plate there than is write here'.[44]

The Duke and Duchess were again at Windsor Lodge in the summer of 1722 when early in June Marlborough had another stroke, from which it became clear he would not recover. The unwelcome daughters came to see him, to their mother's undisguised displeasure. After his death Sarah wrote up in her 'Green Book' (it was bound in green vellum) a detailed justification of her dealings with her daughters, which includes a vivid account of the deathbed scene. (Because of its importance in the history of Cumberland Lodge this is given in Appendix Two.) With the help of Flitcroft's plan (see Figure 12), the setting can be imagined in the complex

41 The Lime-Tree Avenue in winter. The Duke and Duchess seldom saw this sight as they moved to warmer houses in winter.

of rooms to the left of the front door. The entrance led into the hall, from which one would go into the 'outward room', represented by the present anteroom, on the garden side of which was the drawing-room. The area occupied by the present drawing-room can be reconstructed as being divided into bedchamber, dressing-room and closet. On the other side of the hall were the large and small dining-rooms.

Great folk did not die privately in those days, and in the room besides the Duke and Duchess were their daughters Henrietta and Mary, their grandchildren Harriet (Henrietta's daughter), Anne Egerton, Diana Spencer and her brothers Charles, John, and Robert who had become Earl of Sunderland two months earlier on his father's sudden death. In attendance were doctors, surgeons, apothecaries and servants, among whom were Grace Ridley, Sarah's faithful waiting-woman, and Mrs. Kingdon her companion. No wonder she felt the need to clear people out of the room to get some air. After prayers were said, in which he joined, the Duke was blistered (a medical cure-all used to relieve congestion), and then carried from the narrow couch where he lay, perhaps in the drawing-room, into his bedroom. There, Sarah's 'soul tearing from her body', he died early in the morning of 16 June.

There must have been tremendous turmoil at the Lodge to organise the removal of his body to London, where he was interred with great pomp at Westminster Abbey. On Sarah's death his body was removed to lie beside hers at Blenheim.

So ended one of the great love stories of history.

***

After his son's death, Marlborough had arranged by special Act of Parliament that when he died his eldest daughter Henrietta should become Duchess of Marlborough in her own right. This cannot have been easy for Sarah, and it was not made any better when shortly after her father's death Henrietta sent a brief note to Windsor Lodge addressed to 'the Dutchess Dowager of Marlborough' and signed 'Marlborough'. Perhaps writing her Green Book helped Sarah to vent her spleen; she sent copies to friends in the hope of dispelling the bad reports which she was convinced her daughters were spreading about her in London. Lady Portland was one of the recipients, and wrote to Sarah in commiseration with sentiments that have echoed down the ages: 'I cant tell what reign's in this age, for respect and regard for parents seem extinguisht'.[45]

Sarah, then aged 62, lived on another 22 years. Still beautiful and dynamic, as well as being the richest widow in Europe, she could have married again. One of her suitors was the widowed Duke of Somerset (the builder of Petworth House) whose wife had supplanted Sarah as Groom of the Stole and Mistress of the Robes. She rejected his ardent wooing firmly but with kindness and respect:

> I am confydent that there is very few women (if any) that would not be extreamly pleased with what your Grace proposes to me; but I am resolved never to change my condition and if I know anything of myself I would not marry the Emperor of the world tho I were but thirty years old. [46]

Though for a time she enjoyed his attentions, she knew tht she preferred her independence, and was glad when he found a suitable bride elsewhere.

There were a great many practical matters to keep her busy. She threw herself into the completion of Blenheim with more energy than ever before; this together with the memorials to the Duke took another ten years to achieve. She bought estate after estate, so that there was hardly a county in the southern half of England where she did not own land, rightly believing, especially after the South Sea Bubble of 1720, that this was the best investment. Among these estates was Wimbledon Manor, where she started building yet another house, intended eventually for her favourite grand-daughter, Lady Diana Spencer. Lady Diana and her brother Lord Sunderland each had their own set of rooms—chamber, dressing-room and closet—at Windsor Lodge, and it must have been a colourful house, as comfortable as Sarah could make it. One chamber was upholstered in red damask, another in blue; a chamber with a grey bed was painted red; downstairs there was a room 'hung with ye summer seasons' (tapestries), another with green damask. The general effect of this décor can be seen today at Ham House, Richmond. Sarah said that the drawback was that pictures could be hung only over the mantelshelf or door. She liked pictures and had good ones, which she sometimes acquired at auction sales—for example at the sale of Kneller's effects after his death in 1723, where she bought a portrait of Baptist May.[47]

In the drawing-room were tables for cards, or for Sarah to dispense tea from her 'large chiny tea pot blue and white'; when the fire was not lit a large 'chine jar' was placed in the chimney. The new vogue was for articles from the orient, and Cumberland Lodge has examples of lacquered chests from China and Japan. There were plenty of books—Montaigne's *Essays*, Sir William Temple's *Letters*, Plutarch's *Lives*, Defoe's *Robinson Crusoe* and many more in a big press and in a closet.[48] She read Swift whose view of the world was in tune with hers, she quotes from Dryden and Cowley and she knew Voltaire. Later, when she was too incapacitated to go to the opera, Sarah bought a chamber organ with which she was delighted:

> It is a thing that will play eight tunes. Handel and all the great musicians say it is beyond anything they can do; and this may be performed by the most ignorant person and when you are weary of those eight tunes, you may have them changed for any other that you like. This I think much better than going to an Italian opera.[49]

Lady Diana lived with her grand-mother until her marriage, keeping her company and acting as her secretary when her 'Mamma Duchess's' hands were too painful with gout to write, and above all managing to remain on good terms with her through her genuine fondness for her—though even they had their ups and downs. Diana was now in her late teens, and Sarah was careful to keep her under her eye, and particularly away from the influence of her older sister Anne, Viscountess Bateman, as she, Sarah, wished to have no interference in planning a brilliant match for her.

George II had succeeded his father in 1727, and at the beginning of 1729 his elder son Fredrick Louis, who had been left behind in Hanover, arrived in London. He at once became the most eligible bachelor in the land. An inadequate allowance together with expensive tastes and a passion for gambling kept him chronically short of money; these facts together with certain mysterious comings and goings about the Lodge late in 1730 gave Horace Walpole the opportunity to tell a good story:

42   Horace Walpole, by J.G. Eccardt, 1754. Son of the Prime Minister Robert Walpole, he recorded his observations of the passing scene in letters, memoirs and journals. An early champion of the Gothic style, he built his house at Strawberry Hill, Twickenham, to exemplify it; the house can be seen in the background. (National Portrait Gallery)

Old Sarah, Duchess of Marlborough, ever proud and ever malignant, was persuaded to offer her favourite grand-daughter, Lady Diana Spencer, afterwards Duchess of Bedford, to the Prince of Wales with a fortune of one hundred thousand pounds. He accepted the proposal, and the day was fixed for their being secretly married at the Duchess's Lodge in the great park at Windsor. Sir Robert Walpole got intelligence of the project, prevented it, and the secret was buried in silence.[50]

Sarah, however, was unlikely to have breached royal etiquette in this way, and at the time she was on friendly terms with the King and Queen. In 1731 she brought about Diana's marriage to Lord John Russell, who succeeded to the title of Duke of Bedford on the death of his elder brother, husband of Sarah's grand-daughter the former Lady Anne Egerton. Sarah missed her company, and we find her writing even more letters, waiting for Diana to call, and paying her visits, accompanied by Grace Ridley and her little daughter, a woman servant and a footman. Diana's oldest brother Robert, another of Sarah's favourites who also had rooms at the Lodge, died in 1729—Sarah blamed 'murthring Physicians'. She spoke with feeling, as she could get little relief herself from the gout and kidney stone from which she suffered. Without being reconciled to her mother (and having left her husband for the dramatist Congreve), Henrietta died in 1733. Sarah was surprised to find how much she was affected, writing to Diana from Windsor Lodge, 'I can say with Job that my eyes are dim with sorrow, and my nerves are as shadows, and indeed I think my circumstances is more like his, than anybody's that I have heard of or read of'.[51] How much more like him she must have felt when in 1735 her beloved Diana, her 'Darling Angel', died like her mother of tuberculosis. It was a penalty for living so long that Sarah had to endure the deaths of so many of her family; but it did not seem to make her cherish more those left to her. It was so easy to fall from grace.

On Henrietta's death Diana's brother Charles became Duke of Marlborough, Henrietta's only son Willigo having died of too much good living in 1731. Charles asked his grandmother for the lodge in the Little Park which had been Henrietta's, and Sarah somewhat grudgingly agreed. The proximity did their relationship no good. Though she had at some time found many good qualities in him, later she could hardly bear the sight of him. 'His person is very well if he had a Mask on', she said.[52] His main fault was that he had chosen a wife without reference to her, moreover he had chosen the grand-daughter of Lord Trevor, an old opponent of Marlborough. Sarah was furious, thumping the ground with her cane in rage. She blamed Diana's sister, Anne Bateman, whom she had never liked, for aiding and abetting the match. Horace Walpole tells the story in his racy style:

> The grandam's rage exceeded all bounds. Having a portrait of Lady Bateman, she blackened the face, and wrote on it, 'Now her outside is as black as her inside'. The Duke she turned out of the little lodge in Windsor Park; and then pretending that the new Duchess and her female cousins had stripped the house and garden, she had a puppet-show made with waxen figures, representing the Trevors tearing up the shrubs, and the Duchess carrying off the chicken-coop under her arm.

Sarah was nothing if not original in her expressions of anger. There was a lawsuit between herself and her grandson over the possession of a sword set with diamonds, given to his grandfather by the Emperor, which the Duke claimed was his by right. Yes, she had kept it, Sarah said, 'lest he should pick out the diamonds and pawn them'.[53] Charles had become an inveterate gambler.

When Sarah made Charles move out of the lodge in the Little Park in 1738, she added insult to injury by installing in it his younger brother John Spencer—her dear Johnny, who, though just as wildly spendthrift as Charles, was more circumspect where his grandmother was concerned; he had for instance married a wife (who adored him) chosen by Sarah. They lived in a pleasant neighbourly way, visiting each other for a cup of tea or a dish of coffee, exchanging gifts of pheasants and turkeys, and John's children came to play draughts with their formidable great-grandmamma. A charming letter written to Johnny from the Lodge in 1742 survives:

> I find they are mighty fond of coming to me, for I play at drafts with 'em & they both beat me shamefully. I believe they really like to come to me extreamly, tho' I heard they had been told I intended to give them a present; upon which they press'd Grace mightily to know what it was. And after she acquainted me with their curiosity I ask'd 'em if they would have a kiss or Gold, and they both cryd out very eagerly, Mony.[54]

At last in her closing years she had found some comfort in an affectionate family relationship. She also enjoyed the companionship of her dogs: 'I am very fond of my three dogs, they have all of them gratitude, wit, and good sense; things very rare in this country. They are fond of going out with me but when I reason with them, and tell them it is not proper, they submit, and watch for my coming home, and meet me with as much joy as if I had never given them good advice.'

43 Two of Sarah's dogs in the Great Park, by John Wootton. Windsor Castle can be discerned in the background.

Sarah was never reconciled to Blenheim, which she said in 1736 'I never design to see again: in a lodge I have everything convenient, and without trouble'. As for Wimbledon Manor, 'though it stands high, it is upon clay, an ill sod, very damp, and I believe an unhealthy place, which I shall seldom live in'. She preferred the Lodge to Marlborough House, because

> after such an hour in this place I am sure I can see nobody. At Marlborough House it is very different, for there are many visitors, though few that have any sense, or that are capable of any truth. I would desire no more pleasure than to walk about my gardens and parks; but, alas! that is not permitted; for I am generally wrapped in flannel, and wheeled up and down my rooms in a chair. I cannot be very solicitous of life upon such terms, when I can only live to have more fits of gout.[55]

At Marlborough House she entertained, gave parties and went out and about, showing incredible vitality despite her age and infirmity. Though she was glad to have a quieter life at Windsor Lodge, she still enjoyed visitors, among them Lord Chesterfield and Alexander Pope; but she no longer had the influential rôle in public affairs that she had wielded in the past.[56]

Throughout these years Sarah carried out her duties as Ranger energetically, seeing that keepers' lodges were repaired and palings kept in order, the deer protected and hay provided for them, the trees preserved—'I never cut down a tree so long as it will bear a leaf'. She battled continually to maintain the privacy of the Parks; keepers had trouble keeping out carriages then, just as they have trouble with cars today. 'If I should allow this every body would pretend a Right, and it would soon ruin the Park.' She blamed this on the gravelling of roads by Queen Anne.

> There never was any Road in that Part of the Park, unless it were in Oliver Cromwell's time when the King was not in possession of his Crown: and then it is probable there might have been Roads, when it was turn'd into Farms. In Mr. May's time ... there might have been some waggons go thro by bribing the Gate-Keepers; which had done so much hurt to the Park, that my Lord Portland put an end to it.[57]

She always backed up her keepers; through them she heard of trespassers, of deer being hunted too savagely, of the death of a cart-horse: 'One of the poor old cart horses that had the pole evil, is fell into the ditch in Cow pond, and is dead'.[58] Among her keepers were the brothers Robert and Baptist Nunn, whose family had been established in the Park by Baptist May.

She had a long-standing quarrel with the Duke of St Albans (Nell Gwyn's grandson) who, having been made Constable of the Castle with Cranbourne Lodge as his residence, considered

himself entitled to come into the Park when he liked through a private gate. Sarah had the gate nailed up and he broke it down. Arguments with 'that insolent Idiot' dragged on for seven years, when she was at last prevailed upon to allow him a key. No wonder she was called Old Mount Aetna, Her Graceless, and the Beldam of Bedlam.[59]

Another bête noire was Sir Robert Walpole, the chief minister. She made difficulties about concessions Queen Caroline wanted in her Wimbledon estate, and suspected that it was in retaliation for this that he had her Crown grant of £500 a year as Ranger stopped in 1737, together with the allowance for looking after her garden. She had been perennially at odds with the Treasury about her grant, which she said had not been paid since 1725, and was even more aggrieved about taxes from which her predecessors had been exempt. She complained about

> officers for the taxes at Windsor coming to me perpetually to tell me they would seize my goods at the Lodge ... I make no advantage of the park, but to eat sometimes a few little Welsh runts, and I have no more cows than I allow the under keepers, which are to each six, but I have laid out a good deal of money ... and I never was so mean as to bring any bills ... for what I did for my own satisfaction.[60]

44 This key to the Great Park, drawn by Maud Wilson, belonged to Princess Marie Louise. The monogram suggests it was made in the reign of George I.

Years later she wrote to Lord Wilmington, the Lord High Treasurer, in the same vein: 'tis an agreeable place to live in, though tis too much to lay out in what will return to the Crown, and I am sorry I have done it'. Shortly before she died she seemed to become disenchanted with the Park, 'for though tis a great park, it is full of roads and there is nothing beautiful in it but clumps of trees'.[61]

As she became increasingly infirm, from stumping around the house on a stick to being wheeled or carried in a chair and 'lifted about like a child', she had to rely more and more upon her servants. She treated them well, encouraging them to make the best of themselves, and they repaid her with enduring devotion. Commending them in a letter to 'dear Johnny' shortly before her death, she wrote 'I believe nobody ever had so many good ones as I have'.[62] She describes the marriage of 'my maid in the kitchen and one of the carters':

> The procession to church was very fine. His hair was powdered, a flourished cravat, a very good suit of clothes with brass buttons and in short he was better dressed than ever I saw the Right Honourable Horatio Walpole ... As soon as the ceremony was performed, the bridegroom with a very white pair of gloves would lead his lady himself to the lodge, where they are to have a dinner in plenty and state, and these nuptials are to be in my house.[63]

In her last years there were signs of a reconciliation between Sarah and her surviving child, Mary Duchess of Montagu, for they exchanged letters; but mother and daughter never met again. Sarah lived on despite several false alarms about dying. 'Old Marlborough is dying—but who can tell!' wrote Horace Walpole in 1741: 'last year she had laid a great while ill without speaking; her physicians said, "She must be blistered, or she will die." She called out, "I won't be blistered, and I won't die." If she takes the same resolution now, I don't believe she will.'[64] And she did not, living on for another three years and dying very peacefully on 18 October 1744 at Marlborough House.

3: John Spencer 1744-1746

After generous bequests to her faithful servants, Sarah left almost all her vast fortune to her grandson John Spencer. His brother Charles Duke of Marlborough inherited Blenheim, but Sarah left John her estates in a dozen counties, her houses, and the Rangership of the two parks at Windsor. After John, it was all to go to his son, also called John. Sarah did not miss the opportunity of making a last political statement: neither John Spencer nor his son was to take up any employment or pension under the Crown, apart from the Rangership, on pain of forfeiting their inheritance. The Rangership was diverted from her daughter Mary, the third life in the 1709 patent, who would not have been interested in it; when the new patent was issued in May 1745 the grant was for 'John Spencer for his own life, he being by virtue of the will of Sarah Duchess of Marlborough in possession of the said office, and entitled thereto for and during the life of Mary Duchess of Montagu'.[65]

Mary, who belonged to one of the richest families in the land, was left some pieces of heirloom jewellery, perhaps in token of their reconciliation (though the diminutive size of the gifts is in sharp contrast to the vastness of the estates left to her nephew): a gold snuffbox and a pearl bracelet which contained miniatures of her father, and two miniatures of her sisters Anne and Elizabeth.

John and his wife Georgiana moved into Windsor Lodge, where all the furniture had been left for them. He owed everything to Sarah. She had brought him up when his mother died; by her efforts he had become Member of Parliament for Woodstock, a seat which Sarah thought should always be held by a member of the Marlborough family; she had chosen a wife for him, and now she had left him a huge fortune. As she had once said, though he was a younger brother, and her only grandson to be a commoner, she would leave him as considerable a fortune as most elder brothers.[66]

45 John Spencer, by Stephen Slaughter, shown dressed as a young beau with a favourite dog. After his early death his great fortune passed to his son John, who later became the 1st Earl Spencer.

But of his Rangership there is nothing to report, for, as Horace Walpole duly recorded, two years later he was dead:

> Jack Spencer, old Marlborough's grandson and heir, is just dead at the age of six or seven and thirty, and in possession of near 30,000 l. a year, merely because he would not be abridged of those valuable blessings of an English subject, brandy, small-beer, and tobacco.[67]

Chapter Six

Butcher Cumberland— or Sweet William?
1746-1765

1: A Favourite Son

After the anticlimax of John Spencer's brief term of office, the Rangership received an injection of energy with the appointment to it, for the first time in history, of a royal prince; it has remained in the royal family ever since. The new Ranger was William Augustus, Duke of Cumberland, second surviving son of King George II. Born in London in 1721, he was his parents' English son and their darling; his brother Frederick Louis ('Poor Fred'), born in Hanover 14 years earlier, had been left behind when his parents came to London after George I's accession, and was all but ignored until after his father came to the throne in 1727. He reached his majority the following year, and George II was persuaded by his ministers to call him to London as he was, after all, heir to the throne. When he arrived in Whitehall, unannounced, he was not entirely welcome, and his parents were soon at odds with him. They called him 'the greatest beast in the whole world', and scandalised the public with their open disregard for him. His young brother, on the other hand, could do no wrong in his father's eyes for most of his life.

William was created Duke of Cumberland when he was five and Knight of the Garter when he was nine; he was then given his own establishment, with Stephen Poyntz as his governor and steward. An Eton Scholar and Fellow of King's College, Cambridge, Poyntz had travelled abroad with the Duke of Devonshire and later entered the diplomatic service, being sent on special missions to Sweden and to France. The King and Queen must have chosen carefully the man to whom they were entrusting the upbringing of their nine-year-old son, and Poyntz rendered the Duke devoted service, staying with him for the rest of his life.

The young Duke's education was seen to by tutors, among whom was Henry Flitcroft for architecture, who was to reappear at Windsor Lodge. A Cambridge professor of astronomy taught him mathematics, and gave him a lasting interest in astronomy; Handel was attached to his father's court as music-master to his sisters, and William was later to become one of his patrons. As well as all this, he attended classes at Westminster School. His twin passions were for all things military and for hunting. He was given a hunting-lodge in Windsor Forest, where he learnt about horses and horse-breeding. His military career began with experience in both army and navy, and at 19 he was made colonel in the Coldstream Guards.

At 21 William—or 'the Duke' as he was universally called—was made major-general and saw his first active service alongside his father in the campaigns of the War of the Austrian

Succession against the old enemy, France, and in defence of Hanover. In 1743 he fought at the Battle of Dettingen under his father's baton,[1] and their victory greatly enhanced their popularity at home. William showed the dogged courage characteristic of him, particularly when he was shot in the leg by an 'own goal' musket-ball from an allied soldier. He was not a military genius like Marlborough, but he had the ability to win the loyalty of his men, who nicknamed him 'Billy the Bold'. Wootton's equestrian portrait in the large dining-room at the Lodge shows the Duke at Dettingen in commanding pose, already portly, wearing the star and ribbon of the Garter with the red coat originally introduced by Cromwell for the New Model Army.

William had now reached an age when a suitable marriage was being considered. The King tried to arrange a good match for him—one which would be advantageous politically, especially to Hanover. He planned a double wedding, his youngest daughter Louisa marrying King Frederick of Denmark, and William the Danish King's sister. Louisa's marriage took place in 1744, but William was appalled at the thought of marrying a princess he had never seen and who was said to be misshapen. When he protested to the Secretary of State, Lord Granville, the curt reply was that 'he must be taught his duty to his father'. The Duke turned for advice to that shrewd old statesman, Sir Robert Walpole (just in time as he died two days later), who advised him to seem to consent but with the proviso that the King would make a very large settlement. 'The Duke', says Horace Walpole, 'took this sage counsel, and heard no more of his intended bride.'[2] Walpole takes up the tale again:

> Finally the King gave up trying to marry him off. 'William', he said, 'I see you will never marry; it is in vain to think of making a great establishment of a new branch through you; I shall do well for you for your life; yet not so large as I should have done in that case.'[3]

46   The Duke was known to enjoy the company of women. His appearance lent itself to caricature: the comments on the banners are not flattering.

The nearest he ever got to the altar was to stand proxy for his sister Mary's bridegroom, the Landgrave of Hesse-Cassel, at her marriage in 1740. Though disinclined to matrimony, William enjoyed the close company of women and had mistresses from the age of seventeen. Walpole tells us that after the Battle of Fontenoy in 1745 he was as popular with 'the lower class of men as he has been for three or four years with the low women: he will be the soldier's Great Sir as well as theirs'.[4]

By 1745 the Duke was Captain-General of the forces, a post last held by Marlborough, and he was recalled from a campaign in Flanders to deal with the Jacobite uprising led by Bonnie Prince Charlie, which General Wade had failed to quell. In this contest where two princes of the same age faced each other, the son of 'James III', the Old Pretender, opposing the son of the reigning king, each fighting for his father's crown, the greater military expertise of the Duke of Cumberland proved decisive. The final battle was fought at Culloden on 16 April 1746, the day after the Duke's 25th birthday. Horace Walpole wrote to a friend a week later when the news had reached London: 'The defeat is reckoned total, and the dispersion general; and all the artillery is taken. It is a brave young Duke! The town is all blazing round me, as I write, with fireworks and illuminations'.[5]

After this victory Cumberland returned to London amid great rejoicing; he had saved his father's throne, affirmed the Hanoverian succession and averted the horror of another civil war. Both Houses of Parliament joined in giving him a vote of thanks, and, more to the point, added £25,000 to his annual grant of £15,000; he was given the freedom of the City of London; Handel wrote an oratorio *Judas Maccabaeus* ('See the conquering hero comes!') in his honour— a work so immediately popular that it revived the composer's waning fortunes; and the King granted him the Rangership of Windsor Great Park, which once again had fallen vacant at an opportune moment. William was at the peak of his fame:

> Since the Duke's victorious blows
> The lily, thistle, and the rose
> All droop and fade, all die away;
> Sweet William only rules the day.[6]

His hour of glory was short-lived. News of the ruthlessness of Cumberland's treatment of the defeated Jacobite troops took a few weeks to reach London, and it produced a wave of revulsion which was fostered by his brother the Prince of Wales, who had never been allowed to have his own moment of glory. When someone suggested making the Duke a freeman of a City company, an alderman cried out 'Then let it be the Butchers'!' and the nickname stuck. Far from his being Sweet William, in Scotland the rank weed Common Ragwort was renamed Stinking Billy, and his name is still regarded with odium by many Scots people. Whatever the rights and wrongs of his actions may have been—and volumes have been written on the question—for the Duke, who thought he had done what the government wanted and what would please his father, it was bewildering to have his success rebound against him, and to be transformed so rapidly from a conquering hero to a cruel villain. Then, and for the rest of his life, his new interest at Windsor was to prove a solace to him and bring out a different side of his nature.

2: A Royal Ranger

The Rangership was granted to him on 12 July 1746 for his own life and the lives of his unmarried older sisters the Princesses Amelia and Caroline. Amelia sometimes acted as hostess for her bachelor brother and accompanied him to social gatherings; a projected marriage to her

47 Thomas Sandby's 'Lodge and Garden from the Great Lake'. The originals of Sandby's Views of the Great Park are in the Royal Library.

cousin, Frederick the Great of Prussia, never came off, and later she became Ranger of Richmond Park in her own right, finally settling at Gunnersbury Park, where, growing increasingly deaf, she entertained that great socialite Horace Walpole to cards and gossip. Caroline cherished an unrequited passion for Lord Hervey, her father's Vice-Chamberlain, and finally retired into seclusion and died when she was forty-four. The Countess of Portland had a hand in the upbringing of these sisters, since a few years before William's birth his parents were expelled from court by George I (who, like all the Hanoverian monarchs, could not abide his son and heir) and the children were put into Lady Portland's care. When William was born, the King relented and allowed his parents to keep him.

The granting of the Rangership to a prince transformed the life of the Lodge. Though the Duchess of Marlborough was a great lady, she had lived comparatively simply with a small staff in her 'clean sweet house'. Now it had to accommodate a princely retinue: the Duke's household consisted of some 130 persons, from Lords and Grooms of the Bedchamber to 70 liveried servants, dressed in red and green. Of course not all of them were in the same place at the same time, as the Duke had apartments at St James's and Kensington Palace and also his hunting-lodge at Ramslade near Bracknell; but the Great Lodge must have been as busy and full of people then as it is today. The poet Gray wrote in September 1746, 'The Duke is here at his Lodge with three Whores and three Aid-de Camps; & the country swarms with People. He goes to Races, & they make a Ring about him, as at a Bear-Baiting'.[7]

The Duke had gone to Windsor in July 1746, and shortly afterwards the King came on a flying visit 'and view'd the Lodge in the Park there, and that in the Forest, both of which are fitted up for the Duke'. Fitting up the Lodge was made easier by the purchase of furniture

Detail of Fig. 47, showing the west or garden front of the Lodge, the garden sloping gently down towards the Duke's ly-created lake. The range of the new stables is visible above the trees to the left of the house.

'The Great Lake', by Sandby. The Doric Temple can be seen left of centre, and the Chinese bridge on the right; the Lodge at of sight to the left.

belonging to John Spencer, and repairs were at once put in hand. In September 1746 an account for £1,380 11s. 6d. was rendered 'To repairing the Great Lodge, rebuilding part of the Offices, building Sheds for Cattle and rebuilding a Cowhouse'. There was also an account 'To building stabling for 50 horses according to a plan and Elevation approved by his Royal Highness the Duke of Cumberland ... £1534'.[8] Though the account does not specify where the stables were, it seems certain they were at the Lodge. For the planning of his new stables the Duke turned to his old tutor Henry Flitcroft who had already done work for him at Ramslade. By 1747 he was being paid regularly, and handsomely, for his architectural services to the Duke.

Flitcroft cleverly designed the additional stabling to fit in with the existing stable block, which as we have seen was separated from Groom's House by a gap of a few yards. This space was now used up with an addition allowing stabling from front to back, and a companion building to the whole was put up on the right, joined to the old block by an arched entrance topped by a pediment and surmounted by a handsome turret. To this a clock was added in 1750, engraved with the name of J. Davis, a Windsor clockmaker, and the date. Anyone looking today at the front of the Mews and Groom's House can see how the building was planned to take advantage of the space available. Indeed Groom's House and the Mews are the most authentic buildings at Cumberland Lodge, having escaped fires and demolition. The hooks for tying up the horses outside are still in place, and the graffiti of idle grooms using their stirrup-wheels to carve their initials can be found about the building.

Like Hugh May and others before him, Flitcroft did not confine his architectural interests to buildings. His father had been a gardener at Hampton Court in William III's time when its gardens were redesigned along classical lines by London and Wise; but he became a pupil of

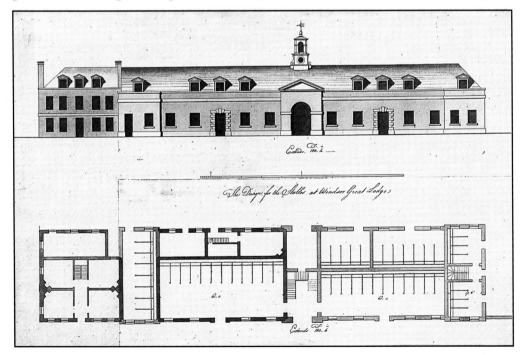

50   Flitcroft's design for the new stables, with Groom's House on the left. The darker shading indicates the older buildings, seen better on the lower plan.

William Kent, and his colleague at the Office of Works. Kent, along with others, was moving away from the idea of gardens as plots, parterres and terraces, and instead seeing the house in relationship to the wider landscape. Grandeur was no longer to be suggested by avenues proceeding from the great house like the rays of the sun, but by the amplitude of the surrounding parkland with unexpected views as the eye is taken to rest on some distant and attractive object. The effect was contrived, but had to appear natural. The difference between the two styles can be experienced vividly by looking down the Long Walk from Snow Hill to Windsor Castle, a magnificent example of the formal style, and then walking towards Bishopsgate to be surprised by glimpses of the Castle, the trees falling away to disclose it.

Flitcroft was ably assisted by Thomas Greening, who was in charge of gardens at the Lodge, and by Thomas Sandby, who as military draughtsman had been associated with the Duke on the Scottish campaign and accompanied him to the Netherlands in 1747. Sandby then worked privately for the Duke as draughtsman, and composed the wonderful series of views which illuminate our knowledge of Windsor and the Great Park at this time. His view of the Lodge from the Great Lake shows the ideal blend of house and landscape which was sought in the new style: the house is situated on a hill, the land falling gently away from it down to the lake, all appearing natural, indeed inevitable. But the Duchess of Marlborough had no such view: beyond her terraced gardens the land sloped down to a boggy hollow before rising up to a horizon of heathland. In the new fashion the park was to reach to the very door, so Sarah's formal gardens were swept away and replaced by an open lawn with oak and chestnut trees (some still thriving) leading the eye down to a lake created for the purpose.

The Great Lake, now called Great Meadow Pond, was designed to be irregular in outline, contrasting with the Cow Pond on the other side of the house which had been given a formal shape by previous Rangers. The soil dug out to form the new lake was used for landscaping the ground around it, and features were added to give charm and interest. A knoll at the southern end was crowned with a Doric temple; this was not visible from the house, but would be discovered by people strolling by the lake. All trace of it has now disappeared. Another feature was the pretty wooden bridge on the right of Sandby's picture. It did not matter that this was derived from China and the temple from ancient Greece; the point was that they were both picturesque. There was another bridge at the other end of the lake, and a boathouse, and a 'riding' made all round it.

For this huge undertaking an army of labourers was recruited—literally an army, as many were unemployed soldiers from the Duke's regiment. For some people in the neighbourhood the Duke was unpopular because he closed the Park to the public, saying they spoiled the trees and disturbed the deer; he liked order and discipline around him, with everything under his control. For others he came to be seen as a benefactor, since he gave regular employment to so many people. The labourers received a daily wage of 9d. to 1s. 6d., which compares well with the £15 a year given to keepers,[9] though these had permanency together with a house and garden (a loaf of bread cost 5d.).

Great attention was given to the planting of trees. Twelve plantations were made in 1747 alone. Smith's Lawn, across which stretched an avenue of limes from earlier days, was furnished with several clumps of trees to give it more interest—oaks, beeches, chestnuts, and firs which were an innovation in the Park. These have all gone as the lawn was levelled in the present century. Between 1747 and 1750 a double row of beeches was planted inside the double avenue of oaks leading from the Lodge to Bishopsgate. This great avenue has now vanished,

51 The Obelisk; a memorial to William Duke of Cumberland, originally erected to commemorate the Battle of Culloden. A pleasant walk along a grassy avenue leads from Cumberland Gate to the monument and the Obelisk Pond beside it.

apart from a few isolated trees—which sometimes lead one, out of the corner of an eye, to imagine one has caught a glimpse of it. The Duke, no doubt advised by Thomas Greening, experimented with different types of trees. His officer friends who had gone to the American colonies as governors were asked to send seeds of unusual and beautiful trees and shrubs, so, as well as cedars, firs, pines, yews and evergreen oaks, more exotic trees appeared in the Park. These were concentrated in the southern area where to this day the greatest variety of trees is to be found. The next lake to be created was Obelisk Pond, though it did not acquire that name until after the erection of the Obelisk—'the focal point of a vista from Cumberland Lodge'. Its inscription reads thus:

> This Obelisk was raised by command of King George II commemorates the services of his son William Duke of Cumberland the success of his arms and the gratitude of his father. This tablet was inscribed by His Majesty King William IV.[10]

Across the shaft was carved the word 'Culloden'; this was discreetly removed later by Queen Victoria and replaced by 'Cumberland'.

The grandest enterprise was the creation of Virginia Water out of the river running south-east from the Great Lake, together with the enlargement of Johnson's Pond to the west of it. It appears in Thomas Sandby's *Eight Views in Windsor Great Park* (published 1754); so all the work of clearing, draining, damming, landscaping and planting was done in an incredibly short space of time. It was said that 100 labourers were employed daily. The result was 'magnificent beyond description'; it was the largest ornamental lake in Europe. Like the Great Lake, it had picturesque features such as China Island, so called from its summerhouse in Chinese style. A hulk was lugged all the way from the Thames at the *Bells of Ouseley* and transformed into a Mandarin yacht (variously spelt in bills as yot, yoat, yote, yout, yott, yatcht, yatch and yacht).[11] There were many plantations of trees in this area and as we shall see work continued on it until the end of the century. It is worth noting that the work carried out by the Duke was done mainly at his own expense, so the Rangership was freed from the quibbling about payments that had gone on in the past.

3: The Lodge Transformed

While all this work was going on in the Park, building operations were in progress at the Lodge. For its new role the house needed enlarging on a grander scale than Flitcroft's early plan for an additional building to house a library at the southern end of the house, which seems never to have been adopted.[12] Instead a palatial edifice, almost certainly designed by Thomas Sandby, was built across the northern end, making the total house T-shaped. The jumble of small buildings at this end of Sarah's house was demolished, and the new structure related to the stables, its façade at right angles to them, its main door (where the side door is today) giving on to a spacious exercise yard. The centre of gravity of the house moved to its north end, and then as now the stables were an integral part of the life of the Lodge. The style of the building was Palladian, and contained state apartments appropriate to the Duke's royal status. Sandby's drawing and the picture of the ruins after the fire of 1869 (see Figure 77) show what the addition was like.

We do not know precisely when this great enlargement took place, but Joseph Pote in his *History and Antiquities of Windsor Castle*, published in 1749, already sees the house being embellished: 'By the great and noble improvements now making by his Royal Highness to this Lodge and Gardens, this most pleasant Villa seems to promise for the future not only to be the delight, but habitation of Princes'. In *Les Délices de Windsor*, published six years later, he says, with a change of tense, that the Duke 'has made this villa, the most delightful Habitation of Princes'.[13] In August 1751, having been made Keeper of Windsor Forest and Warden of Cranbourne Chase on the death of the Duke of St Albans (Sarah's bête-noire), the Duke moved into Cranbourne

52 'The new North Face of the Great Lodge with Barnard Smith lunging a colt', by Sandby. The Duke is to the right talking to two courtiers, Sir Thomas Rich and Lord Albemarle, while Thomas Sandby stands slightly apart.

53 Thomas Sandby (*c.*1721-1798). He and his brother Paul produced many water-colours and drawings of Windsor, the Park and its people. He became the first Professor of Architecture at the Royal Academy, and almost certainly designed the new north front of the Lodge.

Lodge 'when the Great Lodge was being altered'; he celebrated his taking possession with a cricket match—which the Duke's XI lost by an innings. He spent most of 1752 and 1753 at his hunting-lodge in Windsor Forest.[14] Meanwhile the building work went on. Thomas Sandby's view of the Lodge, published in 1754, shows the new stables in place, without any sign of a new wing, but in 1755 there was an influx of residents to the Lodge, suggesting that by then it had been enlarged. An anonymous person is quoted as saying in 1757, 'Windsor Lodge is so out of repair that it is necessary to be rebuilt, and a plan is prepared for that purpose'. This statement follows the story of how the arch of the cellar under the Duke's bedchamber fell in, 'happily with no other accident, not withstanding that he was in bed'.[15] The arch had probably never before borne so great a weight. As the bedchamber was in the old house, which perhaps had been neglected, this statement is not inconsistent with a new edifice already having been built. That year there was a bill for work done (mainly putting in stoves and fireplaces) in both the Old and the New Cellar, and in the New Servants' Hall and the New Kitchen, which suggests the new building was then in existence.[16]

Thomas Sandby, having no doubt assisted Flitcroft from 1748 onwards, seems to have begun to take over from him in the Great Park in the 1750s, and by the end of the decade he was calling himself 'Architect to H.R.H. the Duke'. Farington in his Diary remarks that he was in such favour with the Dukes of Gloucester and Cumberland soon after King George III came to the throne 'that on some occasion when it is usual, pro forma, to make a Knight, He would have been the person', but unluckily for him he could not be found that moment, so someone else was knighted instead.[17] It was under the next Ranger that he came more to the King's notice, through work he did for him at Windsor. As for Flitcroft, his rise from anonymity had been as easy as falling off a ladder, since it was by doing so when working as a joiner on the roof of Burlington House that he came to the notice of Lord Burlington, who took him into his draughtsman's office.[18] By 1758 Flitcroft had reached the top rung of the ladder when he was made Comptroller of the Office of Works; he was also much sought after for private commissions, and so would be content to leave the Windsor work to Sandby.

John Vardy, another employee at the Office of Works, may have been involved in the planning of the gardens; a 'drawn plan of the Gardens in Windsor Great Park belonging to H.R.H. the Duke of Cumberland' of 1747 shows, in pencil, plots marked 'Cabages', 'Raspberys', 'Plants', and seems to have been a draft for Vardy's 1750 map of the gardens and part of the Park. Beyond the stable and farm buildings were the kitchen gardens, behind a high wall still to be seen curving round as far as the present Royal School, which was later built within the gardens. Flitcroft designed hothouses 156 ft. long, with Fruit Rooms, Beds for Pine Apples and Alleys to walk round. Further off was that essential resource of a great house, an ice-house, its most likely situation being on, or in, the north-facing cliff which now forms the edge of the garden of Chaplain's Lodge. In winter ice would be cut from the Ox Pond below the cliff and stored in the ice-house for future use. For entertainment there were nine-pin alleys and a bowling-green. The Wilderness to the south of the house was enlarged by planting more trees of various kinds, and serpentine paths were made in it. There was a 'thatched temple' used as a summerhouse. The Duke was in the forefront of the vogue for having menageries on great estates. Horace Walpole came to see the lions and tigers, finding them 'delicious', though there was an unfortunate incident when a tiger broke loose and killed a child—the animal was sent to the Tower.[19]

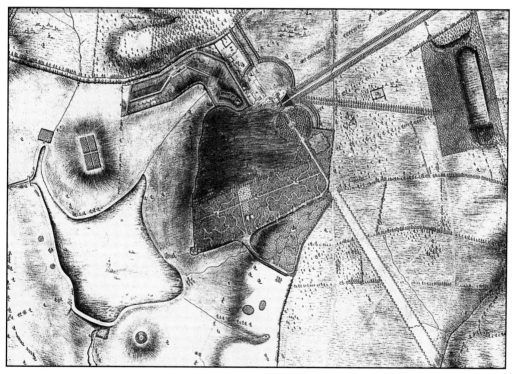

54 John Vardy's Plan of the Gardens (1750). The Cow Pond is on the right and the avenue from it leads to the Lodge; the Wilderness to the south has been developed and includes a bowling-green; the Great Lake is on the left with the Doric Temple at the south end, and Mezel Hill and its plantation to the north. The kitchen gardens stretch round to the north-west. The vestiges of hedges dividing the old fields are still visible. An enlargement of the area about Cumberland Lodge on this map can be seen in Plate VI. (K Top VII 38 2b in the British Library)

55 *Left.* King Herod, by Sawrey Gilpin. The artist was employed to paint the Duke's horses and had a room in Groom's House.

56 *Right.* Eclipse, by George Stubbs. The Duke did not live long enough to know of his horse's amazing success as a racehorse.

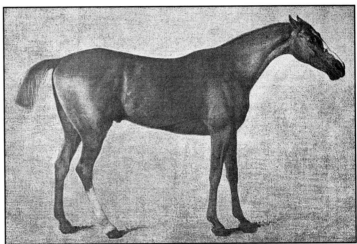

The Duke was one of the leading horse-breeders in the country, and did much to improve the quality of racing. A founder-member of the Jockey Club, he also revived racing at Ascot, which had fallen into abeyance after Queen Anne's reign. Duke's Lane to the West of Cumberland Lodge is named after him, as it is the route he always took to Ascot; it is still used by the sovereign when driving there ceremonially. The most famous racehorses produced by his stud were King Herod and Eclipse, each descended from one of the three great horses from which all thoroughbreds are descended: Byerley Turk, Darley Arabian and Godolphin Arabian (the last so called because it was owned by Lord Godolphin, Henrietta Duchess of Marlborough's husband). Herod, a bay horse by Tartar (Byerley Turk's great-grandson) out of Cypron (a mare owned by the Duke), was foaled in 1758 and won six of the ten races he ran between 1763 and 1767, when under a new owner he began a new career as a stallion. Eclipse, a chestnut horse descended from Darley Arabian, was foaled at the Cranbourne stables on the day of a solar eclipse in 1764, the year before the Duke's death, so he never knew of his horse's phenomenal triumphs. Under his new owners Eclipse ran 18 races in 18 months during 1769 and 1770 and was never beaten: 'Eclipse first and the rest nowhere' as the saying went.[20] A plaque near

V The Great Lodge: the old east front. Thomas Sandby, 1754: pencil, pen and water colour. The Duke is being driven from his new stables in a coach and six. Some of his collection of wild animals are depicted in the foreground.

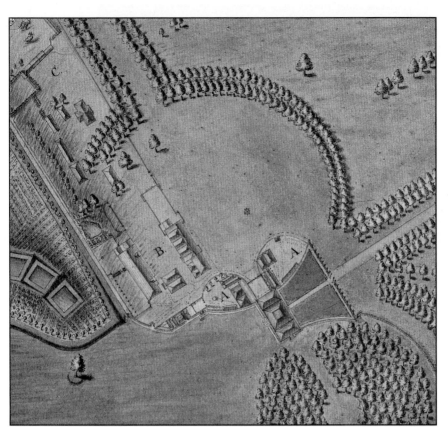

VI Detail of the area
Cumberland Lodge from
Vardy's Plan of the Ga
(1750). (K Top VII 38 2b
British Library)

VII The garden fro
Cumberland Lodge, showi
Gothic alterations carried
James Wyatt. George I
never able to complete the
so the house remained two
classical on one side and
on the other.

Cranbourne Tower commemorates his birth, as do the Eclipse Stakes at Sandown, and the public house at the Eclipse roundabout on the A30 at Egham.

The stud-groom who bred Eclipse was Barnard Smith, who rose through the ranks in the Duke's service, first appearing on the pay-roll as a 'helper' in 1745 when he was one of 11 assistant grooms (paid £20 10s. a year). In 1747 he became groom, in 1749 hunting-groom and in 1751 stud-groom. Though it is often assumed that Smith's Lawn was named after Barnard Smith, this is unlikely as it was known by this name by 1750 (Smith's Lawn Plantation appears on Vardy's map of that date), when Barnard Smith had not yet made his reputation. It is more likely to have been named after some other Smith—and there were several—who had a connection with the Park, just as Johnson's Pond was later called after a keeper living at Manor Lodge. The stables gave employment to a large number of people: Poyntz's accounts list coachmen, postillions, helpers, grooms, footmen, a purveyor, people 'for house-keeping', farriers, a 'sadler' and a harnessmaker, shoeing farriers, coachmakers and 'bittmakers'. Senior people like Smith were on the household staff list. Duke William's personal requirements were catered for by a 'Glover, Belt-Maker, Woollen Draper, Periwig-Maker, Milliner, Taylour, Mrs Kemp for Silk Handker-chiefs, Ribband Weaver, Hatter, Lace-Woman, Linnen Draper, and a Hosier called Woolley'. The Taylour also provided 'the Black Boys livery' for £4 10s. 1d.[21]

The Duke was fortunate—or perhaps it says something positive about his character—in the talented and devoted people he drew around him, who helped him to formulate his ideas and carry them out. The household was run with great efficiency by its Comptroller Stephen Poyntz, as the meticulous accounts which have been preserved bear out. Why this gifted man did not move on to positions of greater public eminence is suggested by Horace Walpole: 'Mr. Poyntz was called a very great man, but few knew anything of his talents, for he was timorous to childishness'. The Duke was generous to his Comptroller's family: he 'secured places for his children, and sends his two sons abroad, allowing them 800 1. a year'.[22] Poyntz's daughter Georgiana married John Spencer's son, and so became the first Countess Spencer. When Poyntz died in 1750 he was succeeded by William Windham who had been his deputy since 1731.

Appointments to the Duke's household usually came through military associations. General Hodgson, who as Gentleman of the Horse managed his stud, had been his

57 Stephen Poyntz, by Van Loo. Poyntz became Governor to the Duke in 1730, and later Comptroller of his Household, dying in his service in 1750. His daughter Georgiana married John, later Earl Spencer.

aide-de-camp at Culloden; Lord Frederick Cavendish and General FitzWilliam, Grooms of the Bedchamber, had also been on the Duke's military staff, as was the Duke's equerry, Colonel Dalling; Sir Jeffrey Amherst, who like Cavendish ended his career as a field-marshal, and Sir Charles Knowles, who had served with Albemarle in the Caribbean and became Governor of Jamaica, were also in attendance. An inventory made on the Duke's death tells us the disposition of the rooms used by members of the household.[23] Those just mentioned, together with Mr. Windham as Steward and Comptroller, had rooms on the first floor of the old house. The rooms in the new building were clearly thought to be superior, for there in the 'new attick rooms' the two Lords of the Bedchamber, the Earl of Albemarle and the Earl of Ancram, were accommodated. The Earl of Albemarle and the Duke had been together at Westminster School, and he had long been First Lord of the Bedchamber. At 21, as Lord Bury, he had commanded the front line at Culloden; he became the Duke's political secretary, and seems to have moved permanently into the Lodge in 1755. Two of his brothers—Admiral Augustus Keppel and General William Keppel—followed him; a third brother was Dean of Windsor. It was a strange twist of fortune that these three should be so comfortably settled in Windsor Lodge, for it was their grandfather who had caused such heartache to William Bentinck.

The library was on the chamber floor of the old house. Its contents as revealed in a separate inventory bear witness to the breadth of the Duke's interests.[24] His official papers were kept there, but the main component was an important collection of geographical and military maps and plans, stored in rolls or flat in portfolios. Besides these there was a large section devoted to history, while other sections covered geography and 'voyages in all parts of the world', classical literature, divinity, sciences and arts—English and French poetry, plays and romances. Books 'of which His Royal Highness did not think it worth while to keep a Catalogue' overflowed onto the landing of the great staircase. There were also two large chests in the library, containing mathematical instruments; 'an Air Pump; an Electric Machine; Telescopes, Theodolites, Microscope etc.' Add to all this the furniture—chairs, reading desks, tables, candlestands—and one can understand why the Duke's first thought was for a larger library; but as the idea of a complete new front to the house took shape, this first plan was abandoned. It is reasonable to suppose that a library was to be included in the new plans.

The librarian, along with Thomas Sandby and the other upper servants, had rooms on the top floor of the old house; it was rather like a 'bachelors' corridor', with rooms for the surgeon, the librarian, the cook, the coffeeman, and one of the pages of the backstairs. These people formed a group which would eat at the house-steward's table.

The Duke's bedchamber was on the ground floor, doubtless the same suite as that used by the Duke of Marlborough. The room was furnished with a four-poster bed in an alcove, a toilette table, an easy chair, nine Pembroke chairs and a 'necessary stool'; there was also a truckle bedstead, for the use of whichever gentleman of the bedchamber was on duty. On the walls of this room and the closet next to it were views by Thomas Sandby, a great compliment to the artist, and indicative also of the Duke's pride in his park. The drawing-room next to this suite was hung with green damask, and next to it was a closet where games were kept: backgammon, chess, dice, draughts, and a board for the game of goose. Beyond the great staircase-hall, which had a large hearth for burning wood, and nine Windsor chairs, was an anteroom, its walls covered with pictures. Among these hung a portrait of 'Sarah Duchess [of Marlborough] after Sir Godfrey Kneller', probably acquired with other effects from John Spencer's estate. From this anteroom one passed into the breakfast-room and the dining-room, adorned with equestrian paintings by Sawrey Gilpin. A passage led to the new building where the state apartments, consisting of an imposing entrance hall leading to a spacious banquet-hall and a grand drawing-room, were located: Figure 61 gives an idea of the splendour of this room. It would be unusual for the Duke to eat with the whole of his court, and the existence of two dining-rooms made divisions easy. It would be the Comptroller's duty to see that the aura of royalty was kept about him. On the other side of the entrance hall there were rooms called in the inventory 'yellow print room' and 'green print room'. Duke William had a large collection of maps, pictures and prints which were liberally displayed around the house, giving these particular rooms their names.

Beyond and below the new rooms were the offices, the house steward's dining-room for the upper servants, and the servants' hall which had five large deal dining-tables with forms to sit on and 47 cloak pins. The servants' great bedchamber had two four-posters, ten bedsteads and nine featherbeds. There was a spare room for sick servants, a room with three four-poster beds for the footmen, and a room of his own for the second page of the backstairs. The numerous servants had to sleep in all kinds of nooks and crannies: there was a bed in the butler's pantry, a camp-bedstead in Lord Albemarle's closet as well as a separate room with a four-poster for his servant, a four-poster in the linen-room and two in the maid's bedchamber next door.

58 The Duke visiting his stud beside the Long Walk, by Sawrey Gilpin (1764). This is most probably the picture which hung over the chimney-piece in the grand dining room, mentioned in *The Windsor Guide* of 1783 (see p. 90 and Appendix Three).

The house adjoining the stables was not yet the groom's house—no room is specifically allocated to Barnard Smith and he may have lived at Cranbourne. It housed an assortment of people including the artist Sawrey Gilpin, painter of animals, whom the Duke had taken under his protection in 1761, hence the number of paintings he made of the Duke's stud. The house had three bedrooms and a billiard-room on the top floor; the chamber floor had four bedrooms, one called the Cheque Bedchamber and another the White Dimitty Room; the ground floor had a bathing-room with a large circular tub, a gun room, and Mr. Sandby's office. The grooms shared rooms above the stables, and there were beds in other outhouses such as the granary and the dog-feeder's room beside the kennels; the gardener had a separate house. There were some 90 beds altogether in the Lodge and its outbuildings.

The heating of this large establishment cannot have been easy, but the best was done to make it comfortable. New stoves and fireplaces were put into rooms that were without them, and at the time the inventory was made in 1765 there were 35 tons of Scotch coal and 50 chaldrons of sea coal in the cellars. Some warmth came also from the many candles and 'lanthorns' used for lighting.

Before returning to the story of the Duke's life, two other undertakings in the Park should be mentioned. One was the building of a Belvedere on Shrubs Hill, beyond the Ascot road which runs past Blacknest Gate and so outside the Park boundary. The idea was rather in the spirit of the 'Banquiting House' of a century before. Designed by Flitcroft, it was a triangular building set on a hill, with fine views in all directions, hence the name. Here the Duke could find a quiet retreat, a place to read or to gaze at the stars using the telescope he kept there. It consisted of three Gothic towers with battlements, one containing a library, where in 1771 John Wesley, viewing 'the improvements of that active and useful man the late Duke of Cumberland', said he was 'agreeably surprised to find many of the books not only religious, but admirably well chosen. Perhaps the great man spent many hours here, with only Him that seeth in secret; and who can tell how deep that change went, which was so discernible in the latter part of his life?'[25]

Many years later, transformed into Fort Belvedere, it was to become the favourite and private residence of King Edward VIII; it is now in private hands.

The other venture was to save the so-called 'Holbein' Gate, a brick gatehouse in Whitehall built for Henry VIII, which was being removed in 1759, and to make use of it as a feature in the Park. The site eventually chosen was at the end of the Long Walk, below where the Man on the Copper Horse now stands; but though with great difficulty it was brought to the Park, it was never set up, and gradually its stones disappeared and were used to adorn local houses. It is said that some were used for the dado and cornice of the new chapel which the Duke started building at the Lodge in 1765, inspired perhaps by the 'change' mentioned by John Wesley. It is remarkable that most of the great innovations in the Park were made in the first ten years of the Duke's Rangership, years during which he was also much occupied with military and political affairs.

4: Resignation and Retirement

In March 1751 Frederick Prince of Wales died at the age of 44. He had caught a chill earlier in the year while planning his garden at Kew, but after seeming to recover he died suddenly after a paroxysm of coughing. His death was attributed to the bursting of an 'imposthume', or abscess, caused three years before by a blow from a tennis-ball (some later accounts say a cricket-ball, and it could have been either, as he was very fond of both games).[26] Their father's open preference for his younger son had not encouraged a happy relationship between the brothers, and this hostility was fostered by Augusta, Princess of Wales. Duke William was not popular with the general public—Culloden had seen to that—and he had a reputation for severity and unyielding military discipline. On Frederick's death the reaction of Londoners was, 'Oh, that it was but the butcher!'[27] Yet Horace Walpole said of him, 'You would have loved him if you had not feared him'.[28] Rumours had been put about earlier that he wished to usurp his brother's place in the succession (and indeed George II would have liked an arrangement whereby Frederick had Hanover and William had Britain). After Frederick's death a new rumour went around that if the old King should die while his heir, Frederick's son George, was still a minor, the Duke could be made regent and even king. William too thought he might be made regent, and the question was much discussed in Parliament. When it was decided that the Princess of Wales rather than himself should be regent, he was deeply mortified. Nevertheless he was respected, and frequently consulted on affairs of state. When in 1751 the news reached London that he had died at Windsor there was great alarm—until the deceased turned out to be a favourite horse called Duke.[29]

In April 1757 he was unwillingly obliged to leave England again to defend Hanover against the French. Faced by an army vastly superior in numbers which defeated his forces at Hastenbeck, the Duke was against pressing on, and was relieved to receive a letter from the King telling him to make the best peace he could with the French. This he did, and the Convention of Kloster-Zeven was drawn up in September; but meanwhile, too late, the King had changed his mind. When the Duke returned to Whitehall in October, satisfied that he had done what was best in a sorry situation, he received a bleak welcome. He found the King at cards with Princess Amelia in her apartment; without a word of greeting the King said, 'Here is my son, who has ruined me and disgraced himself'. The Duke went straight to the apartment of his father's mistress, Lady Yarmouth, asking her to inform him that he was resigning all his military appointments. Much concerned, she said, 'Pray, Sir, don't determine this at once'; to which he replied that he begged her pardon; he was not come for advice; he had had time to think, and was determined. The King was much agitated by this, but his son stood firm, saying he had been 'loaded with the imputation of having acted basely without authority. He would always show the utmost respect to his Majesty, but never would serve him more'. Horace Walpole, to whom we owe this story, comments, 'When the Duke could tear himself from his favourite passion, the Army, one may judge how sharply he must have been wounded'.[30]

The Duke retired to Windsor. Though still only 36, he was in very poor health. He was asthmatic, he had become blind in one eye and his old leg wound was troublesome; but he bore his ailments stoically and made light of them. In addition, as W.H. Pyne delicately puts it, 'His Royal Highness was remarkable for corpulency'. A contemporary observer called him

> the largest prince in Christendom, whose charger ... bore on his back, in the field, somewhere around four and twenty stone! I remember seeing him when a boy, at the house of his royal nephews, in Leicester-square; and distinctly recollect his weighing the carriage on one side, as he raised his ponderous body up on the step.

Another contemporary gossiped that once when he fell down when dancing 'he lay like a tortoise on its shell; his face could not reach the ground.[31]

59 'A Chariot in the yard at Cumberland Lodge'. Water-colour by Sandby. The empty chariot, with a coat of arms on its side, is standing at the back of the stables at the Lodge.

His courage, as well as his corpulency, was legendary. Abscesses in his bad leg necessitated cutting it open, without benefit of anaesthetics. Walpole tells the story:

> Ranby (the surgeon) did not dare to propose that a hero should be tied, but was frightened out of his senses when the hero would hold the candle himself, which none of his generals could bear to do: in the middle of the operation, the Duke said, 'Hold!' Ranby said, 'For God's sake, Sir, let me proceed now—it will be worse to renew it'. The Duke repeated, 'I say, hold!' and then calmly bade them give Ranby a clean waiscot and cap; for, said he, the poor man has sweated through these. It was true; but the Duke did not utter a groan.[32]

In 1760 he suffered a stroke from which he made a good recovery, and was able to attend his father's funeral a few months later as chief mourner. He wore a black cloak with a train of five yards, and was forced to stand on his bad leg in the Abbey for two hours, his face distorted by the stroke, but 'bore it all with a firm and unaffected countenance. Sinking with the heat, he felt himself weighed down, and turning round, found it was the Duke of Newcastle standing upon his train, to avoid the chill of the marble'.[33]

On the King's death William and his sister Amelia moved out of their apartments in St James's; he first lived in Schomberg House in Pall Mall,[34] and then bought a house in Upper Grosvenor Street. The new King, George III, instead of cold-shouldering his uncle as might have been expected, treated him with courtesy and distanced himself from his mother's hostility towards him. When he married Princess Charlotte in 1761, it was the Duke who gave her away, and the King often turned to him for advice; as he now held no official position, he was able to help his nephew through the political minefields of the early part of his reign. In March 1765 the Duke was thought to be dying, but rallied and ordered his equipage for Newmarket; and in April he was called upon by the King to deal with a government crisis. He went to London from Windsor and organised the formation of a new ministry, and, because there were riots in London, the King even asked him to return to his old post of Captain-General of the forces; he confided to him that if he should die, he hoped the Duke would act as regent during his son's minority.

In October the Duke came up to London to attend a meeting of the Privy Council. In the evening he was playing piquet with General Hodgson when he grew confused over his cards; but he recovered, and the next day went to court, dined with Lord Albemarle and had tea with his niece. In the evening he complained of a feeling of suffocation, and his valet was preparing to bleed him when he cried 'It is too late! It is all over!' and died.[35] He was buried with military honours at Westminster Abbey. An eloquent eulogy was given in the House of Lords:

> The many eminent public and private virtues, the extent of capacity, and the magnanimity of mind; the affection to his Majesty's person, and the eminent services performed for this country, which distinguished this great and excellent Prince, have made an impression never to be erased from the minds of a grateful people.

At Windsor, feelings were mixed: some resented his refusal to allow people into the Park to collect firewood, others were grateful for the work he had given them.

> The large sums he yearly expended there, and the numbers of workmen that he daily employed and regularly paid, have rendered that place one of the wonders of England, and make his loss most severely felt by that town and neighbourhood.[36]

We too might have mixed feelings about him in relation to Cumberland Lodge. In enlarging it to create a princely residence, he destroyed the elegant symmetry of Byfield House; but his transformation of the Great Park is worthy to stand alongside the greatest achievements of the 18th-century landscape movement, and provides a happier memorial than his military exploits.

60 'The Duke and Duchess of Cumberland walking in the garden at Windsor Lodge; Lady Elizabeth Luttrell s sketching', by Gainsborough, in the Royal Collection. Duke Henry is wearing the Star of the Garter, and holds l stick aloft as if simulating the baton of authority held up by military leaders. Lady Elizabeth was often in th company, and came to an unhappy end.

Chapter Seven

The Habitation of Princes
1765-1790

Duke William left no will, so the King appointed Lord Albemarle as administrator. He had hoped to be granted the Rangership on the Duke's death, but the King wanted to keep it in the royal family. As a consolation prize he was given the Garter stall vacated by his friend and patron, and in any case he was already Ranger of Bagshot Park. The King's policy was to share out the Rangerships among his brothers: the Duke of York was Keeper of Windsor Forest and Warden of Cranbourne Chase; the Duke of Gloucester was Warden of Hampton Court; so the Rangership of Windsor Great Park went to 'Poor Fred's' youngest surviving son, the harum-scarum Prince Henry Frederick, then aged twenty. A year later, on reaching his majority, he was made Duke of Cumberland.

Prince Henry was six years old when his father died, and according to Horace Walpole his mother kept him locked up with his brother the Duke of Gloucester until he was 21, his education totally neglected. Thence he sallied forth into a life of brothels and drunkenness. Walpole's description of him is restrained:

> Henry, Duke of Cumberland, though not tall, did not want beauty, but with the babbling disposition of his brother York, he had neither the parts nor the condescension of the latter; familiarising himself with bad company, and yet presuming on a rank which he degraded ... His youth had all its faults, and gave no better promises.[1]

He was 'pert, insolent, senseless'. On a more engaging note, this Duke shares with the Duke of Gloucester the fame of having greeted the historian Edward Gibbon, then writing his monumental work *The Decline and Fall of the Roman Empire*, with the words 'So, I suppose you are at the old trade again—scribble, scribble, scribble?'—a variant of the version attributed to his brother.[2]

The young Duke soon got into trouble. In 1770 he was defendant in a lawsuit brought by Lord Grosvenor, who accused him of having had 'criminal conversation' with his wife. Embarrassing letters were read in court—'never was a public regaled with a collection of greater folly'.[3] It was the first time a royal prince had appeared as defendant in such a case, and the King with his strict moral code was deeply mortified, quite apart from his annoyance at having to help his brother to pay the £13,000 compensation required of him. Another affair produced a daughter who called herself Princess Olive of Cumberland for the rest of her life, insisting that her parents had been married.

In October 1711 he secretly married Lady Anne Horton, a beautiful widow, daughter of a disreputable Irish peer called Simon Luttrell. Anne was not to be caught out like Princess

Olive's mother; she 'took special care to be married in the face of day, and have register, certificate, and witnesses all forthcoming'. Knowing that the King would disapprove, Henry kept quiet about his marriage, but at last felt obliged to tell him. This he did by writing him a letter which he handed to him in person. Horace Walpole takes up the tale:

> After walking some time in the garden with the King, the Duke gave him the letter. The King put it into his pocket, saying, 'I suppose I need not read it now'. 'Yes, Sir,' said the Duke, 'You must read it directly.' The King had no sooner read it than he broke out in these terms—'You fool! you blockhead! you villain! you had better have debauched all the unmarried girls in England—you had better have committed adultery with all the married women—but this woman can be nothing—she shall never be anything'. The Duke asked what he would have him do. The King said, 'Go abroad till I can determine what to do'.[4]

So abroad the couple went.

What George III decided to do was to have a bill brought before Parliament preventing the marriage of members of the royal family without the sovereign's consent; if they were over 25 and consent was withheld, the marriage could take place after a year's notice to the Privy Council. After a stormy passage through the House of Lords, during which Duke Henry himself put in an appearance, anxious to discover whether the Bill would set aside his own marriage.[5] The Royal Marriage Act became law in March 1772 and is still on the statute-book. It took several months for Henry's elder brother the Duke of Gloucester to pluck up courage to tell the King of his own secret marriage, a few years previously, to the widowed Countess Waldegrave, illegitimate daughter of Sir Edward Walpole, a Whig politician (which made matters worse), and incidentally a niece of Horace Walpole who was thus well-informed. The King's reaction was to ban both brothers from court, and to forbid his courtiers to visit them, a ban which lasted for eight years and caused great scandal in the nation.

> As the King was going about this time in his sedan to a service at St James's Chapel, one of the crowd through which he passed thrust a paper into the royal chair, on which was written— 'First go and be reconciled to thy brother, and then come and offer thy gift'.[6]

Even Walpole had to concede that the new Duchess had charms:

> The new Princess of the Blood is a young widow of twenty-four, extremely pretty, not handsome, very well made, with the most amorous eyes in the world, and eyelashes a yard long. Coquette beyond measure, artful as Cleopatra, and completely mistress of all her passions and projects. Indeed, eyelashes three quarters of a yard shorter would have served to conquer such a head as she has turned.[7]

She affected not to care about being banned from court, ridiculing the King and Queen and making 'whatever appertained to rank, birth, or dignity, the object of her contemptuous sarcasms'. In any case the royal court was dull, and the Duchess's style was for wild and noisy parties; if those who frequented court refrained from visiting her, she was 'better pleased that tag, rag, and bobtail should flock in than that numbers should be wanting'.[8] Her younger sister Lady Elizabeth Luttrell, wilder even than herself, lived with them, presiding over the gaming-table they kept at Cumberland House in Pall Mall, where 'she played high and cheated much' according to the diarist, Joseph Farington; 'a noble harvest they made of the opulent pigeons that frequented it'.[9] Though most of these parties took place at their London house, the Lodge was no doubt also the scene of revelries of a kind unknown since the days of Charles II and Baptist May.

61 'His Royal Highness the Prince of Wales, with a Lady of Quality, going to Ascot Races'. He initiated the custom of the royal drive in carriages to Ascot which is still followed today.

After eight years the King relented, and the two Dukes—though not their wives—were allowed to attend court; but the reconciliation was only formal. About this time the Cumberlands took up with the 18-year-old Prince of Wales. Their entourage provided much more fun for the young Prince than his parents' stuffy court. They led him on in drinking, gambling, horseplay and sexual adventures: the King suspected the Duchess of having introduced him to the pleasures of the flesh. When the Prince was of age, he was given Carlton House, which with its gardens adjoining those of Cumberland House was all too convenient for the furthering of this disastrous association. Perhaps the saddest thing for the King was that they taught the Prince to be contemptuous of his father.

As it happened, it was through the Cumberlands that the Prince became familiar with two places that were to become important to him in later life: Brighton and Windsor Great Park. He was invited to stay with them at a house they rented on the Steine at Brighton, and he revelled in the celebrations organised in his honour. As for the Great Park, the Duke gave him a key of his own: 'I enclose a key of the Park', he wrote in 1780, 'Shall be happy at all times that the Park may afford you every amusement you can wish'.[10] The Cumberlands were in the secret of the Prince's marriage to Mrs. Fitzherbert in 1785, though who better than they knew that it contravened the Royal Marriage Act? Eventually the Duke became too presumptuous in his attitude to his nephew. He found it amusing to call him Taffy, an allusion to his principality, which so irritated the Prince that this as much as anything else caused their friendship to wane.

The Great Park and Lodge were not the inspiration to Duke Henry that they had been to his predecessor: his London house was his main base; but he frequently went to Windsor Lodge, mainly for hunting, or for a partridge shoot, or, as reported in *The Times* of 7 November 1787, to celebrate his birthday. He kept up the Ascot tradition, instituting a cup which later became the Gold Cup. Duke William had given enough impetus to the development of the Park for work to go on until the end of the century, in the devoted hands of Thomas Sandby. In

62 An old engraving showing the new north front and stables, probably copied from Sandby's pictures. A hunt is assembling.

1764 Sandby had become House Steward at Windsor Lodge and by the same token acted as deputy to the Duke as Ranger; he lived at the Little Lodge, or Dairy, which was later to become Royal Lodge. Here his gifted artist brother Paul often came to stay, and they both recorded Windsor and its Park in a number of charming paintings. As a new steward with a new Ranger, Sandby pressed for the carrying out of repairs which had awaited a Treasury grant for ten years. As a result, the Lodge was repaired, painted and whitewashed, together with outbuildings and the garden sheds where melons and mushrooms were grown; fences were repaired and painted, including the 'Ha Ha fence round Pleasure-ground and Gardens'.[11] The drop today from the lawn behind the house to the field below suggests that the ha-ha went along here to prevent animals from straying in, without interrupting the view.

The Lodge itself was much as Duke William had left it, his furniture having been bought by the King and for the most part left there. *The Windsor Guide* of 1783 gives a description:[12]

> The great park lies on the south side of the town, and opens by a very noble road, called the long walk, on each side of which runs a double plantation of stately trees, to the summit of a delightful hill (called Snow Hill) at near three miles distance from the entrance; this leads to the ranger's lodge, the seat of his royal highness the duke of *Cumberland*, and formerly the residence of his late royal highness, the duke of *Cumberland*, who greatly improved the natural beauty of this delightful park, by large plantations of trees, extensive lawns, new roads, and spacious canals, which have rendered this villa an habitation worthy of a prince.
>
> The first room of the lodge is neatly hung with plain paper, ornamented with prints, among which are improvements made by his royal highness in the park,—*Sanby* Esq.
>
> In the dining-room, over the chimney-piece, is his royal highness's stud, by *Gilpin*, 1764.
>
> The drawing-room. The ceiling, cornice, and pilasters of this room, are most superbly gilt; over the chimney is a portrait of her royal highness the present duchess of *Cumberland*, by Miss Reid.
>
> In the first passage is an excellent painting of the crossing of the Rhine, and in another passage are two pagodas.
>
> The pages waiting-room is ornamented with several good sea-pieces, among which is the *Monmouth* engaging the *Foudroyant*.
>
> In the music-room are several of the late duke's breeding-mares, and over the chimney is marshal *Saxe*.

The breakfast-room is hung with paper of a lilac ground, ornamented with curious painted lime-trees, which have a very pleasing effect.

In the apartments above stairs, are several paintings by the best masters; but these rooms being bedchambers, are not shewn to strangers.

An earlier description, from which some of this is taken, is to be found in Appendix Three. In the 1770s George III became more and more drawn to Windsor, but the Castle had been unused since Queen Anne's day and was uninhabitable. He looked about for a suitable residence until it could be repaired, and the obvious answer seemed to be Windsor Lodge. Accordingly he offered his brother (who was always short of money) an annual pension of £6,000 if he would give up the Lodge and Rangership.[13] Henry and his Duchess were in no mood to oblige the King, and the offer was refused. Instead, at great expense, Queen Anne's House near the Castle and Burford House (built for Nell Gwyn) were renovated to house the King and Queen and their large family, the two houses becoming known as the Upper, or Queen's, Lodge and the Lower Lodge.

As he spent more time at Windsor, the King took so much interest in the Park that those working in it were confused by receiving instructions from both King and Ranger. In 1768

63 'The Queen's Drawing Room, Cumberland Lodge'. Pencil drawing by T. Kearnan, 1816, in the Royal Collection. The ceiling, cornice and pilasters were 'superbly gilt'. The connection with the Queen was probably a compliment from Duke William rather than Duke Henry, of whose way of life Queen Charlotte disapproved.

Virginia Water flooded over its inadequate dam of sand and clay (earning for Sandby the nickname Tommy Sandbank), and after this disaster much attention was given to this area of the Park for the next 20 years. After another serious flood in 1782, the lake was enlarged, the great cascade constructed, and a huge programme of landscaping carried out, with hills, lawns, and woods offering surprise views of the lake which still delight us. The plans were submitted to the King rather than to the Ranger, the Surveyor General of Woods and Forests seeing himself as directly responsible to the King, whereas Sandby was responsible to the Ranger. One would inadvertently undo the work the other had ordered, as when the Duke, seeing grass ten inches high, ordered it to be mown, thus destroying the oak and beech seedlings planted on the King's orders. 'I fear it will not escape His Majesty's Eye', the Surveyor General wrote ruefully to a colleague.[14] These misunderstandings did not improve relationships between the two brothers and, according to William Menzies, at one point things reached such a pass that the Duke threatened to lock the gates to keep the King out.[15]

These differences were abruptly resolved one day in September 1790. The Duke came up to town from Windsor Lodge to attend a concert at his London house, intending to return to the Lodge the next day to go hunting. He had been suffering from an 'eating ulcer', and stepping out of his coach he felt excessively weak and exclaimed, 'I feel now that I am going', which he did that same night. Reporting this news, *The Gentleman's Magazine* did its best to commend him:

> The loss of the Prince will be much regretted by those who had an intimate acquaintance with his character, in which many amiable qualities predominated over the frailties incident to human nature. His domesticks, in particular, and all those who were employed by him, will have great cause to lament the melancholy event.[16]

His funeral was as flamboyant as his life, taking place at 10 o'clock at night with a torch-light procession. The King was not present.

Chapter Eight

A House in Abeyance
1790-1865

1: Farmer George and Gothic Additions

After Duke Henry's debts were paid, there was nothing left to provide for the Duchess. The King offered her an annuity of £4,000 which she considered far too small, complaining to the King, to the Prince of Wales, to Prime Minister William Pitt, and to anyone else who would listen; but, as the Prince said, it was like trying to whip blood out of a post.[1] She continued to 'throw herself on the mercy' of the King, in vain, and wore out the Prince's patience with her protests. A valuation of the effects at Windsor Great Lodge was made for Pitt shortly after the Duke's death, and amounted to £8,440, but there was no question of a sale, the King sharply reminding Pitt that he had bought the furniture on his uncle's death: 'The late Duke had certainly only the loan of it'.[2] The King, however, allowed the Duchess to stay on at Cumberland Lodge, though she was there only intermittently, often going abroad where she said it was cheaper to live.

On his brother's death, George III took on the Rangership himself, and the intimate connection between Lodge and Rangership ceased for 80 years. The King's friend General (later Earl) Harcourt was appointed Deputy Ranger, living in his own house at St Leonard's Hill. Little was done to the Lodge while the Duchess remained its tenant; it is surprising therefore to find Nathaniel Kent, the King's agricultural adviser, recording that on 5 October 1794 he arrived at the Lodge and 'had the satisfaction to observe that Divine Service had been performed for the first time to upwards of seventy persons that morning in the Chapel with great propriety by Dr. Oglander; who in his sermon stated his Majesty's goodness in the present establishment, which gave them the opportunity of attending to their religious duty with more ease than they could do before'.[3] The chapel which Duke William had begun shortly before his death was left unfinished during Duke Henry's time—it would scarcely have ranked high in his priorities. There is a Sandby drawing of the unfinished building, which was situated beyond the present kitchen courtyard. Efforts were made in the early years of Duke Henry's Rangership to make something of it by converting it into a Doric temple; there were also plans for a colonnade linking this to the garden front of the house, but these never materialised. Today Studio Cottage, a charming house with a glass turret, is situated in this area. On the King's initiative, the chapel where Dr. Oglander officiated was contrived out of a room in the service area which later became the servants' hall. The arched entrance and apsidal shape of the present staff parlour bear witness to its past use.[4]

64   King George III (studio of W. Beechey, on loan to Cumberland Lodge from the National Portrait Gallery). This attractive portrait shows the king wearing the Garter Star, and dressed in military uniform. The horse suggest mettle and power. (National Portrait Gallery)

One of the King's main interests in the Rangership was the opportunity it gave him to put into practice his progressive ideas about agriculture. The Norfolk and Flemish farms were created for his experiments in farming methods, and still exist today (see back endpaper). In his farming capacity he gave himself the name Ralph Robinson, using it in correspondence about the farms, and earning him the nickname 'Farmer George'. Nathaniel Kent had permission to use the outbuildings at the Lodge in the service of the farms, and several were taken over or taken down, including the suttling-house, which had become a public house, 'liable to great abuse'. The Lodge itself provided rooms for some of the Park officials, including Kent.[5]

The kitchen gardens attached to the Lodge were looked after irrespective of who lived in the house, as their produce was needed to serve the royal table. An innovation at this time was the planting of the Cumberland Great Vine in a vinery near to the present Royal School. It came from the same parent as the Hampton Court Vine, both being grown from cuttings from a vine grown at a famous nursery, Valentine's in Great Ilford; it was known as the Black Hamburg, or Hambro, Grape Vine, having been imported from Hamburg in 1758. The vine at the Great Lodge yielded a greater weight of fruit than either of these, averaging in its hey-day some 2,000 bunches. Its stem was 3 ft. 8 in. round, and its roots reached Great Meadow Pond, a quarter of a mile away. From time to time throughout the Victorian period the vinery had to be enlarged, until it reached 138 ft. in length and 20 ft. in width. The grapes were sent to hospitals all over the country. The vine survived until World War Two, when patriotic fervour caused it to be discarded in the interest of growing tomatoes in the Food for Britain campaign. The Royal Gardener wisely made some cuttings, so young plants from the Cumberland vine are still being cultivated. Another Black Hambro is flourishing at Dartford, where Mr. Leslie Stringer has nurtured it to a yield of over 7,000 bunches and well over 1,000 lbs., winning it a place in the *Guinness Book of Records*.[6]

In 1803 the Duchess seems to have given up the Lodge to live abroad permanently, and *The Times* of 10 March 1809 briefly reported her death 'at her retreat in Switzerland'. Her departure in 1803 opened the way for a burst of activity. The King had always liked, indeed coveted, the house, and he now decided to enlarge, modernise and beautify it, presumably with the intention of using it himself. During most of his reign he was affected by bouts of apparent insanity, now thought to have been caused by a disease called porphyria; today this is controllable by drugs, but then it was treated, even in the case of a king, by the unmerciful methods of the day. Small wonder that the King longed to have a place of quiet retreat, and the Lodge was ideally suited to his purpose. It was near to one of his experimental farms, the Norfolk Farm, which he frequently visited, walking five miles from Windsor to the southern end of Great Meadow Pond where it is still situated. He liked drawing and painting, and a local belief persists that he used Studio Cottage for that purpose. The Lodge therefore was convenient for two of his greatest pleasures.

The King's chosen architect for the changes he wanted to make at the Lodge was James Wyatt, master of the Gothic style which harked back to Horace Walpole's Strawberry Hill, and had become fashionable in architecture and in literature, when the nation discovered its medieval past. Wyatt was supervising alterations to Windsor Castle, and he had designed additions to Cranbourne Lodge for the Duke of Gloucester, who succeeded his brother the Duke of York as Keeper of Windsor Forest and Warden of Cranbourne Chase; by 1799 he had also built Sandpit Gate and Lodge in the Gothic idiom (see Figure 69). The Castle was ready for occupation in 1804, and work had already started at the Lodge, which now acquired its present name of

65 A perspective view of the back part of the chapel at Windsor Great Lodge, by Thomas Sandby, 1765. This puzzling composition suggests an architect's test-piece in perspective rather than a picture, the figures introduced to give a narrative element. The unfinished chapel was eventually converted into a 'temple' as a feature in the grounds of the Lodge.

66 Studio Cottage now stands where the unfinished chapel is thought to have stood.

Cumberland Lodge. Wyatt rebuilt the garden side of the house in Gothic style, building a square central tower with ornamental turrets spaced out on either side, and furnished with battlements and pointed windows. This probably involved moving the staircase northwards to the adjoining room. We are unable now to tell how much of the house it was intended to embellish in this way, because the money ran out. By July 1804 £2,209 0s. 11°d. was needed for work done at the Lodge and at the Windsor gardens, and the Treasury made heavy weather, telling the Office of Works to curb its expenditure:

> No alteration, addition or repair may henceforth be commenced at any of His Majesty's Palaces or Houses but such as the Surveyor-General may deem absolutely and indispensably necessary for the prevention [preservation] of the Building.[7]

The money was not produced for at least a year and no more was forthcoming, so the King's project remained unfinished. The result of Wyatt's work was to impose yet another element on the original shape of Byfield House, which had already been aggrandised by Duke William's palatial extension.[8] In August 1804 the King's illness manifested itself again in erratic and extraordinary behaviour: he took a violent dislike to the Queen, saying that he was going to have the Great Lodge fitted up entirely for himself, together with one of her ladies and the two youngest princesses. One of his sons reported that

> on going to see the lodge the other day with two of the Princesses he accidentally met a housemaid called Sally and appeared in ecstasies at seeing her—that he desired the Princesses to stay above stairs when he came down and went into the room where she was and locked himself in with her for three quarters of an hour.[9]

By November he was in a more stable mood, and *The Gentleman's Magazine* reported that 'his Majesty, the Dukes of Kent and Cambridge, and Princesses Sophia and Amelia, with their usual attendants, went to Cumberland Lodge to see the great improvements making there'.[10] In December 1804 Lord Essex wrote to Lord Lowther, 'His buildings go on at Windsor, Kew, the Duke's Lodge in the Great Park, and what was called Sandby's lodge; at all these he has extensive plans for improvement ... This is magnifique, mais qui payera?'[11]

The King's plans to 'live snug' at the Lodge never materialised, for from 1805 onwards his health deteriorated steadily and he began to go blind. By 1811 it was apparent that no great improvement could be expected, and George Prince of Wales was declared Regent. 'Prinney', as his friends called him (though not to his face), was delighted, and at once embarked on plans for a residence near Windsor consistent with his new status. What could be more suitable than Cumberland Lodge? As for several years it had not been lived in except by 'a few domestics', it had fallen far below the standards the Prince Regent would require. Plans were made for its improvement.[12]

2: John Nash and the Royal Cottage

The Prince's favoured architect was John Nash, whose star was now in the ascendant. Rumour had it that his career took off after 1798, when it seems he made a marriage that obliged the Prince, and fortune and favour followed.[13] Wearing his hat as surveyor to the Office of Woods and Forests, Nash thought that the refurbishment could be paid for by the sale of 'top and lop' from the trees in the Forest. While repairs were going on, the Prince could be housed in Dairy Lodge where Sandby had lived as Deputy Ranger, provided a modest amount of work was done

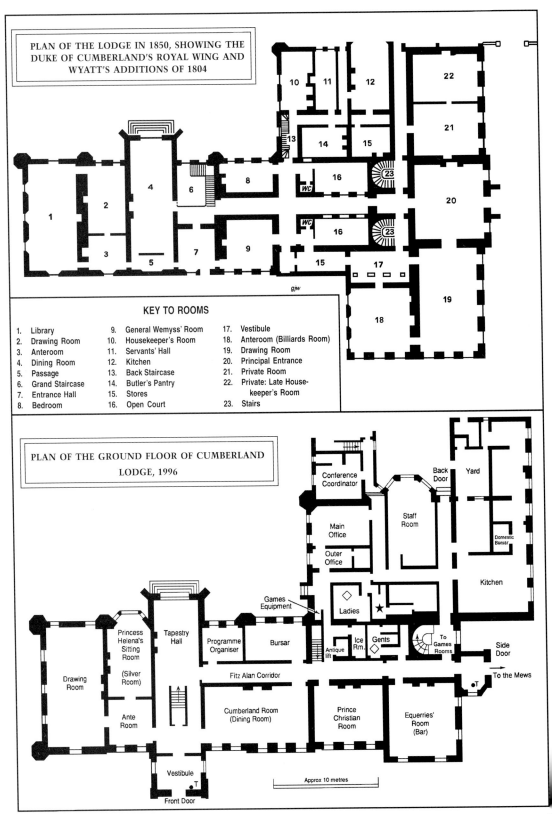

PLAN OF THE LODGE IN 1850, SHOWING THE DUKE OF CUMBERLAND'S ROYAL WING AND WYATT'S ADDITIONS OF 1804

KEY TO ROOMS

1. Library
2. Drawing Room
3. Anteroom
4. Dining Room
5. Passage
6. Grand Staircase
7. Entrance Hall
8. Bedroom
9. General Wemyss' Room
10. Housekeeper's Room
11. Servants' Hall
12. Kitchen
13. Back Staircase
14. Butler's Pantry
15. Stores
16. Open Court
17. Vestibule
18. Anteroom (Billiards Room)
19. Drawing Room
20. Principal Entrance
21. Private Room
22. Private: Late House-keeper's Room
23. Stairs

PLAN OF THE GROUND FLOOR OF CUMBERLAND LODGE, 1996

67 *Top.* Plan of the Lodge in 1850, showing the Duke of Cumberland's Royal Wing and Wyatt's additions of 1804 (After British Library MPE 586). *Bottom.* Plan of the Ground Floor of the Lodge, 1996.

on it. This plan was agreed by the Treasury, but when Cumberland Lodge was examined more closely, it was found that it would cost much more than Nash's guessed estimate had suggested, and the Treasury decided it would cost less to enlarge Dairy Lodge than to put Cumberland Lodge into good order. They could not have been more mistaken: the Regent's Cottage, which grew into the Royal Lodge, became a bottomless pit into which tens of thousands of pounds were poured, and which even then was not completed when he died in 1830.

Meanwhile Cumberland Lodge still had to be maintained, and in 1814 Nash specified repairs 'absolutely necessary to be done'. By this time he had been promoted to fill the gap left at the Office of Works by Wyatt's death, and was busily engaged in the development of Regent's Park and the grand new street linking this to Carlton House; Brighton Pavilion was soon to be on his agenda. The conversion of Dairy Lodge suited him perfectly—had he not made his name as the architect of the *cottage orné* ?—and while working on the cottage he could live at Cumberland Lodge. He had a way of falling on his feet which did not endear him to his colleagues, and if they could find fault with his recommendations they did so, thus causing delay. One item for repair was 'the unfinished Temple near the Kitchen Buildings' where he recommended 'such repairs as will secure it from falling', but nothing was done and two months later a report from the site announced that 'the Temple roof is fell in'. This building separated the kitchen area from the gardens, and after its demolition Nash was rebuked for putting up a wall to serve this purpose instead, without prior sanction. He was also found to have included the same washhouse, brew-house and farrier's shop on separate estimates for both the Lodge and the Cottage. As a result the Surveyor-General refused to authorise any more work for three months.

68 John Nash, by Landseer. Favoured by the Prince Regent, he lived at Cumberland Lodge while directing the transformation of Dairy Lodge into the Royal Cottage. He is better known for developing Regent Street in London.

Another 'absolutely necessary' repair arose from the removal of the King's book-cases, which had lined the walls of 'the new Rooms altered by the King'. The walls had been cut away to receive them and, when for some reason they were removed, no making good was done. The wall of the rooms above, without their support, was in danger of collapse, and the place where the bookcases had stood had been left open to the ground and the walls left 'naked'; the chimney-pieces had not been replaced. In short, a thoroughly bad job had been done. Though not much given to answering letters, Nash sprang to defend himself against the charge that he was repairing the interior of the Lodge for his own use. His usual response to criticisms was to invoke the authority of the Prince Regent:

> Your last letter makes it necessary for me distinctly to state that however H.R.H. may graciously permit me to occupy any of the apartments at Cumberland Lodge as a personal convenience whilst I am transacting H.R.H. private business that the fitting up of those apartments at the Lodge is not done for my private accommodation but for that of the visitants at the Cottage, which I have no doubt H.R.H. will satisfactorily explain.

The following year he was in trouble for having made a doorway through the east front of the Lodge without authority; he referred the Surveyor-General to the Prince Regent. Responsibility for the management of the Park was shared confusingly by the Office of Works, the Commissioners of Woods and Forests and the Deputy Ranger; the joker in the pack was the Prince Regent, who driving around the Park would give orders off the cuff. Nash was adept at playing this card.[14]

He made the most of his privileged situation, entertaining his friends at the Lodge. The painter Romilly and his family spent their Whitsun holidays there: 'Our time was spent very delightfully ... I enjoyed the fine knolls and groves of beeches which form the enchanting scenery of this part of Windsor Park'. Meanwhile the Prince Regent was urging Nash to get the repairs done so that the Lodge could be papered and furnished ready to receive his guests for Ascot Week, 'there not being any convenience in the Cottage for lodging H.R.H.'s company'. The result of all these pressures on Nash and his workforce was that the work in both houses was hurriedly done, leading to constant need for more repairs.[15]

In the neighbourhood there was a general expectancy that the Lodge was going to be rebuilt; but this was not to happen for another half century, and then only as a result of a catastrophe. The 1827 edition of *The Windsor Guide* describes the house as being of 'stuccoed brick'; Nash was known to be partial to stucco, so perhaps this was his way of leaving his mark upon the Lodge. After the Prince Regent became King, Nash fell out of favour, and it was James Wyatt's nephew Jeffry (who gentrified his name to Wyatville) who received the commission for yet another restoration of Windsor Castle, which he did in the romantic and Gothic style he had learnt from his uncle.[16]

3: King George IV and the Park

King George III died in 1820, and George IV was crowned king in Westminster Abbey in July 1821, his estranged wife Princess Caroline banging on the door to be let in. The previous year, when he refused to receive a letter of complaint from her, she had sought the support of the press by sending it to *The Times*, which had shown sympathy for her cause, as had the general public. *The Times* more than doubled its circulation; the King remained obdurate; Caroline died

69 King George IV at Windsor, from a drawing by G. Scriven in the Royal Library. He could still cut a fine figure, as long as he remembered to wear his stays.

70 'George IV taking his favourite exercise near the Sandpit Gate, Windsor Park', a drawing in the British Library. One of the oldest gates in the Park, Sandpit Gate and its Keeper's Lodge were redesigned in Gothic style by James Wyatt.

71 The statue of George III on Snow Hill, commissioned by George IV. Known today as 'The Man on the Copper Horse', it provides a favourite walk from Cumberland Lodge, and a magnificent view of Windsor.

three weeks after the coronation.[17] Their only child, Charlotte Princess of Wales, who had married Prince Leopold of Saxe-Coburg, had died in 1817 giving birth to a son, who also died. Had she lived, she and not her cousin Victoria would have become Queen. Her mournful memorial is to be seen in St George's Chapel, Windsor.

In the early days of his reign, the King used the Royal Cottage only for special occasions such as Ascot week, putting up his guests at Cumberland Lodge. At the races he still sometimes showed his old style. Creevey in his diary describes an occasion in 1823:

> Another charming day we had. Prinney came as before, bowling along the course in his carriage and four. In passing the young Duchess of Richmond's open landau he played off his nods and winks and kissing his hand, just as he did to all of you 20 years ago on the Brighton racecourse.[18]

That year he stayed on for his birthday on 12 August, when he gave a great ball at the Lodge for his Windsor tradesmen, and another the next night for his liveried servants; splendid occasions these must have been, using the now vanished grand rooms at the north end. Cumberland Lodge and the Royal Cottage were now contained in one big enclosure, so it was a special privilege for the townsfolk to be invited in.

The King used to drive over to St George's Chapel to Sunday services, but soon changed to the nearer and more private chapel at Cumberland Lodge. Then he decided to have a new chapel built in the grounds of his cottage, and this was completed by Wyatville in 1825; the chapel at Cumberland Lodge was used to extend the kitchen area so that it could serve the stable lads. The King went driving daily in the Park in his phaeton, using avenues from which the public were excluded: as he grew older he began to shun the public gaze, becoming virtually a recluse in his last years. A favourite halt was at Sandpit Gate, where, following his great-uncle's example, he kept a menagerie. There, 'seated in his pony-chaise with his favourite cockatoo on his arm, [he] enjoyed his glass of cherry gin, which was always kept in preparation for him'.[19] As well as the chamois, wapitis and gazelles and the much-loved giraffe which died, there was presumably an elephant, as the 'elephant-boy' lived in the stables of Cumberland Lodge.

Another favourite place was Virginia Water, where the King would go fishing and entertain his friends in the fantastic Chinese Fishing Temple he had built on the island where Manor Lodge had once stood. One of his visitors was Princess Victoria who, in August 1826 when she was seven years old, came to stay at Cumberland Lodge for three days with her mother, the Duchess of Kent. Victoria tells the story many years later. They were invited to the Royal Lodge to see the King; he took her by the hand, saying, 'Give me your little paw', and gave her his picture set in diamonds. 'None of the Royal Family or general visitors lived at the Royal Lodge,' she remembered, 'but only the Conyngham family.' Everyone else was at Cumberland Lodge. Next day she was out walking with her mother near the Lodge when the King drove by, stopped, gave orders to 'pop her in', and swept her off on a fishing expedition to Virginia Water—to her mother's consternation as she never let her daughter out of her sight.[20] Lady Conyngham, the King's favourite, was well established at the Royal Cottage; her married son Lord Mount Charles had rooms at Cumberland Lodge, but in 1829 was told to leave—to his great indignation—because he had transgressed by talking outside of a political matter heard privately.[21]

Meanwhile Cumberland Lodge was moving ahead with the times. In 1825 the Master of the King's Household wrote respectfully to the Surveyor-General, saying that, 'It would be a great accommodation to a branch of His Majesty's Household residing at Cumberland Lodge if the Surveyor-General would sanction the erection of a water closet within the house'.

In 1824 an orangery had been authorised; in 1825 a new mess room 'for Single Servants' was built on the site of the old brewhouse; and in 1826 an ice-house was approved; the Treasury could not see its way to providing new stables at a cost of £12,000, but 20 temporary coach-houses were put up in 1829. There were also constant requests from John Aiton, head gardener at Windsor (son of the first curator of the Botanic Gardens at Kew), who needed forcing-houses for peaches, cherries and figs, brick pits for early vegetables and fruits, and 'a fruiting pine pit'. He was hard-pressed to meet the needs of royal entertaining.[22]

In the course of his rebuilding work at Windsor Castle Wyatville had built the George IV gateway, splendidly terminating (or beginning) the Long Walk. 'On Saturday afternoon,' the *Windsor and Eton Express* reported on 1 January 1825, 'his Majesty came to Windsor Castle in a coach and four, and went through the new gateway for the first time.' The King proposed to put up an equestrian statue of his father at the other end, on Snow Hill. This was commissioned from Richard Westmacott, who modelled it on the statue of Marcus Aurelius in Rome. In 1829 the King celebrated his birthday by laying its foundation stone inscribed

GEORGIO TERTIO
PATRI OPTIMO
GEORGIUS REX

Age had mellowed his feelings for his father, as a century earlier it had mellowed those of Sarah Churchill for Queen Anne. The enormous statue, weighing 25 tons, and large enough (according to the local story) for the workmen to sit eating their sandwiches inside it, was not ready to be put up until 1831, by which time George IV was dead.

4: A Redundant House?

George IV was succeeded by his brother William IV, who at once showed himself to be a man of the people. He put himself across as a bluff sailor, having entered the navy at the age of thirteen and made a career in it. The local paper reported that 'the moustaches of the Horse Guards are to come off; and the French Cooks have received marching orders'.[23] People warmed to his genial manner, finding him an improvement on his predecessor; even his nickname, 'Silly Billy', was affectionate rather than scornful. He assumed the office of Ranger himself, and promptly opened up all his brother's private drives and avenues. He was already Ranger of Bushey Park and, being comfortably settled in Bushey House, he had no use for the Royal Cottage. When the first requests for repairs came in he ordered most of it to be demolished, its stones being used to build Adelaide Cottage at Frogmore for the Queen. Some of the late King's furniture from the Royal Lodge and many of his books and pictures were sent to Cumberland Lodge to be stored; it was already being used as a repository for royal pictures, especially equestrian paintings by Stubbs. Much of the racing stud was sold off, and the menagerie animals were sent to the new zoo in Regent's Park.

The fate of the Lodge remained undecided. The new King offered it to his brother the Duke of Sussex, who had been appointed Lord Steward of Windsor, but he did not take up the offer. Then it was rumoured in 1832 that the Duke of St Albans, Hereditary Grand Falconer, was to make it his official residence, build a mews and revive the ancient art of falconry; but this did not happen either. The King's view as reported to the Prime Minister was that it was 'perfectly useless' as a royal residence, but 'admirably calculated for a cavalry barracks'; but this was not (yet) to be its fate.[24] The house continued to be used occasionally for royal guests, such as Lord and Lady Falkland who came for their honeymoon in December 1830. Lady Falkland was Amelia Fitz-clarence, the King's youngest daughter by his former 'common-law wife' the actress Mrs. Jordan. It was also used as a convenient residence for royal pensioners who had small apartments in it.[25]

Lord Harcourt had died a week before King George, and he was succeeded as Deputy Ranger by Sir William Fremantle. He lived at Holly Grove, near Sandpit Gate, which was bought as a residence for him. It is in a letter from him to the Surveyor-General of the Office of Works that we come across the first mention of a fire engine at Cumberland Lodge. He asks for it to be repaired as it is in 'a state of great neglect ... we should regret extremely in case any fire took place in the immediate Neighbourhood of the Park to find that there was an engine which could not be used'.[26] This is of interest to us today, as it may well have been the same as the rediscovered fire engine now on view in the Mews, which experts say dates back at least to the 1840s (see Figure 126). Sir William considered the fire-engine to be the responsibility of the Surveyor-General, and he embarked on a lengthy correspondence with the latter and with the Commissioners of Woods and Forests about their respective duties in the management of the Great Park. It was the sort of discussion Sarah Churchill would have carried on with zest, though with less urbanity and more passion. The correspondence, all hand-written by the principals concerned, without benefit of secretaries and word-processors, went on for years, until its flow was halted by the appointment of Prince Albert as Ranger.

5. A new era

Queen Victoria succeeded her uncle in 1837, and married Prince Albert in 1840. She wished her appointment of him as Ranger to be seen as a mark of special favour. The announcement was made in April 1841:

> The Queen has been pleased to appoint His Royal Highness Prince Albert to be Ranger of the Great Park at Windsor, with all such Powers and Authorities, and in as ample a manner as the Queen is enabled to grant the same.[27]

The Queen granted Cumberland Lodge to Henry Paget, Earl of Uxbridge, who was Lord Chamberlain early in her reign. With his young wife and children from two marriages he lived in some style, having 20 living-in servants as well as grooms and gardeners in the outbuildings.[28] He was in office for the Queen's wedding, but a general election in 1841 brought Sir Robert Peel and the Tories to power, which occasioned a change-over of senior staff in the Royal Household. Uxbridge ceased to be Lord Chamberlain, to Prince Albert's satisfaction as he disapproved of his scandalous private life and was determined to clean up the Court. He was replaced at Cumberland Lodge by the Prince's Clerk-Marshal, General William Wemyss, who looked after the Prince's equestrian and agricultural establishments, for like George III Prince Albert was interested in farming. The farm bailiff was installed in what remained of the Royal Cottage.

General Wemyss lived more modestly than Lord Uxbridge, occupying only part of the house with a mere half-dozen servants living in.[29] He died at the Lodge in 1852, and Prince Albert appointed Alexander Nelson Hood, son of Lord Bridport, to succeed him as Clerk-Marshal, and he moved into the older part of Cumberland Lodge in 1853. A Colonel in the Army, he had been Groom-in-Waiting to Queen Victoria since 1841, and in 1858 was appointed Equerry. By the time of the 1861 census he and his wife had six children at home with them, a governess, and a staff of 17 resident servants, as well as the usual contingent of grooms, gardeners and other servants living in and around the stables. In 1850 Sir William Fremantle died and was succeeded as Deputy-Ranger by Prince Albert's Equerry, Major-General Francis Seymour, who like his predecessor lived at Holly Grove. Prince Albert, as Ranger, now had people of his own choosing in all the significant positions in the Park.

72 Alexander Nelson Hood, later Lord Bridport, took over the management of the farms in the Park in 1851, and came to live in the Lodge with his large family when Prince Albert appointed him Clerk-Marshal.

73 Group at Cumberland Lodge on the occasion of the wedding of the Hon. Mary Hood, daughter of Lord and Lady Bridport, and the Hon. Captain Hugh Seymour, son of the Deputy Ranger, General Francis Seymour, 16 April 1868. This is the earliest known photograph taken at Cumberland Lodge.

Standing, from left to right: Lt. Col George Ferguson; Hon. Rosa Sandys; General Francis Seymour; Lady Emily Seymour; Nina, Hon. Mrs. George Ferguson; Hon. Mrs. Wellesley; Hon Anna Maria Sandys; Prince Christian of Schleswig-Holstein; Mary, Lady Filmer; Lord Bridport; Miss Mary Seymour (bridesmaid); Hon. Alexander Hood; Miss Georgina Seymour (bridesmaid); Rev. St John Blunt.

Seated, from left to right: Hon. Victor Hood; Hon. Adelaide Hood; Col. Hon. Dudley De Ros; Lady Bridport; Mrs Erskine; Mr. Erskine; Princess Christian; the bride and groom; Hon. Victor Seymour; Capt. Arthur Hood; Hon. Rosa Hood; Miss Constance Seymour; Hon. Albert Seymour; Hon. E. Hood.

The attitude of Queen Victoria and Prince Albert to the Park was quite different from that of their predecessors, although King William IV must be given some credit for preparing the way for them by opening up the Park after his brother's death. Though they enjoyed riding in it—and the Queen had little tea-houses placed at various vantage points for her refreshment while taking the air—they were not concerned to use it solely for their own pleasure, but also for the benefit of all who worked and lived in it. They had various philanthropic projects. In 1845 they established a school for Park children, realising it was not easy for them to travel to schools in the neighbourhood. The gardener's house in the Lodge kitchen gardens was fitted up as a school house, and a schoolroom built next to it.[30] The Royal School still thrives a short distance from the Lodge. Cottages for employees were built in the Park, and in 1853 Prince Albert set up a library and reading-room in two large rooms in the state apartments.[31] The rooms came to be used for Park meetings and for entertainments such as slide shows and conjuring performances. What a revolution in outlook all this represented can be measured by trying to imagine Charles II and Bab May—or indeed George IV only a decade before Victoria—making provisions of this kind.

The setting up of the Royal School went along with the dismantling of many of the garden buildings at the Lodge. In 1838 an enquiry had been carried out into the management, or rather mismanagement, of the royal gardens, as a result of which it was decided to concentrate the Windsor Gardens in the Home Park and do away with the kitchen gardens at Cumberland Lodge.[32] So the hothouses and pineapple beds, the melon ground, the peach and strawberry houses, the fruit rooms and mushroom sheds, cherished over the years by a series of gardeners, all disappeared. The Queen and Prince Albert came in person to inspect the gardens and decide what should go and what might still be useful. The orchard and the Great Vine were spared, and the orangery was reprieved with the intention of fitting it up to provide loose boxes for horses. The stables were still much used, and in 1849 a new granary was built at the end of the stables, and is now incorporated into the Mews buildings.

During these years the Queen and Prince Albert were providing the royal nursery with a succession of children—nine altogether between 1840 and 1857; by the time the youngest, Beatrice, arrived, the marriage of Vicky, the eldest, was being discussed. The Great Exhibition of 1851 had been a personal triumph for Prince Albert, who was created Prince Consort in 1857. But 1861 was to prove a fateful year for the Queen. In March her mother the Duchess of Kent died at Frogmore. The Royal Chapel in the Great Park was rebuilt as a memorial to her, the drawing-room at Cumberland Lodge serving as a temporary chapel during its rebuilding. Then in December, while she was still reeling from the shock of the loss of her mother, beloved Albert died of an illness she had not at first thought serious. Life for Victoria and for her court became black-edged like the royal notepaper, and the brunt of coping with Mama fell upon the unmarried children still living at home. Her middle child, Helena, was to stay close to her for the rest of her life; and she provides the next chapter in the story of Cumberland Lodge.

74 A statue of Prince Albert, Ranger of the Great Park on the western side of Smith's Lawn, a short walk from the Lodge. The inscription reads:

Albert Prince Consort; Born August 26 1819; Died December 14 1861. This statue was presented to Victoria Queen and Empress; A token of loyalty from the Daughters of Her Empire In remembrance of Her Jubilee June 21st 1887.

75 Queen Victoria and Prince Albert at Osborne on the Isle of Wight (photograph by Miss Day, 1859, in the Royal Photographic Archives).

Chapter Nine
An Unsung Princess
1865-1923

1: Princess Helena

On 25 May 1846, 'just after three in the afternoon a plump good-sized little girl was born'. So Queen Victoria recorded in her diary the birth of her fifth child and third daughter, who was christened Helena after her godmother Hélène d'Orléans (Albert's cousin), Augusta after Aunt Cambridge, who was also her godmother, and Victoria 'to mark her having been born the day after my birthday. I am so thankful', she went on, 'to be so strong and well this time, and my nerves so much better, so that I am more fitted to cope with worries and anxieties.' Helena was a 'pretty, fat and most thriving child darker than any of the others and has a great deal of dark brown hair'. A few days later she wrote 'the little Baby wore short sleeves for the first time today, and looked very dear and pretty'.[1] After Louise replaced her as 'baby' she was called Lenchen in the family.

As she grew up, overshadowed by her more vivacious sisters, 'dear and good' and 'poor dear' replaced 'dear and pretty' in her mother's references to her. 'Poor dear Lenchen, though most useful and active clever and amiable, does not improve in looks and has great difficulties with her figure and her want of calm, quiet, graceful manners.'[2] This was written by the Queen in a letter to her eldest daughter Princess Victoria—her beloved Vicky—in 1864 when the question of arranging Helena's marriage was being discussed in the family. She felt she must have a daughter living with her, and this was to be Helena's rôle; she would have kept Helena with her, unmarried, had not the Prince Consort indicated before his death that she should marry at 18 or 19. So a way must be found whereby Helena would marry but still live with her. Her mother would look out for

> a young, sensible Prince ... who can during my lifetime make my house his principal home. Lenchen is so useful, and her whole character so well adapted to live in the house, that ... I could not give her up, without sinking under the weight of my desolation.[3]

Helena, gentle, dutiful and unambitious, did not demur. When Frederick, Crown Prince of Denmark, seemed to be taking an interest in her the Queen warned him off, thus offending his sister Princess Alexandra, the Princess of Wales, and stirring up the strong feelings Helena's marriage was to arouse in the royal family.

It was through Princess Victoria that Christian Holstein came into the picture. Prince Christian of Schleswig-Holstein-Sonderburg-Augustenburg (the longer the title the smaller the territory actually attached to it) was a friend of the Princess and her husband Frederick (Fritz),

76 Engagement picture of Princess Helena and Prince Christian, December 1865 (photograph by Hill & Saunders, in the Royal Photographic Archives).

the Prussian Crown Prince, who had been a student with him at Bonn University. He was in a hopeless situation politically. The history of the duchies of Schleswig and Holstein was immensely complicated, and had presented a problem off and on for centuries. It was of the Schleswig-Holstein question that Palmerston said he knew of only three people who had ever understood it: the Prince Consort, who was dead; a German professor, who had gone mad; and himself—and he had forgotten. Now the suzerainty of the King of Denmark over the duchies of Schleswig and Holstein was disputed by Prussia, and Christian's elder brother the Duke of Augustenburg also laid claim to them. In this triangular situation victory went to the strong, and Bismarck annexed both duchies. Christian and his brother lost their family home and property and became exiles; Christian joined the Prussian army as a cavalry officer. However, his homelessness was a positive advantage in Queen Victoria's eyes, since he would surely be glad to come and live in England and Lenchen would be at hand to look after her. Lenchen met him in 1865 and by the end of the year they were engaged.

None of the marriages of Queen Victoria's children caused more dissension in the royal family than this one; at first it seemed as if only the Queen was in favour of it. The Prince and Princess of Wales took it as a personal slight since Christian and his brother had opposed the Princess's father, the Danish King, over the Schleswig-Holstein question; Princess Alice felt that Lenchen was being sacrificed; the younger children objected on the grounds of Christian's age (he was 15 years older than Helena and looked it) and his lack of distinction—he seemed to do nothing but smoke, eat and shoot birds. Among the general public scandalous rumours circulated: one made out that Christian was a lunatic, another that he had 15 children, one of whom would be coming to live with Helena. Queen Victoria however was determined to make the best of things. It was indeed a pity that Christian looked old for his 35 years, but she would have his cough seen to, and his teeth, and if he ate less and coddled himself less and had more fresh air he would look fresher and younger. It was too late to do anything about his colouring: 'Only I wish his mother had been dark for that constant fair hair and blue eyes makes the blood so lymphatic'.[4] Later she was to attack his 'filthy habit' of smoking. Lenchen at any rate seemed happy with him; they were

HRH Princess Helena, Princess Christian of Schleswig-Holstein. Painting by Heinrich von Angeli in the Royal
ction.

IX Edmund Bernard FitzAlan-Howard, lst Viscount FitzAlan of Derwent, by Oswald Birley. He is seen in Garter r
having been made a Knight of the Garter in 1925, after coming to live at Cumberland Lodge.

genuinely fond of one another and that was a great comfort. Helena wrote to Lady Augusta Stanley, close friend and confidante of the Queen and her family:

> I am intensely happy—what he is I cannot find words to say, so noble, precious, loving and such tact and discretion, never shrinking from saying what he thinks right—to you I say all this what I would not do to others.—I cannot say how happy I am—God has indeed richly blessed me and my heart is filled with gratitude.[5]

At last things were smoothed over, and despite earlier threats none of the family boycotted the wedding. In the end, Helena was probably the most happily married of all the family.

The wedding took place in the private chapel of Windsor Castle on 5 July 1866. The Queen made a point of giving the bride away herself, as none of her sons could replace 'dear Papa'. 'I led Lenchen, who walked between Bertie and me, and I gave her away.'[6] After the service Christian 'was much overcome when I told him with what confidence I gave our darling good Child to him'. It is heartwarming to find that Queen Victoria shared the anxieties of all brides' mothers: she wrote to Vicky, 'Lenchen looked extremely well, and so did Christian, but certain relations (an old Aunt especially) made one uncomfortable'.[7]

In June Christian had been created Royal Highness and was given British nationality; he was made a major-general in the army (an appointment which caused some controversy), and on his wedding-day the Queen 'gave him the Garter', as she expressed it. His banner is now displayed in the dining-room at Cumberland Lodge. After the Prince Consort's death the Rangership had been left vacant, so the Queen now appointed him Ranger of Windsor Great Park 'during our pleasure'. Cumberland Lodge would have been the obvious residence for the new Ranger, but the Queen had already settled on Frogmore House, where her mother had lived and where 'Bertie and Alix' had begun their married life. It was available, and moreover within easy walking distance of the castle.

2: The Great Fire

As it turned out this was a fortunate arrangement, because of the Great Fire three years later at Cumberland Lodge. Colonel Hood, who in 1868 became Lord Bridport, was still living in the old part of the house. In the newer part, two rooms were used for meetings for Park employees, and a five-roomed flat had been made for Mrs. Thurston, retired housekeeper of Windsor Castle. One Sunday morning in November 1869, as this lady was getting ready for church, Lord Bridport burst in to tell her the roof was on fire; the flames were spreading so fast that she had to leave all and flee. Lord Bridport ordered out the Lodge fire engine and sent riders to summon other engines. The Windsor Fire Brigade heard the news at 10.30, an hour after the fire had been discovered, and having got four horses from the *Castle Hotel* they reached the Lodge 'within 40 minutes after the information was received'. The local newspaper reporter clearly thought they had made very good time. He goes on to describe the operation:

> The Cumberland Lodge engine was supplied from a well, with buckets; the Great Park engine obtained a supply of water from a large tank in the stableyard, and pumped it into the Windsor Brigade engine, the hose being taken across the garden on to the roof of Lord Bridport's residence, which the flames were likely to reach, owing to the wind driving them in that direction.

By this time four more fire engines had appeared on the scene, together with over 100 troopers of the Royal Horse Guards and a company of Grenadier Guards, 'but the difficulty of getting water considerably impeded their operations'. Prince and Princess Christian and

77 'Ruins of Cumberland Lodge, Windsor Park, after the Fire'. This contemporary sketch shows the damage done to the royal apartments, the old house remaining relatively unscathed.

78 The garden front was undamaged by the fire. This view shows Wyatt's garden elevation before the roof was raised in 1912, to make a second floor out of the former attic floor.

many others had come over from the Castle and every one helped to get furniture out of the house. The report went on,

> At noon the interior of the building was a mass of flames, confined within the shell formed by the massive walls. At this time the excitement which prevailed was intense. Throngs of spectators crowded upon the open park in front of the burning building, the crowd increasing every moment as the day wore on.

Mrs. Miles in Groom's House was in a state of hysteria nearly the whole day, as her husband, the Queen's stud groom, was unable to move because of a broken leg. By one o'clock 'the interior of the fine old building was gutted completely, and the beautifully decorated apartments destroyed'. The cause of the fire was thought to have been 'a beam carried into a stack of chimneys'.[8] So the grand pavilion built for the Duke of Cumberland lay in ruins, having lasted for just over a century.

Queen Victoria arrived rather late on the scene, and she now takes up the story as she recorded it in her Journal:

> Nov.14. Heard after breakfast that Cumberland Lodge was 'on fire'... After luncheon drove off to Cumberland Lodge with Leopold, Beatrice and the Duchess of Roxburghe ... There was a great crowd there and still much smoke, but it was hoped the fire had got under. The wing in which old Thurston lived, was entirely destroyed, with most of her things, though it is hoped Ld. Bridport's have been saved. It was a dreadful scene of confusion, things lying about in every direction, and Ld. Bridport, the Governess and maids, all going about disconsolately for the many things which had been too hurriedly thrown out of the windows ... Got wet and were shown by Ld. Bridport over the house, which was completely gutted and a very melancholy sight, reminding one of the uncertainty of earthly things. In the Nursery, which was quite destroyed, Ld. Bridport and I were pumped upon and got very wet. Drove back to the Shaw Farm, where we took tea.[9]

The Queen did not seem in the least put out at having been 'pumped upon'. She went into action immediately to organise rebuilding. That same day she saw Mr. Gladstone (then Prime Minister) 'and spoke of the fire, and that the wing would have to be built up again, which he promised should be done'.

There was much discussion about how the house should be rebuilt. The Queen, the Treasury officials, the Keeper of the Privy Purse, and the Surveyor-General of the Office of Works all had their opinions. The Queen wanted a 'commodious residence' suitable for a member of the royal family; the Surveyor-General favoured a new block in Gothic style, with the east front of the old building altered to harmonise with it; the Treasury wanted whatever cost least. In the end the Treasury got its way; a new block about half the size of its predecessor was built, set back to continue the line of the east front; The architect was Anthony Salvin, a pupil of John Nash. The old house was ivy-covered, and much of the ivy had been burnt. When this was removed the walls were found to be insecure and they had to be strengthened by facing with new brickwork. The opportunity was taken at the same time to improve the kitchens, and the water supply, and to introduce 'heating by hot water pipes in the large rooms and passages', long requested by Lord Bridport who suffered from the cold.[10]

By the summer of 1872 the house was ready, and the Queen had worked out plans for it involving Prince and Princess Christian. By this time they had three children. In April 1867 the first baby was born, and was christened Christian Victor Albert Ludwig Ernst Anton, which in the family was reduced to Christle. In February 1869 there was a second son, Albert John Frederick Charles Alfred George (Abby for short), and in May 1870 the first daughter, Victoria

79   The children of Prince and Princess Christian in 1877; from left to right, Princess Helena Victoria, Prince Albert, Princess Louise, Prince Christian Victor (photograph by Hill and Saunders, in the Royal Photographic Archives).

Louise Sophie Augusta Amelia Helen (Princess Helena Victoria), known as Thora. Having three children in four years took its toll on Princess Christian's rather fragile health and this was giving cause for concern—she had constant coughs and colds and nervous trouble. The doctors thought Frogmore was unhealthy for her as it was 'low-lying and the drains were bad'; and the house was not large enough for the growing family. An ideal solution lay only two miles away: Cumberland Lodge was larger, had just been rebuilt and modernised and stood on higher ground (260 ft. above sea level). After a long holiday abroad, Helena and Christian could spend six months there to see how they liked it. Accordingly Lady Bridport was asked to place Cumberland Lodge at Their Royal Highnesses' disposal for the autumn and winter of 1872 (the worst season for Frogmore), and to prepare for their moving permanently into the Lodge in autumn 1873. The Bridports took this edict graciously—how indeed could anyone argue with Queen Victoria? A corollary of the move was that the Prince's Equerry Colonel Gordon moved from Frogmore Cottage to Royal Lodge. Meanwhile the Deputy Ranger, General Seymour, had left on becoming Marquis of Hertford, and was succeeded in 1810 by Colonel Augustus Liddell.[11]

3: A Family Home

On 6 July 1872 the Queen drove to Cumberland Lodge, 'where I went over the rooms with Ld. Bridport, to see where Lenchen is to live when she goes there'; and on 17 July Lenchen moved in.[12] Thus it was that Franzisca Josepha Louise Augusta Marie Christina Helena, Princess Louise, known later as Marie Louise, and as Louie in the family, was born at Cumberland Lodge on 12 August 1872, and christened in the Royal Chapel, Windsor Great Park, in September. The local newspaper reported that the royal party made the short journey in a carriage and pair; the Princess led her little son by the hand, and the baby, in white hood, feathers and cloak, was carried by a nurse. The Christians wanted none of the Park employees to be excluded, so there was a big crowd.[13] Helena was to have one more child, a boy called Harold born in May 1876, who died eight days later. This infant Prince is commemorated in the Royal Chapel in the Great Park by a memorial window made at the Royal Windsor Stained Glass Works.[14]

By December 1873 they were settled into the Lodge, when the Queen recorded in her Journal:

> Dec.10. Drove with Alice and Beatrice to Cumberland Lodge, where Lenchen and Christian received us, and took us over their rooms below and upstairs, which are beautifully arranged with their things from Frogmore, as well as new ones they have got. They really are splendidly lodged.

A member of the court wrote to his wife, 'The house is charming, everything quite new (at the Queen's expense) and in very good taste'.[15]

The Queen also paid for a housekeeper and two housemaids, and she helped her daughter to decide upon the livery for her servants—indeed she enjoyed organising Lenchen's household. Christian spoke out of turn when he made a number of additional requests: for a telegraph (which was granted), for 13 new coachhouses, a laundry, a dairy, all with rooms above for servants. He received a sharp rap over the knuckles:

> The Queen is obliged to remind the Prince that all outlay on Royal Residences—when of a nature to attract public attention—places Her Majesty and indeed the whole Royal Family in a very invidious and disagreeable position. There is nothing more likely to wake the attention of the House of Commons than a demand for Coach Houses for thirteen Carriages, particularly as more than £10,000 has been lately expended on Cumberland Lodge, if the demand should be known.

80 The Staircase Hall before later alterations, showing the tapestries and the walls bedecked by Prince Christian's hunting trophies: an illustration from *The Graphic*, 11 July 1891.

However, two years later she approved the addition of four rooms on the upper floor for the family; these are probably the rooms now known as the 'bachelors' corridor'. The children, coming in muddy from walking and riding in the Park, could reach them by the back stairs, as they must never be seen on the main staircase unless they were clean and tidy.[16]

At Cumberland Lodge their life settled down into a pattern of attendance upon the Queen, family life, public duties and philanthropic interests. For the children it was an ideal place to grow up: they had the freedom of the Park, with space to play, to ride, to hunt, and to go shooting and fishing. A footman taught Christian Victor how to play cricket when he was six, and he developed a lasting devotion to the game; he played in the Park, at school, at Oxford, at Sandhurst, on the North-West Frontier and in Africa, organising teams wherever he went. Albert followed him in this pursuit; each in turn captained his team at school. In 1881 Christian Victor went away to Wellington, and Albert to Charterhouse in 1884. They were the first royal children to be sent away to school, and their parents insisted that they were to be treated 'just like anyone else'.[17] The young Princesses had a German governess and three maids—one English, one French and one German; all the children were fluent in both English and German. Prince Christian had a Prussian valet, and German as well as English newspapers were delivered to the house.

As for the household, the 1881 census lists a housekeeper, a cook, four housemaids, one stillroom maid, one kitchen-maid, one scullery-maid, an under-butler, three footmen and one under-footman, and a coal porter; these all lived in the house, and other servants came in daily. They all felt great affection for Princess Christian. According to a former footman, 'she was a dear lady, and like a mother to us. If one had a cold, or was not well, she immediately detected it, and you were told to go to her dresser, Miss Moorhouse, for some remedy'.[18]

In and around the stables there were five grooms and other stablemen, four gardeners, a coachman and a wheelwright, a farrier and a farmer; and the stud groom, the much respected Josiah Miles, living in Groom's House. The western row of stables (where the grace and favour

81 *Right.* Princess Christian's sitting room, 1900, with a portrait of Prince Christian over the fireplace.

82 *Below.* Menservants at Cumberland Lodge, c.1906. The footmen are in livery, 'breeched and powdered'. Seated in front are the house steward and Prince Christian's valet, A.T. Palmer (on right), who had succeeded the Prussian valet and continued to serve the family until his death in 1932. His son, the late Ronald Palmer, donated this photograph to St Catharine's.

houses are now) was used by the Prince of Wales, and there another eight grooms lived. A bell at the Lodge summoned them to meals; it was rediscovered recently during repair work, and is now in the entrance to the mews. It appears that the menservants in the house received an allowance to make their own meals; they were therefore delighted when, for instance, Prince Arthur of Connaught brought to their pantry a gift of rabbits he had shot in the Park. The house was lit by paraffin lamps, and each evening it was the duty of one of the footmen (nicknamed Aladdin) to carry out the ritual of trimming and lighting them, and placing them in the rooms. Mishaps occurred now and then, causing small fires.[19]

A visitor to the house in 1897 described it as 'a comfortable, unpretentious home'. The drawing-room was the most formal room, but was not much used as the family preferred their smaller sitting-rooms. The furniture was mostly mahogany, and there were comfortable chairs with embroidered cushions, pictures interspersed with antlers on the walls, a great many books, family portraits, knick-knacks and curios, and flowers everywhere.[20] Lord Ribblesdale, when he was Master of the Queen's Hounds towards the end of the century, gives an attractive picture of the Lodge and its outbuildings as he saw them:

> A comfortable range of warm-toned red brick, with a high-pitched gabled roof, and all sorts of proper and sympathetic things about it—wide lawns, spreading trees, a cricket ground, and at the back a very remarkable kitchen garden. The stabling has all the dignity and character of a royal and ancient establishment ... We always had a lot of horses there, 25 or 30, and yet there always seemed to be plenty of room ... Most of it is stall stabling, but of the wide, long, generous sort, with old oak divisions and posts.[21]

Almost every day Prince and Princess Christian spent some time with the Queen, either attending her at a function or keeping her company at home, and the Queen visited them at the Lodge, calling in to see the children while driving in the Park. When she went to Osborne or to Balmoral, they were with her for at least part of the time. Princess Christian, with her kindness and easy manner, was a godsend to nervous new ladies-in-waiting whom she initiated into their duties, helping along the conversation when it flagged, even though as one lady-in-waiting remarked she seemed to be somewhat in awe of 'dear mama'.[22] The Queen tended to speak plaintively about her, saying she was inclined to coddle herself, and that Christian spoilt her; but when she was away she 'missed her terribly'. Living at Cumberland Lodge, together with her increasing involvement in charitable work, helped Princess Christian to distance herself a little from the Queen, a fact which did not pass unnoticed: when Princess Beatrice married in 1885, the Queen made it a condition that the couple should live under her roof.

Princess Christian had the accomplishments of a well-brought-up Victorian lady: she played the piano, sang, talked well and was a good hostess; her skill as a needlewoman led her to be Founder-President of the Royal School of Needlework, where examples of her work can be seen. She took an interest in the neighbourhood, singing with the local Madrigal Society and supporting the Windsor and Eton Opera Group. She visited the sick and poor, and so found out how ordinary people lived and what their needs were. Mothers who had to go out to work needed a place to leave their children so she founded a crêche. Medical help often did not reach people at home, so she set up a branch of the newly founded St John's Ambulance Brigade to equip people to help themselves; but she did not stop there: she attended classes herself, took her examinations, and gained the medallion. In 1894 she founded a Nursing Home in Windsor,

Above left. Princess Helena's bookplate, showing Cumberland Lodge, a bouquet of national emblems, and examples of various interests: music, piano, books, and a representative of Prince Christian's doves from Augustenburg, together with father's motto, which she chose for the banner of The Royal British Nurses' Association.

Above right. Medals for HRH Princess Christian's Trained Nurses, with a larger one for HRH Princess Christian's Army ing Service Reserve (worn by the nurses in the picture), a ribbon and medallion for HRH Princess Christian's Nursing e, with its motto 'Charity Never Faileth'; the small one is for Queen Alexandra's Imperial Military Nursing Service rve, which was created later. (Pictures and information by courtesy of Kathleen Whelan, former Matron of the Hospital).

'Princess Christian's Army Nursing Service ve Sisters receiving Christmas mail, 1900'. e onset of the Boer War in 1899, many s left HRH Princess Christian's Hospital ndsor to serve in Princess Christian's Army ing Reserve at hospitals in South Africa, on board hospital ships and trains. This e of nurses formed by Princess Christian forerunner of the corps of nurses that ne Queen Alexandra's Royal Army ing Corps. The Reserve uniform consisted rk blue serge dresses, cloaks faced with t and hoods lined with scarlet.

where nurses could be trained to go out and treat the sick in the community. She also carried on the work started in the Crimea of providing nursing services on the battlefield, raising a Red Cross fund for the Sudan campaign, founding the Princess Christian's Army Nursing Reserve and equipping hospital trains to serve in the South African War. Indeed it was said of her, 'Florence Nightingale planted, Princess Christian watered'.[23]

Though because of her particular sensitivity to the needs of the area she was thought of as 'Windsor's Princess', her name crops up in other places connected with other enterprises: a college for nannies in Manchester, a church in Bayswater, a scout troop in Surrey, a girls' school in Hertfordshire, a holiday home for crippled boys in Englefield Green, the Helena Club in London for 'girls of slender means'. What was characteristic was the thoroughness of her personal interest in all these concerns. She was never a mere figurehead, but everything was done unostentatiously, so that the range of her activities, and the influence she exerted, were never fully recognised.

Prince Christian supported the Princess in her various undertakings. On his own account, he was closely concerned with the foundation of the King Edward VII Hospital in Windsor, and also that of Royal Holloway College in Englefield Green, where he helped to plan the gardens.[24] He was made a Privy Councillor, a Bencher of the Inner Temple, and a governor and later President of the Royal Agricultural Society; he was involved in its Jubilee Show in the Great Park in 1899. His genial personality created a friendly community in the Park, and he took an interest in its affairs. There was an annual sports day hosted by Cumberland Lodge on the Lawn, as the ground to the north-east of the Lodge was called. There too cricket was played by the Great Park Cricket Club of which he became President; his sons played for it, both Christian Victor and Albert in turn serving as captain. They organised 'cricket weeks' at the Lodge, and in 1885 planned the laying down of a new cricket ground. Prince Christian was not a player, but he became an enthusiastic spectator. It was while watching a match at the Oval with his father that Christian Victor first met the famous cricketer W.G. Grace, and they met again at Oxford in 1886, where Christian Victor spent 18 months at Magdalen College before going to Sandhurst. Dr. Grace became a friend of the family and frequently took part in matches at the Lodge (see Appendix Four).

Prince Christian's personal interests were those of a country gentleman and sportsman. In Cumberland Lodge the walls were decked with hunting trophies. He was a follower of the Garth Hounds and enjoyed shooting-parties. One of these he enjoyed less than others, as his left eye was caught by a ricochet from a shot fired by his brother-in-law the Duke of Connaught.[25] Thereafter he wore a patch over it, or, it is said, one of a set of five artificial eyes, whichever matched his good eye best on any particular day.

Under his Rangership tree-planting continued: one of the pleasures of rambling in the Park is to come across plaques commemorating this or that family event. There are planta-tions named after Prince and Princess Christian to the north-west of the Lodge, near the school; four splendid cedars were planted by the four children near the Lodge in 1875; in 1888 an oak was planted near to the Lime-Tree Avenue to celebrate Prince Christian Victor's coming-of-age; and again in 1888, Princess Louise planted a tree in the Deer Park near to the Bishopsgate entrance to celebrate the silver wedding of the Prince and Princess of Wales. In 1887, to mark her Jubilee, Queen Victoria laid the foundation stone for the statue of Prince Albert the Prince Consort which stands on the side of Smith's Lawn, and unveiled it three years later.

86 *Above*. Cricket at Cumberland Lodge in Prince Christian's day. It will be noted that there are women players as well as men.

87 *Right*. Dr. W.G. Grace, the most famous of all cricketers, became a friend of Prince Christian and his son, and played at Cumberland Lodge. He is seen here walking across the cricket ground with Prince Christian on the occasion of Prince Albert's Veteran XI's match with Charterhouse in June 1911 (see Appendix Four). Dr. Grace is wearing a black arm band as he was in mourning for a brother who had recently died.

88   Prince Christian Victor as captain of cricket at Wellington School, 1885.

89   Prince Albert joined the Hessian Dragoons in 1889.

Meanwhile the children were growing up. After leaving Sandhurst in 1888 Prince Christian Victor joined the 1st Battalion of the 60th King's Royal Rifles, and went abroad on active service, first to India, then to Africa, where he took part in the Ashanti and Sudan campaigns, followed by South Africa and the Boer War.[26] Prince Albert left Charterhouse in 1888, and the following year joined the Hessian Dragoons, transferring two years later to serve the German Emperor in the Lieb Garde Husaren Regiment (Life Guards).[27] Throughout their boyhood there was a fairly frequent exchange of visits between the family at Cumberland Lodge and their relations in Germany. The German Emperor William II ('Kaiser Bill') kept in close touch with his cousins; he was Princess Christian's nephew, his wife the Empress Augusta Victoria was Prince Christian's niece.[28] There were also visits to the Grand Duke of Hesse, widower of Princess Christian's sister Alice; he seems to have been a favourite uncle for the two young princes, as they all loved hunting. With these connections Prince Albert's choice is understandable. He was at home in both England and Germany, and could not have imagined the convulsion that was to overtake Europe 25 years later.

Princess Victoria became the daughter who stayed at home, helping her mother in her charitable work, and taking on a good deal on her own account. A particular interest was the YMCA, and in the First World War she became Founder-President of the YMCA Women's Auxiliary Force. She enjoyed her private pursuits of reading, playing the piano, painting and needlework, as well as riding in the Park. The present chapel was her private-room, and gave her an enchanting view across the garden to the lake and beyond. She had no wish to marry into foreign royalty and go abroad to live, and so she became the devoted companion her grandmother had always looked for among her daughters.

90 Princess Helena Victoria succeeded her mother as President of HRH Princess Christian's Hospital.

As for Princess Louise, the year after planting her tree she was to meet and fall in love with His Highness Prince Aribert of the small German principality of Anhalt, and in July 1891—the day after her parents' silver wedding—they were married in St George's Chapel, the Anhalt family being guests at Cumberland Lodge for the occasion. Prince Christian Victor noted the main events in his diary:

July 4 [1891]. The Emperor arrived at Windsor today. Went down to meet him at the station.

July 5.   Papa and Mother's Silver Wedding Day. Service at 11.30. We had a big luncheon at 2.30. Family dinner at Windsor Castle at nine.

July 6.   Louise's wedding day. Wedding took place at four o'clock, and went off very well indeed. She had a great reception from the crowd.

July 8.   Garden party at Cumberland Lodge. The German Emperor and Empress were present, and also the Queen. We had a match v. Household Brigade. We dined with 2nd Life Guards in the evening ...

July 10.   Went to the Eton and Harrow match. State Concert in the evening.

July 11.   Wimbledon Review. I was galloping for Uncle Arthur. It was a great success. We all went to the Crystal Palace for dinner, where there were the most splendid fireworks.[29]

Sadly, after several years it was accepted that Louise's marriage had been a mistake: she was too adventurous a girl to be happy in the restricted environment of a small German court.

91 Princess Marie Louise was born at Cumberland Lodge in 1872; she became an adventurous traveller and wrote several books.

Princess Marie Louise movingly tells the story of her marriage in her book *My Memories of Six Reigns*, and of its ending. When visiting Canada in 1900 she received a peremptory summons to return at once to Anhalt. The reason, she learnt later, was that her father-in-law, exercising his sovereign right, intended to annul her marriage. To her eternal credit Queen Victoria, knowing what was afoot, at once sent a telegram to the Governor-General saying 'Tell my grand-daughter to come home to me, V.R.'. Louise never returned to Anhalt and her marriage was annulled that December. In 1908 it was announced that in future she would be called Her Highness Princess Marie-Louise, to avoid confusion with her aunt, Her Royal Highness Princess Louise, Duchess of Argyll (she later dispensed with the hyphen). Her marriage had given her more independence, and she was to become an indomitable world traveller, visiting North and South America, Asia and Australia, as well as Europe and Africa, where she travelled widely; her book *Letters from the Gold Coast* gives a lively account of one of these journeys.

92   Princess Marie Louise and Prince Aribert of Anhalt—a photograph taken in July 1891, at about the time of their marriage.

93 *Above.* The memorial to Prince Christian Victor on Castle Hill in Windsor.

94 *Below.* A drawing by R.T. Pritchett of the unveiling of the Prince Consort's statue on Smith's Lawn in May 1890.

4: Darker Days

The century did not begin auspiciously for the family. Out in South Africa Prince Christian Victor, who had come unscathed through numerous battles and was now serving as aide-de-camp to Lord Roberts in Pretoria, was looking forward to his return home on 10 November 1900. After playing in a cricket match (and scoring a century), he felt feverish and attributed this to over-exertion in the match; but it was enteric fever, and he died on 29 October. The Queen was at Balmoral when the wire arrived from Lord Roberts, and it fell to Princess Victoria, who had always been close to her brother, to break the news to her: 'Grandmama, he is gone'.[30] At Cumberland Lodge, where Prince Albert was staying on leave, the household was plunged into grief. The Prince, at his own wish, was buried in Pretoria alongside his men, with whom he had been extremely popular. From school onwards he had won golden opinions everywhere he went for his straightforward, unaffected and kindly nature. At home there were memorial services in various places, including St George's Chapel, Windsor, where a monument was erected by his 'devoted Grandmother, Victoria R.I.' in the Bray Chapel—not far from Baptist May's last resting-place. In 1904 Princess Christian and Princess Victoria made the journey to Pretoria to visit the Prince's grave.

Princess Christian's reaction to this bereavement was a positive one. Finding that two houses next door to her Nursing Home in Windsor were available, she bought them and converted them into a small hospital in memory of her son; so HRH Princess Christian's Hospital was founded, and still functions today.

It had been a bad year for the aged Queen. The Boer War in South Africa and the Boxer Risings in China were depressing events; her second son Prince Alfred had died in July, and her eldest daughter Vicky, now Empress Frederick of Germany, was seriously ill.[31] Christle's death seemed to be the last straw. Her strength failed, and though she lived to see out the old year she died early in January 1901, Princess Helena and her elder daughter being her constant attendants to the end.

**

In 1911 it was decided that Cumberland Lodge should be modernised by having electricity installed.[32] When work started on this, extensive dry rot was discovered in the old building and deemed by the Sanitary Adviser to the Office of Works to be a danger to health, and also to present a serious fire risk because of the large amount of timber used in the house's construction. The only satisfactory solution was to rebuild the whole of the interior of 'Byfield House'. The cost was estimated to be in the region of £10,000, and the family was asked to move out for a year; Frogmore House again became their Windsor home. Princess Christian was very insistent that they should be able to move back in October 1912: she wrote to the Surveyor-General on 3 September 1911:

> Both the Prince and I think the domestic measures recommended by Dr Packer should be adopted and not half measures which in the end always cost more! But please may we entreat the matter should be taken in hand at once—for I do not think we could arrange to be longer away than till October 1912.[33]

But the work got off to a slow start as Prince Christian was in Germany, the Princess in France, and all the officials away in Scotland.

The general upheaval provided the opportunity to make a number of internal alterations. The most important of these were the relocating of the main staircase, the creation of the present dining-room and consequent changes on the floor above. As the roof had to be renewed it was raised and the dormer windows replaced, giving more light and air to the rooms on the top floor. Additional bedrooms were made for servants so that there was less sharing of rooms: people were no longer packed in as they had been in Duke William's day. The wooden floors were replaced by concrete floors covered with parquet in the main rooms and passages. (See Appendix Five for further details of the alterations.) When new basements were constructed, there was some excitement when underground passages were found leading towards Great Meadow Pond—probably the origin of the local legend that the Lodge is connected to Windsor Castle by an underground passage 'big enough for a man on horseback to ride through', as a Park resident remarked.

A belated request was for the installation of a small hand-powered passenger lift for the 81-year-old Prince Christian. This was provided, but he found it 'practically useless' as it was too slow and cumbrous; so then as now the lift was more for show than use. Another after-thought was the provision of extra lights outside, deemed 'necessary for caretaking purposes during a period when suffragette raids were expected'.[34] The inevitable result was that the cost of all this reconstruction rose to more than double the original estimate, and that the family was not able to return until June 1913. Princess Christian had a moment of panic in 1912 when she heard a rumour from the officials in charge of the alterations that 'they think they are rebuilding Cumberland Lodge for some other Royalty ... as they consider Prince Christian has not much longer to live!' She had always understood that the house was given to her by Queen Victoria for her lifetime, but had no written document to prove it. The matter was put before King George, who firmly said that when Cumberland Lodge was finished, the Christians would occupy it, and 'no one but His Majesty himself has anything to do with future occupancy'— an important statement of principle.[35] Prince Christian wrote to the Surveyor-General:

> We cannot thank you sufficiently for all your exertions to bring the question of Cumberland Lodge to a satisfactory end. It would have been a perfect disgrace if the idea of pulling down Cumberland Lodge and building a vulgar Villa instead had been carried out.[36]

***

95   Princess Christian at home in her new sitting-room with her lady-in-waiting, after the 1912 renovation. The room was smaller prior to 1912 when a side staircase was removed. It is now the Principal's study.

96 Prince Christian at home. When his family had to leave Augustenburg, his mother took a pair of her pet pigeons and doves with her to her new home in Silesia; Prince Christian brought descendants of these to Cumberland Lodge. Each morning a bowl of peas was put out in the dining-room for him to feed them.

The outbreak of the First World War in 1914 had cataclysmic effects for Queen Victoria's family scattered throughout Europe and on different sides of the conflict. Princess Helena might have been considered lucky to have stayed in England, but it caused painful division in her family too. Prince Albert had retired from the German army with the rank of major in 1910, and had claimed the family estates in Silesia (then part of Prussia). He remained in close touch with his family, and visited Cumberland Lodge often enough to remain captain of the Great Park Cricket Club until 1914, when the club was suspended for the duration of the war.

When war broke out, Prince Albert was recalled to serve in the German army; he did so on condition that he would not be sent to fight on the Western Front. It must have been a painful and difficult position for all of them, emphasised in a publicly shaming way when Prince Albert's banner of the Order of the Bath was removed from Westminster Abbey. The King tried to resist this, saying it was part of history, explaining unconvincingly to Prime Minister Asquith that Albert was not really fighting on the side of the Germans, but was in charge of a camp for English prisoners; finally, faced with the threat of riots, he was obliged to agree.

97 Golden wedding portrait of Prince and Princess Christian, 5 July 1916 (photograph by J. Russell & Sons in the Royal Photographic Archives).

98 Cycling in the Great Park at the turn of the century. The cyclists are standing in the Lime-Tree Avenue with the Lodge showing in the distance.

Nearer home, the Sunningdale Golf Club, of which Prince Albert had been a long-standing member, and captain in 1910, had a similar debate about whether his name should be erased from the board listing the captains of the club. The argument was pursued via the Suggestion Book throughout the war, until finally it was decided in July 1918 to repaint the board, omitting the year 1910.[37] The situation improved after the war, when calmer views prevailed. Albert became Duke of Schleswig-Holstein in 1921; and in 1927 his name was restored to the list of captains of Sunningdale Golf Club; but his death in Berlin in 1931 passed unrecorded in *The Times*.[38]

Over the years, Prince Christian had become staunchly patriotic to his adopted country. He was not in fact German, though his homeland had been annexed by Prussia and he had served in the Prussian army. In 1870 during the Franco-Prussian War he had had to be restrained from rushing off to Germany to fight, Queen Victoria reminding him that he was now British, and her son-in-law, and they were neutral; but old Park residents tell how during the Great War Prince Christian would read the daily war reports in *The Times*, protesting in guttural tones 'Zese blody Germans'. If he saw a soldier around the Lodge, he would call him in, give him half-a-crown and stuff his pockets with cigars and cigarettes. Nearby, Canadian Army forestry units were encamped on Smith's Lawn, engaged in providing timber for military use; American nurses were thrilled to be invited to tea at the Lodge.

In 1916 Prince Christian, whose health was failing, was able to celebrate his jubilee as Ranger with a great party at the Lodge to which all the Park employees were invited. The same year there were golden wedding celebrations, with the King and Queen and Queen Alexandra being entertained at the Lodge; the German Emperor sent his congratulations via Sweden. The following year, with the de-Germanising of royal titles, Schleswig-Holstein was dropped from the family name, and George V adopted the surname Windsor, creating a new dynasty. That same year Prince Christian died at Schomberg House, cared for by nurses from HRH Princess Christian's Hospital in Windsor.[39]

King George V succeeded Prince Christian as Ranger, and he, with the consideration he always showed to his aunt, allowed Princess Christian and her daughters to remain at the Lodge. She continued her good works until her death, at Schomberg House, in 1923. The Dean of Windsor, paying tribute to her, said: 'Practically every single movement she started for the benefit of Windsor had become universal, and accepted as the normal thing in the charitable and philanthropic life of England.'[40]

Chapter Ten

Lord FitzAlan of Derwent
1924-1947

Rumours about what was to become of Cumberland Lodge were ended by the announcement in *The Times* of 8 October 1924 that the house had been 'loaned' by the King to Lord FitzAlan of Derwent. This led to speculation that he might also be made Ranger, but King George V retained the Rangership, passing it on eventually to his second son, the Duke of York, from whom it passed to the latter's son-in-law Prince Philip, Duke of Edinburgh.

Lord FitzAlan was born in 1855 into one of the great aristocratic families of England, being the third son of the 14th Duke of Norfolk. He started life as Edmund Bernard Fitzalan-Howard, but when he was 21 he took the name Talbot in accordance with the will of the 17th Earl of Shrewsbury by whom he was left property in Worcestershire, and was known as Lord Edmund Talbot. His education at the Oratory School, Birmingham, under the tutelage of Cardinal Newman, deepened and affirmed his faith. His subsequent service in the regular army took him into action in South Africa where, like Prince Christian Victor, he served under Lord Roberts, and was awarded the DSO. From his army training came the erect carriage which gave him 'presence' though he was short and stocky in build. He was both soldier and politician, as he had been elected to Parliament in 1894, representing Chichester, and there developed an abiding interest in politics. During the South African War he had been Assistant Secretary of State for War, thus playing a part in guiding events. After holding several junior governmental posts, he served for eight years as Conservative Chief Whip until in 1921 he was created 1st Viscount FitzAlan of Derwent; at the same time he reverted to his original surname of Fitzalan-Howard.

This honour marked his appointment as Viceroy of Ireland, an appointment the King had to persuade him, somewhat reluctantly, to accept. A special measure, the Government of Ireland Act, had been passed by Parliament in 1920 to allow the appointment of a Roman Catholic. Presumably it was thought this would be pleasing to the Irish, but an Irishman is reported as saying that a Catholic Viceroy was no more welcome than a Catholic hangman; however, no doubt some were pleased to see a Viceroy attending mass. Lord FitzAlan had the political wisdom to see that a negotiated solution to the 'Irish problem' rather than a military one was needed, and after much arduous discussion the Anglo-Irish Treaty of December 1921 brought the Irish Free State into being. After the hand-over to the first Irish Governor-General took place in 1922, Lord FitzAlan returned to England and took his seat in the House of Lords.[1]

His country home was Derwent Hall in a lovely Derbyshire valley, a 17th-century house which had been bought by his father as a shooting-lodge. In 1927 the Hall was bought by the Derwent Valley Water Board in preparation for creating a new reservoir to serve the growing

99 Lord FitzAlan of Derwent during his service in Ireland, with Queen Mary in Belfast, 22 June 1921.

needs of Sheffield. After an interim period when the Hall became a youth hostel, the dam was inaugurated by King George VI in 1945, and the whole village disappeared beneath the water as Ladybower Reservoir came into being.[2] This was foreseeable from 1920, when the Derwent Valley Water Act authorised the construction of the reservoir, and it may have been in recognition of the loss of his country house that George V decided to grant Cumberland Lodge to Lord FitzAlan, who was a personal friend. For him it was a splendid resource: after spending the week in his town house in London, and in Parliament, he could relax and entertain in a place of great beauty less than an hour's journey away. The tempered landscape of the Park suited him better than the wild northern moors, for he was essentially a metropolitan man, who liked to be close to the centre of events.

Like every occupant of Cumberland Lodge, he wanted to bring his own improvements to the house. Some fittings could be rescued from Derwent Hall; others were brought from another house, Badge Court, near Bromsgrove, which had come to him through his Talbot inheritance. Seventeenth-century oak panelling was removed from Badge Court to be fitted on to the walls of the dining-room and the study next door (now the Prince Christian room, used as a second dining-room). Some of the panelling may also have come from Derwent Hall, as it too had originally come from Badge Court.[3] The upper part of the walls was covered with squared panels and the lower with older linenfold panelling; there were also pilasters, carved angels, and arched panels over the fireplaces. Some of these items came from the canopies of four-poster beds, about which Lady FitzAlan wrote from Derwent Hall, hoping they could be made use of at the Lodge.[4] The marbled markings in the squared panels show that the best wood, heart of oak, was used. The fireplaces were also brought from Badge Court, with their Tudor bricks and early Tudor hearth tiles of heraldic design, which give evidence of

100   *Above.* 17th-century fireplace surround in the main dining-room at Cumberland Lodge, brought to the house by Lord FitzAlan.

101   *Below.* Hearth tile showing the hound of the Talbots and the name of Sir John Talbot, ancestor of Lord FitzAlan.

the Talbot connection. Old oak doors from Badge Court were fitted into the existing doors of these rooms. A hatchment of the Wintour family with the motto *Omnia desuper* ('Everything comes from above'), from Badge Court, was displayed in the dining-room, and a panel bearing an earlier coat of arms of the same family was placed in the study.[5] The décor was completed with tapestries from Derwent Hall, which were about 10 ft. square, and hung in the dining-room, where wall-space was left for them.

The coat-of-arms above the door in the Prince Christian Room is of particular interest as it is probably that of George Wintour, who died in 1594; his three sons Robert, Thomas and John, and his son-in-law John Grant, were involved in the Gunpowder Plot, drawn in by their persuasive and hot-headed cousin Robert Catesby, who master-minded the whole affair. It was Thomas Wintour who had brought Guy Fawkes over from Flanders to give technical advice. However, the plot was leaked and discovered in the nick of time. Catesby was shot resisting arrest, but the others were tried and suffered public execution in January 1606. The hatchment in the dining-room belongs to Robert Wintour's grandson, Sir George Wintour (1622-1658), who must have redeemed the family name by services to the Royalist cause, as he was made a baronet in 1642.[6]

102   Hatchment, in the main dining room, of Lord FitzAlan's ancestor, Sir George Wintour (1622-58), whose grandfather Robert Wintour, and his brothers, were put to death for their involvement in the Gunpowder Plot. A second armorial board hangs in the Prince Christian Room, and is thought to show the arms of an earlier George Wintour, father of Robert.

The carpets in the main rooms were dark red, the walls kept plain to show up the family's oak furniture of the Jacobean and Stuart periods. There were four-poster bedsteads, court cupboards, coffers, hall settees, refectory tables, carved Restoration chairs, gate-legged tables, and several long-case clocks.[7] One carved oak bedstead had a secret cupboard in the back, and the four-poster in the master bedroom was said to have belonged to Mary Queen of Scots. It was so large that it had to be taken to pieces to get it into place. These changes of furnishing must have given the house quite a different character from the one it had in Princess Christian's day with its mahogany furniture, patterned carpets and papered walls laden with pictures and antlers. Outside, improvements were made to the garden; the semi-circular border round the front lawn was planted with shrubs and rhododendrons which flowered in sequence, together with red-leafed Japanese maple, so that there was colour for most of the year. These can be enjoyed to this day, though lack of care over the years has allowed the rhododendrons to become overgrown. The grounds then extended right down to the road to Bishopsgate and along to Cumberland Gate. The lime-tree avenue across Smith's Lawn was cut down to provide a flying-ground for the Prince of Wales who was living at Fort Belvedere.

As devout Roman Catholics, Lord and Lady FitzAlan wanted to have a chapel in their new home. The room first chosen for this was the one used as the present chapel, in a key position at the head of the stairs. This had been Princess Helena Victoria's bedroom, with a door through into her bathroom and wardrobe. Some adjustments were needed, and Queen Mary, always the careful guardian of royal houses and their contents, expressed some disquiet on hearing that alterations were taking place—she had perhaps heard of the havoc wrought by the removal of George III's book-cases. What would happen to the panelling now being installed, when Lord and Lady FitzAlan died? She was reassured to hear that it was removable, being fixed to a framework on the walls, though in the event it has remained permanently. What was being done to Princess Victoria's bedroom and bathroom?[8] In the end Lord and Lady FitzAlan decided to leave them alone and instead use as a chapel the former schoolroom in the west wing, which possibly was the upper part of the chapel provided by George III (see p. 93). The small room next door would serve as a sacristy, and beyond this there was a bedroom where the priest could stay. The chapel was furnished with simple panelling, a red plush carpet, an altar in the window, a confessional, and rows of prie-dieu facing the altar.

James Lees-Milne, who as a young man often visited Lord FitzAlan at the Lodge, describes in *Ancestral Voices* the celebration of Mass in the chapel at 9 a.m., an aged priest from Beaumont College officiating:

> Lord FitzAlan served in spite of his 87 years, shuffling about and genuflecting like a two-year-old. The priest ... is a cripple with arthritis and can barely move with a stick. I was in agonies lest he or Lord F. should collapse and have to be propped up. As it was each supported himself upon the other. Yet the scene was impressive and the recollection of it fills me with pleasure.[9]

Each evening the Rosary was recited at 6.30; any member of the household could come, but all the family were expected to attend, even if they were not all as devout as Lord FitzAlan, who said prayers aloud while driving his car.

The story is told that when Lady FitzAlan died in 1938 her body awaiting burial was laid in the chapel, surrounded by candles, while two nuns kept prayerful watch. It so happened that a burglar chose this night to break into the Lodge. Creeping upstairs he saw a dim light through a slightly open door, peeped in and was aghast at the sight that met his eyes; the nuns were hidden from view, and hearing a low voice saying 'Come in', he thought the dead had spoken, dropped his loot and took to his heels in fright.

***

The two great passions of Lord FitzAlan's life were his church and politics; in both spheres he wielded influence and his advice was sought by princes and leaders of both church and state. He and Lady FitzAlan were charming hosts, and his wide contacts meant that people of significance in public life met at Cumberland Lodge. One weekend in mid-October 1936, the guests were the Prime Minister, Stanley Baldwin, and Mrs. Baldwin, Lord and Lady Salisbury, Mr. J.A. Herbert M.P. and Lady Mary Herbert, and Lord FitzAlan's nephew the Duke of Norfolk. The Prime Minister had just returned to London after two months away to take care of his health, and this house-party had been arranged before he went away. On returning to London he had been immediately confronted by the problem raised by King Edward VIII's association with Mrs. Wallis Simpson. This must inevitably have been a topic of conversation at the Lodge.

These people were all influential and had a particular interest in the course events might take. The Duke of Norfolk as Earl Marshal was in charge of arrangements for the coronation in May, and needed to know whether a queen as well as a king was to be crowned. Lord Salisbury, as Under-Secretary of State at the Foreign Office, was aware of the interest taken in this affair abroad. The Prime Minister, always hopeful that tricky problems would go away, had had it impressed upon him by the King's private secretary, Major the Hon. Alexander Hardinge, that this one would not disappear and that as Mrs. Simpson's divorce petition was pending at Ipswich Crown Court, the time-scale was such that the King could be free to marry her in April, in time for the coronation in May.[10]

103   The Duke and Duchess of Windsor (photograph by Cecil Beaton, 1937).

Norfolk.

J.H. Hubert

Stanley Baldwin

Lucy Baldwin

Mira Sutherland

Salisbury

Mary Herbert.

Philippa Stewart
Edward Stewart
Minnie S.C. Anson

Oct. 16th – 19th.

104 A page in Lord and Lady FitzAlan's visitors' book signed by those spending the weekend of 16-19 October 1936 at Cumberland Lodge.

105 Stanley Baldwin, Prime Minister, later 1st Earl Baldwin of Bewdley. Portrait by R.G. Ives, in the National Portrait Gallery.

106 Major the Hon. Alexander Hardinge, later 2nd Baron Hardinge of Penshurst, private secretary to King Edward VIII.

Baldwin had suggested to Major Hardinge that he should come to see him at Cumberland Lodge on the morning of Saturday 17 October, where they could talk privately, and Lord FitzAlan obligingly invited Major the Hon. and Mrs. Hardinge to lunch, and included the press baron Lord Kemsley, who lived nearby. We can imagine the conversation between the Prime Minister and Major Hardinge taking place amid the smoke from Baldwin's pipe in the study next to the dining-room. The most urgent step that needed to be taken was for Baldwin to see the King and persuade him to have the divorce proceedings stopped; the King could not marry a woman already married, and a delay at least until after the coronation would give everyone time to think. Baldwin was still undecided, and suggested the Hardinges should return for dinner. Meanwhile he took Lord Kemsley aside and asked his opinion. Kemsley gave the now famous reply, 'Prime Minister, the Non-Conformist conscience is not dead'. Whether the whole group discussed the matter together after dinner over port and cigars (the ladies of course having withdrawn) history does not relate; but the collective wisdom emerging was that the already twice-divorced Mrs. Simpson would not be acceptable to the nation as queen; the King should be deflected from marrying her; if he insisted, the end of the road would be abdication. The Prime Minister agreed to seek audience with the King as soon as possible, and after some difficulty in tracking him down they met at Fort Belvedere the following Tuesday. From then on events took their course until that wintry day in early December when the King drove from the Fort past Cumberland Lodge to the Castle, and movingly broadcast to the world his own announcement of his abdication.

CUMBERLAND LODGE
WINDSOR GREAT PARK

(Nearest Stations: Egham (S.R.) 3 miles, Windsor (S.R. and G.W.R.) 4 miles. Green Line buses to Englefield Green "The Barley Mow")

THE VALUABLE ELIZABETHAN AND JACOBEAN FURNITURE OF THE MANSION

including numerous FOUR-POST BEDSTEADS, COURT CUPBOARDS, COFFERS and HALL-SETTLES, Stuart RESTORATION and YORKSHIRE CHAIRS, REFECTORY and SERVING TABLES; GATE-LEG, DINING and WRITING TABLES, William and Mary LONG-CASE CLOCKS and others in Chinese lacquer and oak. CABINETS, CORNER-CUPBOARDS, CRADLES, SPINNING-WHEELS. Also GLASS, CHINA and MISCELLANY, which

Messrs. TURNER, LORD & RANSOM
in conjunction with
Messrs. PHILLIPS, SON & NEALE

are instructed to Sell by Auction on the premises on WEDNESDAY, OCTOBER 1, 1947, and following day, at ELEVEN O'CLOCK PRECISELY each day.

May be viewed Saturday, September 27, and Monday, September 29 (10 to 4 o'clock each day). *No view Tuesday, September* 30. Admission to View and Sale by presentation of Catalogue only, PRICE **2/6**, obtainable of the Auctioneers, Messrs. TURNER, LORD AND RANSOM, 127, Mount Street, W.1 (GRO. 2838), and Messrs. PHILLIPS, SON & NEALE, 7, Blenheim Street, New Bond Street, W.1 (MAY. 2424).

107 Notice of the Sale by Auction of the contents of Cumberland Lodge which appeared in *Country Life*, 26 September 1947.

***

Because of all the entertaining they did, the FitzAlans were seldom on their own at the Lodge at weekends, and Ascot Week was the occasion of a big house-party.[11] Their daughter Magdalen lived with them, and their son Captain the Hon. Henry Fitzalan-Howard and his family often came to stay. Lady FitzAlan had made a set of rooms on the north-east corner of the second floor into a nursery for her first grand-daughter Alathea, and later for Alathea's sister Elizabeth Anne. They spent many holidays with their grandparents, so that it became a second home to them. Visits were exchanged with Princess Elizabeth and Princess Margaret when they were at Royal Lodge, and they always came over for birthday parties, simply walking through the grounds, without the elaborate precautions found necessary today. During the war Alathea came to live permanently at Cumberland Lodge with her governess, and must have provided a cheerful presence for her grandfather after Lady FitzAlan's death. Later Alathea is remembered cycling down to Egham to catch a train to London or down the Long Walk to her war work with the Red Cross in Windsor. Some excitement was caused when Life Guards and Grenadier Guards came to patrol Smith's Lawn, which it was feared might be used as a landing-ground for German parachutists; while on duty they were quartered in the mews. King William IV would have thought this a very suitable arrangement. Boys from Beaumont College, evacuees from the Cardinal Vaughan School in London, were billeted on the top floor of the Lodge, no doubt astonished to find themselves in such surroundings, each with his own room, a four-poster bed, rush mats on the floor and a brass water-jug. When they left each was given a copy of *The Imitation of Christ*, inscribed in memory of their stay at Cumberland Lodge.

For the domestic staff things were different. Senior staff moved from house to house with the master and mistress. There was a butler who grew old with his master, two footmen and an odd man; the housekeeper had a room on the top floor near to the linen-cupboards and the sewing-room; the four housemaids and four kitchenmaids shared rooms, and other servants such as the chauffeur and gardeners lived in the outbuildings. The maids had to rise early to see to the fires, the coal-scuttles being taken upstairs by the 'odd man' using the hoist near the kitchen. The downstairs rooms had to be cleaned before the family appeared, and maids must never be encountered on the main staircase. Those who cleaned the top floor never set foot on the 'gentry floor'. Though Lord FitzAlan would genially lead off the dancing at staff parties even at a great age, in their daily work servants had to be invisible.

The housekeeper and visitors' maids had meals at the butler's table; the other servants had meals in the kitchen, warm with the cedarwood that was used in the stove to kill cooking smells. There were two kitchens, one of which was more for show than use, with its shelves of copper pans cleaned on Thursdays with a mixture of sand, salt, and vinegar, made in the house. Below in the cellars, home of numerous cats, coal and wine were stored and mushrooms grown. A few years ago when the crowded cellars were cleaned out, great excitement was caused by the discovery of a heavy suitcase. Did it contain some forgotten treasure? On being opened it was found to contain mushroom compost. During the war the cellars were used as an air-raid shelter, and the house had a near miss when a V2 rocket came down in the Great Meadow.

Lord FitzAlan lived through the war, becoming very deaf and so arthritic that, like Sarah, he had to be lifted about and carried to bed by two menservants. He died at Cumberland Lodge in May 1947, and was buried in the Cathedral graveyard at Arundel.[12]

X Amy Buller in later life, by Helen Wilson, 1970. This picture hangs in the drawing-room above the place where she always sat when attending talks there.

XI Colour aerial photograph of part of The Great Park taken in September 1996 (Aerofilms). Cumberland Lodge is at top of the photograph. The diagram on the facing page indicates the main features of the photograph.

Not being Ranger, Lord FitzAlan had not had the close relationship with the Park which Prince Christian had so much enjoyed; but changes were taking place. Chief among these was the rebuilding of Royal Lodge in 1931 to provide a Windsor home for the Duke and Duchess of York. The Rangership passed to the Duke, who loved gardens, and the second great phase of landscaping in the Park took place. Unlike others such as William III and William Bentinck who also loved gardens, the Duke laboured with his own hands and wellington boots to create a garden at Royal Lodge, helped by the Duchess. When Major (later Sir) Eric Savill started in 1932 making the Bog Garden, he had the Duke's enthusiastic support; and later, as the project grew and the Duke had become King, the latter insisted that the glorious result should be called the Savill Garden. After the War the project extended to the Valley Gardens beside Virginia Water, its masses of azaleas and rhododendrons thriving on the acidity of the Bagshot sand which forms the soil in that area of the Park.

Under the Rangership of King George VI conditions improved for workers in the Park. The reading-room and library instituted at the Lodge by the Prince Consort had long since migrated to the upper floor of Studio Cottage; then a clubhouse was put up on the green near the Mews. When a model village was built about a mile from the Lodge, this temporary clubhouse was superseded by the new York Club. The transformation which was to take place at the Lodge belongs to another chapter.

FitzAlan

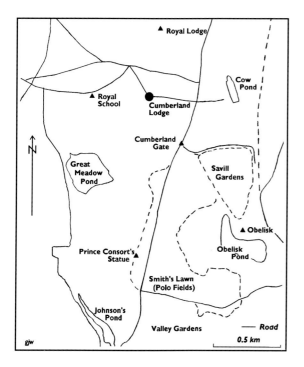

(a) Baptist May (1628-97)

(b) William Bentinck, 1st Earl
of Portland (1649-1709)

(c) John Churchill, 1st Duke
of Marlborough (1650-1722)

(d) William Augustus, Duke
of Cumberland (1721-65)

(e) Henry Frederick, Duke of
Cumberland (1745-90)

(f) Prince Christian of
Schleswig-Holstein (1831-1917)

(g) Princess Helena of Great Britain and
Schleswig-Holstein (1846-1923)

(h) Lord FitzAlan, 1st Viscount Derwent
Derwent (1855-1947)

(a)

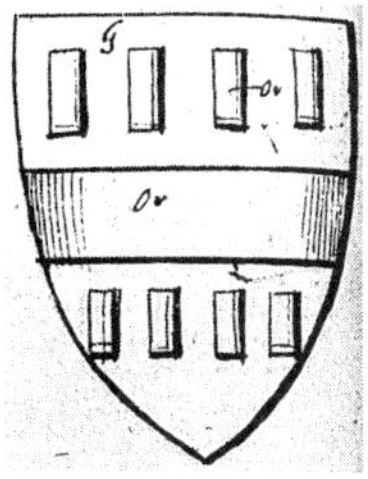

(b)

(c)

(d)

(e)

(f)

(g)

(h)

108 Coats of Arms of the occupants of Cumberland Lodge, 1671-1947.

Chapter Eleven

The Miracle
1947-1988

1: The Dream

The person who succeeded Lord FitzAlan at Cumberland Lodge was unlike everyone who had lived there since Charles II took over the house. She was not rich, not aristocratic, and powerful only in personality and determination. Amy Buller was born in London in 1891, and was brought up in South Africa where the family emigrated. She returned to England in 1911, and shortly afterwards went to Germany to study the language. Thus began a great love of that country and its people; she decided to study for a degree in German language and literature, and went up to Birkbeck College, London University. Here she experienced to the full the drawbacks of being a student in a non-residential institution, and a part-time student at that, working her way through by being a governess in General Wingate's family. This experience of a student life far removed from the Oxford and Cambridge model was to have a profound effect.[1]

She graduated in 1917, and after the war took a post with the Student Christian Movement (SCM), an interdenominational organisation with an international outlook, which was in the process of becoming the liveliest and most attractive society in the student world. The SCM was always perceptive in recruiting its staff, who were deployed in the universities with the aim, not of gaining converts, but of making students think about their beliefs. This was done by getting alongside students and organising study groups in different areas of Christian concern. Amy was just the kind of lively, enthusiastic and thoughtful person who would be excellent at this work. She had the good luck to be sent to work as SCM secretary in Manchester University, in the diocese where the future Archbishop William Temple was bishop; he was to have a deep influence on her thinking, and became a staunch friend.

As well as organising study groups within universities and colleges, the SCM organised conferences in vacations, the biggest of these being held in the summer at Swanwick in Derbyshire. Here students had the chance of listening to and meeting great Christian leaders, and mixing with fellow-students from different disciplines and other universities, including many from overseas, applying their brains to matters of life and death not normally broached in their academic courses. It is difficult to convey to those who did not experience them the excitement of these conferences, and the profound influence they had on the participants. Many students felt that their thinking, from being confined and restricted in their academic curricula, was liberated and energised in a away which remained with them for life. Amy was part of all this as one of the vital forces in the Movement.

In 1931 she moved to Liverpool to be Warden of University Hall, a residence for women students, where she had the opportunity to try to give her students something of this experience. Writing a few years later, Sir Walter Moberly, then Vice-Chancellor of Manchester University, was to define the function of the hall and its warden as he saw it. For him hall life was a fundamental part of university education. The warden

> must care passionately for the things of the mind and ... should have outside contacts which may help to open windows ... A Hall in which there is frequent coming and going of visitors from the great world ... can contribute notably to the real education of students.[2]

Amy, knowing by now a wide circle of people, with her visits to Germany and her outside commitments, was eminently fitted to provide a stimulating hall life for her students.

Through her visits to Germany between the wars she witnessed the rise of Hitler and the Nazi movement, seeing it as having grown out of the humiliating peace treaty of 1918 and the subsequent depression. At first Hitler seemed to have produced some good results—a sense of purpose, employment, and pride in country; but ordinary Germans, blinded by this, had failed to see the evil underside of the movement.

Between the years 1934 and 1938 Amy took over to Germany groups of educationists, economists and theologians who talked to leading Nazis in the hope of trying to understand their way of thinking, and to challenge it. At the same time they made contacts, in a rather cloak and dagger way, with people who were critical of the régime, and they became more and more aware of the stranglehold the new 'philosophy' had on intellectual life. Amy set herself the task of discovering why this takeover of people's hearts and minds had happened.[3]

After these exciting excursions in the company of some of the leading minds of the day, back she would go to her hall: no wonder her students found her presence stimulating. Later, during the bombing of Liverpool in the war, when she and her students were sheltering in the cellars of the hall, she would share with them her impressions of Germany and the Nazis, and try to answer their repeated question, why? It was through these conversations that she came to write a book about her experience of Germany. Commiserating with a student leaving hall about the dismal life she must have had there, spending so much time in air-raid shelters, the student engagingly replied that on the contrary it had been marvellous to hear her talking about Germany; why did she not write a book about it so that others could benefit? So *Darkness over Germany* came to be written.

109   Amy Buller, whose concern for students, and determination, brought St Catharine's into being.

Amy had been particularly dismayed to find how easily people who had graduated through the great German universities had been seduced by the brutal philosophy of Nazism, and she was shocked at the suppression of free speech which had helped to make this possible. In her opinion the universities had failed in not training students to use their critical judgment on the world around them, and western civilisation was in decline because of the weakening hold of Christianity, so that people had no defence against false gods.

She thought that if this could happen in Germany, a highly civilised nation, it could also happen in Britain, and she set about finding ways of serving young people by making them more aware of the forces at work in the world around them. From her own experience she knew how difficult it was in a huge non-residential university like London for students to meet one another and share their opinions. So several strands of her experience and thought converged in the idea of a sort of college, not attached to any university, where students could come with their teachers and, in a relaxed atmosphere, to use her own words 'examine the fundamental

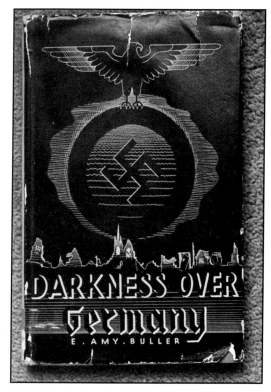

110   The Right Book Club edition (1945) of Amy Buller's book *Darkness over Germany*, first published in 1943, which had a great impact upon people in high places.

assumptions underlying the springs of political or economic or scientific action; and in so doing be given an opportunity of examining the Christian philosophy of life in relation to all this', but there would be no propaganda purpose.[4] She believed that the 'Christian philosophy' was eminently reasonable, and it only needed to be well expounded to prove convincing. Perhaps Amy's chief failing was in not coming to terms with the power of the feelings and giving them their due.

By the end of 1942 she felt that the time had come to devote herself fully to the realisation of her dream. Her amazingly generous and loving friends, Francis and Frieda Scott, made it financially possible for her to leave her hall and live in London without a paid job. Francis Scott was chairman of the Provincial Insurance Company founded in Manchester by his father, and from Amy's SCM days he and his wife had kept open house at their home near Windermere for Amy and her friends. Their unstinting support continued over many years, and he was to become one of her founding trustees. Once settled in London, she recruited other influential friends to her project, among them Archbishop William Temple, the greatest Christian interpreter of his generation and possibly of the century; Lord Halifax, who had been involved in her visits to Germany; A.D. Lindsay who, in the founding of a new university at Keele, was to put into effect his own experiment of giving students an integrated education; Walter Moberly, whose thinking was strongly in sympathy with Amy's, having been nurtured in the SCM and the Christian Frontier

Council; Dr. Eddie Bennet and Dr. Leonard Browne, Jungian psychiatrists; Canon Tissington Tatlow, general secretary of the SCM, and Edward Talbot, Superior of the Anglican Community of the Resurrection at Mirfield, who was to become her dearest and most trusted mentor. But her most influential and unexpected support came from quite a different quarter.

The Bishop of Lichfield, Edward Woods, had been a friend and spiritual adviser of King George VI and Queen Elizabeth for many years, and from time to time he recommended books they might like to read; in 1943 the newly published *Darkness over Germany* was on his list. The Queen read it, was impressed by it, and the Bishop suggested she might be interested to meet the author, so Amy was duly invited to Buckingham Palace.[5] This meeting was what Amy called 'my miracle'. One can imagine the excitement when the totally unexpected summons came. After the initial fuss over 'What'll I wear?', Amy sallied forth to the Palace one day early in March 1944. The conversation was first about the book, and when it was time to go the Queen asked whether Amy would be returning to her students. This gave Amy the opportunity to talk about her new project, which she could be counted on to do with volubility and enthusiasm. The Queen expressed great interest in the project and her willingness to help, and asked Amy to keep in touch. Already, though 1944 was a dark year in the war, buzz-bombs and austerity combining to lower morale, the King and Queen were looking to the future, to the kind of nation which must be built when peace came, and particularly the rôle of the young in it. Amy's was a scheme which appealed at once to their hearts and hopes. Of course she kept in touch, and Queen Elizabeth's 'willingness to help' was no mere form of words. She followed it up with well-judged action—writing a letter here, placing a word there, facilitating negotiations, and strengthening Amy's resolve by her own vision.

The extent to which the Queen had made the cause her own is illustrated by an incident recorded by Professor Ulrich Simon, which happened when he was a curate at Slough. He had cycled through the Park to the Savill Garden, and was resting on a bench when

> my meditations were interrupted: a man, tall and serious, accompanied by a lady, short and vivacious. This was the Queen of England, accompanied by Sir Stafford Cripps. They stopped by my bench and asked after my affairs. My clerical dress gave me credibility, and I ventured to ask them about their business. It turned out to be the scheme which later produced Cumberland Lodge, as a meeting place for all sorts of matters affecting public life, moral issues, and cultural progress.[6]

The problem Amy was faced with at this time was to find a suitable place for her college. She was a good fund-raiser, and was confident that once the place was established and her idea had become reality, money would be found. She was living at this time in a flat made available to her in the Precinct, Regent's Park, property owned by the Anglican Royal Foundation of St Katharine, and hearing that the future of this property was being discussed, she formed the plan of getting it for her college. She had a battery of powerful churchmen to support her, and the Queen facilitating negotiations whenever she could, and of course her own enormous drive, but after two years of protracted discussions the scheme was finally turned down. By this time her project had come to be called 'St Katharine's' and the name stuck. Amy liked it because St Katharine was the patron saint of philosophers, and this title side-stepped more controversial descriptions which had been suggested, such as 'College of Christian Philosophy'.

The project suffered another setback and Amy a personal loss when Archbishop Temple died in 1944. The death of this great leader and thinker was a loss to the whole nation. For a time after the ending of the war in Europe Amy concentrated on other interesting opportunities which came her way, such as lecturing to the troops and to German prisoners of war, but a year later she returned to the St Katharine's idea. Early in 1946 she had a piece of luck in meeting the Queen's niece, the Hon. Elizabeth Elphinstone, who at once took to Amy's ideas and became one of her strongest and most loyal supporters.

By this time another possibility had appeared in the shape of Hatfield House. There followed long negotiations with Lord Salisbury (who had been present at Cumberland Lodge on that fateful week-end in 1936), and it at last began to look as if Amy's dream was going to come true. But the scheme foundered on the question of whether it was to be avowedly Angli-can, which is what Lord Salisbury had understood, or simply Christian, which was what Amy now wanted. In April 1947 Lord Salisbury died suddenly, and his heir brought the negotiations to a close.

This was yet another severe blow for Amy (even though with hindsight one can only feel relief at escaping from the problems of heating and maintaining Hatfield House). Her friends urged her to give up the idea of a residential college

111   The Hon. Elizabeth Elphinstone, niece of Queen Elizabeth The Queen Mother, who played an important role in the beginning of St Catharine's, and its establishment at Cumberland Lodge.

and to find some other way of carrying out her aims, to which she stoutly replied, 'I'll give up anything you like in November, but I never give up anything in the spring'. With renewed energy she and Elizabeth Elphinstone investigated other possible great houses: Lacock Abbey, Audley End and Forde Abbey were but a few.

It was at this point that a second miracle occurred for Amy. Lord FitzAlan died in May, so Cumberland Lodge became free. It demonstrates how much the King and Queen had taken the St Katharine's project to their hearts, that, as Miss Elphinstone who was present told the story, one day early in July they were in the saloon at Royal Lodge, talking about the problem of finding the right house, when the King looked out of the window across to the Lodge and said, 'Now I think that's the house you ought to have for your experiment. It's not a house anyone is likely to want to live in as a private house any more. I think it might suit very well'.[7]

Suiting the action to the words, on 6 July the King and Queen went over to look at the empty house, shown round by Magdalen Fitzalan-Howard, who was clearing up. They signed the FitzAlan Visitors Book for the last time, and all agreed the house had great possibilities for Amy's project. Elizabeth Elphinstone brought this exciting news and the plans of the house to Amy, telling her she was to study these and then go to Buckingham Palace the following day.

112 'Conversation Piece at Royal Lodge' by James Gunn. Here a conversation vital to the future of St Catharine's took place in July 1947. A portrait of the Prince Regent hangs over the fireplace.

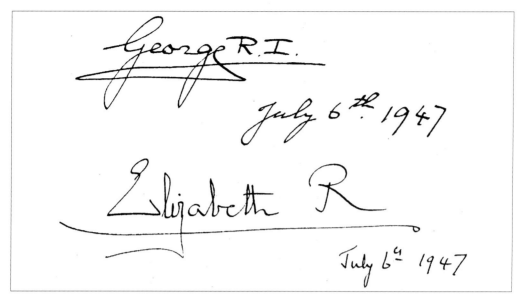

113 The last signatures in Lord FitzAlan's visitors' book, when King George and Queen Elizabeth came over from Royal Lodge to see if the house might be suitable for Amy Buller's project.

There the Queen told her, as Amy wrote in a letter to Father Talbot, that 'they proposed to offer us the use of Cumberland Lodge for the College' and the Queen had even decided which room she wanted Amy to have. He replied at once, 'This is indeed wonderful—a royal offer in every sense. It is glorious that the Queen has the vision, courage and generosity that it manifests'.[8]

A Council for the project had already been set up, with Lord Halifax as chairman, and they set about completing the formalities of the grant. The following notices appeared in *The Times* of 5 August 1947:

THE KING has granted Cumberland Lodge, Windsor Great Park, as a residence for St Katharine's Foundation. This grant has been accepted with deep gratitude on behalf of the Council of St Katharine's Foundation by the Earl of Halifax (Chairman), Dr. Tissington Tatlow (Deputy Chairman) and Miss Amy Buller.

THE COUNCIL recognises that an ideal home has been provided for their experiment and they are greatly encouraged by this indication of the interest and understanding of the King and Queen in the work which the Council wishes to undertake.

By October the Trust Deed was drawn up (see Appendix Six), hammered out through many discussions over the previous five years; it is still the basis of the Foundation. There was a hitch in that Queen Mary, Patron of the other St Katharine's—of which Sir Walter Moberly was chairman at the time—pointed out that confusion could be caused by having two Christian foundations dedicated to St Katharine. Amy was not one to give up something she had set her heart on, even for a Queen; but the matter was resolved by changing the K to C, and dropping the word 'Foundation'. In 1968 another change was made to mark the cardinal rôle played in its origin by the then King and Queen, when it was given the title it now has, The King George VI and Queen Elizabeth Foundation of St Catharine's, Cumberland Lodge. One can but admire the verbal adroitness that crystallised so much history into this final version.

2: The Realisation

The next step was to prepare the Lodge for occupation. When Lord FitzAlan's furniture was finally sold by auction in October, the house was 'empty, uncarpeted and uncurtained' and everything was needed for it. An appeal letter went out over the signatures of Amy Buller as Honorary Warden and Elizabeth Elphinstone as Honorary Assistant Warden (both refused to accept a salary), asking for 'any gift, from a box of tools to a doormat, a lawn mower to a reading lamp'. Chairs, carpets, chests of drawers and tables would be required in very large numbers. They felt that the house

> should provide a background which in itself will be an enrichment of the life of the students who visit the College. Those who know something of the cramped and ugly conditions under which many students in the modern universities have to work will sympathise with the Council desiring to achieve simplicity and beauty in the first country house set aside to serve these students.[9]

They were unable to get any official grants or permits (furniture was in very short supply after the war), so they depended entirely on gifts or loans. It was a disarming letter, and was accompanied by someone's brainwave: a set of drawings of the principal rooms, showing these as they would like to see them furnished. They had had fun preparing this, sticking little bits of paper marked 'chair', 'table' etc. on to a set of plans which they were using to allocate rooms.

DINING ROOM

114   Sketch of the dining-room from the first appeal brochure. On the back were listed items needed to furnish the room. Many large pieces of furniture found a new home at the Lodge, as people moved into smaller homes after the war.

Amy took the appeal in person to the United States, and thanks to the English-Speaking Union was given a large donation of soft furnishings, linen, blankets, glass and cutlery (all hard to come by in Britain) from American colleges. That is why, in the early years, students at the Lodge sometimes found themselves using blankets marked 'Yale University'. The Queen held a party at Royal Lodge (the first of many) for the good and the great, who were invited to donate items of furniture or money. Many were moving at that time into smaller houses, and so could spare large chests and tables for which they had no room, and even a set of handsome chairs, used by peers at the coronation of Queen Victoria.

The appeal was successful and gifts and loans started flowing in, by far the largest being from the King and Queen. In this royal loan are items of furniture which can be identified by the royal stamp on them (e.g. VR CL 1865) as having been in the Lodge in Princess Christian's time and before. VR is sometimes superimposed on GRIIII, which in turn may have been altered from GRIII. This arouses the intriguing speculation that there may be items going back as far as Sarah Churchill. Sarah bequeathed the furniture in the Lodge to John Spencer, from whose executors a large amount was bought by William Duke of Cumberland; George III bought all his uncle's furniture on the latter's death, leaving it in the Lodge for the use of his brother Duke Henry; it therefore became Crown property, and was either stored at Windsor Castle and brought out again to furnish the house for Princess Christian, or left at the Lodge. After Princess Christian's death it was again stored, and found its way back to the house for the use of St Catharine's.

The Tapestry Hall is graced by Soho tapestries which were there in Princess Christian's time.[10] Originally a set of six based on paintings by Teniers (Village Wedding, Harbour, Game of Pall Mall, Domestic Life of Farmers, Fortune-Teller, and Harvest), these three remaining panels have been repaired by joining to them parts of other panels which presumably were beyond repair; only one, the Harvest scene, is complete. They belong to the fashion followed by Sarah Churchill with her tapestries of the summer seasons; similar tapestries can be seen at Blickling Hall in Norfolk.

Queen Mary did not forget St Catharine's; among her gifts was a set of lithographs of the Crimean War, and the loan of several pictures. These and many other such gifts were welcome, as there were yards of bare walls to be adorned. Queen Mary was known to disapprove of ivy on houses, so in deference to her the ivy was cut back, leaving the front looking bare and stark, but no doubt with healthier brickwork.

It was remarkable how the random collection of furniture thus assembled combined to form a gracious setting. It was hoped to furnish the drawing-room elegantly, and this was helped by a later grant from the Pilgrim Trust; the room was to be used for talks and discussions, as well as for sedate parties. The sitting-room next to it was used as a formal lecture-room; Lord FitzAlan's study became the library. Upstairs, the royal bedroom became a student dormitory, and Princess Helena Victoria's bedroom had four beds. Many of the rooms were big enough to take four or five beds without appearing crowded, so that up to 50 students could be accommodated in the Lodge. At first Lord FitzAlan's chapel continued to be used as a chapel, Lord Halifax and the Sheppard Trust giving money to provide furnishings for it. There was to be a daily service, but no one was to feel pressurised to attend. Amy used the room opposite the dining-room (formerly 'Princess Christian's boudoir') as her office, and Elizabeth Elphinstone had the room next door to it. The spacious room above the present bar was Amy's combined bedroom and sitting-room, and Miss Elphinstone had a room on the top floor. A large room

115 The Tapestry Hall as it is today, showing one of the 18th-century tapestries. The ceiling was painted by teenagers from Berkshire Youth Action.

116 The east front of Cumberland Lodge, ivy-covered as in Lord FitzAlan's day. In the renovation of 1912, the roof was raised to allow for better accommodation on the top floor, so the dormer windows of John Byfield's house have disappeared.

on the first floor, now the principal's study, was designated the senior common room; this had once been Princess Christian's sitting-room (see Figure 95).

Another concern was staffing. Amy was to run the place as Warden, assisted by Elizabeth Elphinstone. A distinguished person was needed to preside over the academic activities, and Sir Walter Moberly was an ideal choice. He was about to retire from his post as Chairman of the University Grants Committee, and his book, *The Crisis in the University*, was soon to be published. This was derived from Christian thinking in the SCM and the Christian Frontier Council, from which the initiative for writing the book had come. His thinking was much in line with that of Amy Buller:

117 Sir Walter Moberly, the charismatic first Principal of St Catharine's, author of an influential book *The Crisis in the University*.

> This book is the product of a conviction that much ails universities today, that what is wrong with them is closely connected with what is wrong with the whole world; and that the chief seat of the malady is to be found in the underlying assumption, largely unconscious, by which their life and work are determined. Owing to the confusion of purpose which they share with the modern world, universities are at present crippled in performing their most important function.[11]

In the book he proceeded to examine critically the rôle of the universities from a Christian standpoint, and to pose the question, 'What can Christian insight contribute to enable the university to be the university?'. The vital question, he said, is not 'whether the university does or does not include certain religious activities. It is concerned with the university's raison d'être and with the whole of its life and work'.[12]

118 Amy Buller in typical stance in front of the Lodge in 1951, talking to Ralph Davis (later Professor of History at Birmingham University): 'My attitude to everyone is a challenging one'.

Walter Moberly and Amy Buller were grappling with the same problems; Moberly's response was to write a book which it is hardly an exaggeration to say took the universities by storm. Many people who have since held senior academic posts were deeply influenced by what he had to say, and their work has been enlightened by its teaching; but to read the book today is to realise how far higher education has moved away from Moberly's terms of reference to new ones based on productivity, cost-effectiveness and pragmatism.

The students coming to Cumberland Lodge in those early days, from 1948 onwards, were privileged to have two people of such vision and insight as their mentors: Amy with her dynamism and challenge ('My attitude to everybody is a challenging one', she once said); and Walter Moberly with his quiet charm, his intellectual modesty, and his talent for drawing people out in discussions. He had an endearing absent-mindedness, as when, alighting at Egham Station with his umbrella hooked over his arm, a fellow-traveller approached him saying, 'Excuse me, you've got my umbrella'. 'Oh no', said Sir Walter, patting the umbrella on his arm. 'But what about this one?', said the stranger, indicating a second neatly-rolled umbrella also hooked over Sir Walter's arm.[13]

These two high-powered individuals could not have run the place effectively without the help of Elizabeth Elphinstone; indeed without her labour, for as well as overseeing the household she toiled single-handed to bring the garden to order and beauty. She was also a remarkable person, who saw her rôle as providing a setting which would allow the enterprise to function properly. For this, staff must be efficient and contented, and visitors must be comfortable and at ease. With her country house background, she set a more appropriate model than that of a hall of residence or an Oxford College, though the modest high table where students were invited to join Amy or Sir Walter showed some influence from the latter. Visitors were welcomed at the door, and flowers were put in the main rooms. A certain decorum was expected: people might dress casually by day but they should be 'respectable' for dinner. Thus something of the style which the house had known for generations was kept, despite this invasion of young people coming for short periods so that there was a constantly changing population. Nothing underlines more the generosity and indeed courage of the King and Queen in opening up a house so near to their own, in a place which for centuries had been jealously kept as a private preserve, than this willingness to allow unknown young students to come and possibly disturb its peace. The King and Queen had caught Amy Buller's vision, and, sharing her hopeful belief in young people, had confidence that the gains outweighed the risks. They have been proved right, and part of the magic is that very trust. In 1952, when Queen Elizabeth II came to the throne, she showed that she too shared that trust by renewing the grant of the Lodge to St Catharine's.

The charge was made that the atmosphere was too remote from what was thought of as the 'real' world for people to be able to discuss the contemporary scene in a realistic way. An Australian scholar, writing in these early days, wondered, after listening to a particularly esoteric discussion, whether 'a bombed-out warehouse in the East End might be a far more appropriate place to get a grip on such subjects as life and death'.[14] A few years later a principal's wife was heard to exclaim, on seeing *West Side Story* for the first time, that this was what life was all about, not madrigals on the lawn at Cumberland Lodge.

The St Martin's Singers used to come to give recitals by candlelight from the grand staircase in the Tapestry Hall; this was part of Amy's endeavour to give the young an experience of beauty which was lacking from their lives in cheap bedsitters often in the dingier parts of

119 A group discussion on the south lawn, at the foot of a very old sweet chestnut tree; the shapely tree on the right is a copper beech, planted in 1920 by the Duke of Connaught, who was a frequent visitor to the house when his sister Princess Christian lived there.

London. People would open up and think better if they were relaxed, and the changed, even charmed, setting would be more conducive to calm discussion than the grim institutional environment of their colleges. Primarily they would be able to meet one another. 'All real living is meeting,' said Martin Buber, whose ideas were in the air at the time: and Amy said, 'When people meet in this way and across academic disciplines they begin to ask fundamental questions', and all kinds of new insights emerge.[15] So at a week's reading-party a topic such as Criminality might be discussed by a physician, a magistrate, a psychiatrist, a sociologist and a theologian; or Symbolism from a historical, philosophical, literary and theological point of view; the nature of evidence might be discussed by scientists, historians and lawyers. Another way Amy used to shake people up was by bringing in her 'lions': Stanley Spencer might come to talk to a group of scientists about his pictures, or T.S. Eliot to read his cat poems; Stephen Potter and John Heath-Stubbs came; the names of Paul Tillich, Iris Murdoch, Karl Popper, R.H.S. Crossman, A.J. Ayer, and many others more often seen on bookshelves, are to be found in the visitors' books which have been kept from the beginning. Students were able not only to listen to them, but to talk with them informally at meals or walking in the Park. Sir Ernst Gombrich, a frequent visitor over many years, has spoken warmly of his own experience:

> There is a nice institution, here in England, called Cumberland Lodge in Windsor Great Park where university teachers and undergraduates can meet for informal weekend conferences devoted to various topics. I think I met Colin Cherry there. I also met Peter Medawar who became a very great friend. These meetings were a great inspiration when good people came and talked.[16]

Postgraduate students or graduates who wanted to pause before embarking on a career were recruited as tutors, to provide someone nearer in age to the students. The first of these was Roger Young (later to be Sir Roger and a distinguished headmaster), who showed unusual tact in dealing with all kinds of different people, and resilience in coping with many different demands. He was the first of a long line of tutors who have spent a year or so at the Lodge before moving on to their careers. Amy decided to have a Christmas house-party mainly for overseas students, and Roger Young played a large part in making it a success—such a success that the Christmas party became an annual feature.

In 1949 Amy was deeply grieved when Father Talbot died. He had been the only person she allowed to accept her as she really was, and his departure meant the loss of one of the pillars of her life. Roger Young left in 1951 to embark on his teaching career, and Elizabeth Elphinstone left shortly afterwards, when the place was on its feet and running smoothly, though she served as a trustee until 1973. Sir Walter Moberly retired in 1955. The next ten years had their difficulties, though Dr. Harry Judge, who became Director of Studies in 1959, gives a sympathetic glimpse of St Catharine's in the early '60s, in his book *A Generation of Schooling*. Amy, having realised her dream, lacked any great new goal to which she could direct her drive and energy, and so turned it towards people at the Lodge, with sometimes unhappy consequences. Her life work was too precious for her to entrust easily to other hands, but eventually she retired in 1964, maintaining a lively interest as a trustee. She died in 1974.

***

In the next ten years there were three Principals (as well as two Acting-Principals for long periods). One of these, Professor Geoffrey Goodwin from the London School of Economics, having lived through the times of student unrest in the 1960s, reminded the Trustees that a different kind of student—anti-Establishment and anti-formality—must be welcomed to the Lodge, if it was still to serve the real student community. In 1968 he also first mooted the truly radical idea that the Lodge should have a bar—if only to forestall students from breaking the spell exercised by the Lodge by trooping off to the *Fox and Hounds*.

This innovation was not made until 1971, and under the skilled barmanship of George Nolan and Eric Moakes became a very effective agent for social mixing. There were other changes over the years. Groom's House, which had been divided into three flats and occupied by estate workers, was made available to St Catharine's in the early years, and became the Principal's residence. Inside the Lodge, the chapel was eventually moved to its present ideal position at the top of the main staircase, and the former chapel became a second library. Then in yet another change, this second library was moved to its present home, the former royal bedroom, and the washroom next door to this was converted into a bedroom. The former chapel, later the library, became a bedroom and was large enough for several beds; it has had a mixed history, having been the schoolroom in Princess Christian's day, and is now one of the most attractive bedrooms in the Lodge.

In 1966 St Catharine's suffered one of the financial crises that dogged its existence; it seemed for a time as if the whole enterprise was going to fold up. But the approval by Her Majesty The Queen of the change of title to 'The King George VI and Queen Elizabeth Foundation of St Catharine's, Cumberland Lodge', though with the proviso that it was not to be assumed until a new financial appeal was successful, inspired everyone to redouble their

120   *Right.* The large room
at the top of the main
staircase was made into a
chapel; it is furnished with
chairs designed for peers at
Queen Victoria's corona-
tion.

121   *Below   right.*   Her
Majesty Queen Elizabeth
The Queen Mother, Patron
of St Catharine's, at the
Lodge in June 1978. She is
accompanied   by   the
Principal, Walter James, and
the Chairman of the Board
of   Trustees,   Sir   John
Thomson (to the left).

efforts to raise money. The following year
the possibility of acquiring the Mews
concentrated these efforts on a clear
objective. A further great encouragement
came in 1968 when Her Majesty Queen
Elizabeth The Queen Mother, never
faltering in her support, agreed to become
Patron of the Foundation under its new
name. In 1969 Lord Denning, Master of
the Rolls, resigned as Chairman of the
Trustees and became Visitor, and Lord
Glendevon succeeded him as Chairman.
The sum needed for the conversion of the
old stables, latterly a grain store, was raised,
and in June 1971 the Royal Patron Queen
Elizabeth declared it open. While retaining
an outward appearance that the Duke of
Cumberland would have recognised, the
new annex was altered to contain a fine
conference room on the ground floor and
22 study-bedrooms above, with a link to
the cottage beyond; this became a residence
for a senior academic staff member. The
addition of the Mews meant that larger
student groups could be accommodated,
and it was hoped that long-stay postgraduate students might be attracted by the
new comfortable single rooms.

122   The use of the Mews (the old stable block) was passed to St Catharine's in 1971, and in the 1990s the ground floor was converted into a series of modern conference and seminar rooms. The clock, by J. Davis, a Windsor maker, is dated 1750.

123   Cumberland Lodge from the west. In 1980 the conversion of the western range of buildings into grace and favour houses was completed.

There came a period of stability lasting eight years when in 1974 Walter James, whose distinguished career in journalism had included many years as editor of *The Times Educational Supplement*, was appointed Principal. He set himself the task of understanding Amy Buller's ideas and tracing the history of the founding of St Catharine's, which he wrote up in his monograph *A Short Account of Amy Buller and the Founding of St Catharine's, Cumberland Lodge*, an invaluable sourcebook. By 1974, most student groups were organised departmentally, and tended inevitably to be subject-bound, thus, he felt, not always fulfilling the aims of the Foundation. He asked all organisers to devote at least one session to some matter of general concern, some serious moral issue, or a questioning of the grounds of their subject, so that they did not remain imprisoned in their own curriculum. The response to this was positive, some groups devoting a whole weekend to discussing different aspects of a theme, in a way that Amy Buller would have welcomed. The underlying aim has always been to encourage students to use their critical faculties, not only on their own subjects, but on matters outside of these, and to help them to form judgments based on facts and on reasonable thought, rather than hearsay and emotion.

As students took jobs or went abroad in vacations, the vacation reading-parties lasting a week or more in which fundamental questions such as Responsibility, Authority, Prejudice and so on were thrashed out, were no longer practicable; so instead six to eight weekends a year were (and still are) set aside for such discussions, often as in the past drawing together professionals from different areas of the community to examine a common theme. A 'St Catharine's Weekend', as they came to be called, on 'Official Duty and Individual Responsibility', with soldiers, policemen, lawyers and doctors participating, was well within the Amy Buller tradition.

Walter James retired in 1982, and here reminiscence takes over from history, as in September Lord Vaizey (who had been a trustee for many years) went to Cumberland Lodge as Principal, and I took up the post of Director of Studies. We were joined by Douglas Wilson as General Manager and Bursar, who was professionally trained in catering and hotel management. We found ourselves at once in the midst of a serious financial crisis. Again the Lodge seemed faced with closure. News of the oil crisis and inflation had been slow to reach the Great Park, and rigorous economies together with fund-raising appeals alone were not sufficient to keep pace with the inexorable rise in the cost of living. It was useless to blame the recession and wait for better times. As a money-wise trustee, Erwin Klinge, said, 'Stop talking about the recession; this is how things *are* now'. A completely new approach was needed.

An initial inspection of the building by the Executive Committee and ourselves was depressing in the extreme; every door seemed to open on to a vast room or yet another immensely long and dreary passage. How could such a place ever be made viable? John Vaizey set to work immediately to find a solution. What followed was due to his energy and administrative shrewdness, which harnessed Douglas Wilson's flair and practical skills in a remarkably creative interaction of personalities. Hours were spent hammering out policy. First, it was necessary to reduce costs, and the most expensive item was wages. In comparison with London halls of residence the place was overstaffed, so the painful process of reducing the staff from 45 to 25 had to be undertaken. To compensate for the heartache, this resulted in an efficient and purposeful workforce and the discovery of hidden talents.

This alone would not solve the financial problems. Income must be earned beyond what was produced by appeals and donations; these would always be needed to fulfil the charitable aim of the Foundation, by bridging the gap between what students could be expected to pay and what their visits actually cost (about three times as much). But the times of the year when students were not using the Lodge—in vacations, and often midweek—must be fully used for conferences 'of an educational and training nature' as permitted by the trust, in order to meet running expenses. Conference centres were springing up all over, and the Lodge must be able to match them in the facilities it could provide. To achieve this the house would have to be refurbished; but how could this be financed? Then out of the blue came another miracle, in the form of a generous gift from Erwin Klinge, to be followed shortly by another which came through Major T.C. Harvey, two trustees who supported St Catharine's through many ups and downs. We could start.

We decided to begin by carpeting the wooden passages and floors, so expensive to maintain, and also noisy. For the next few weeks we spent a great deal of time on our knees, comparing different carpet samples. At last the house was carpeted, making it warmer and quieter. The next item was redecoration, for which we were given the services of Anne Harwood, a talented designer. The colour themes in the rooms were dictated by the colour of the fireplace tiles, and though to some eyes bold and unexpected, with the white paint of the woodwork they were refreshing for students coming from the gloomy corridors of London colleges. Local salerooms were scoured for furniture suited to the house, comfortable armchairs came as gifts, beds were reduced to two per room, with bedcovers related to the décor. A laundry was equipped so that bedlinen did not have to be sent out; during its installation an excited electrician discovered Prince Christian's lift which had been walled in. Gradually the equipment taken for granted by conference-goers was acquired. The administration was streamlined. If some groups were dismayed at a rise in fees, they were disarmed when they found themselves well-fed, comfortable, and warmly welcomed in a house of compelling interest.

Lady Vaizey—Marina Vaizey, art critic of *The Sunday Times*—was an approachable and stimulating person for students to meet. She made a unique contribution to the artistic education of visitors by lending her fine collection of contemporary prints, which enlivened the walls and provoked discussion. These were supplemented by loans from the Arts Council and the Contemporary Art Society. Exhibition posters from leading art galleries brightened rooms and passages on the upper floors and in the Mews. From the Royal Archives came family photographs of Prince and Princess Christian and of the house in their day. After a visit by Lord Vaizey to the Royal Lesotho Weavers in South Africa, several magnificent tapestries woven there to designs by European artists were acquired. Today the walls offer young artists the chance to exhibit their works.

Another artistic endeavour was the painting of the plasterwork of the ceilings of the main rooms, most of which dated from the renovation of 1912. This was undertaken for the Foundation by groups of teenagers from Berkshire Youth Action (part of the Youth Training Scheme of that time), who perched on scaffolding like Michelangelo in the Sistine Chapel and produced beautiful colour effects of fruit and flowers. The Prime Minister, Mrs. Thatcher, paid an unofficial visit to see them at work. Another group worked outside, making tables and benches from fallen trees, so that in meditative mood one can rest on a seat made by today's unemployed school-leavers and admire the lake created by the Duke of Cumberland's unemployed soldiers. The Deputy Ranger suggested that a neglected spinney, part of the old Wilderness, now a tanglewood no-man's-land between gardens and park, should be included in the Lodge grounds (as it had been in Lord FitzAlan's day); this provided a quiet wild area, once its overgrowth of brambles and polygonum had been cleared. Another group of young people— pupils of Theale Green School—came to the rescue of the fire engine, which was discovered in a shattered state in a barn in the Park. They repaired it as a school project and returned it resplendent to its present place in the Mews.

124 Young people from Berkshire Youth Action painting a ceiling. They worked on the ceilings of the Tapestry Hall, the drawing-room and the main dining-room, adding colour to the interior.

125 Here they are reclaiming a spinney to the south of the house, part of the old Wilderness.

126 & 127   The fire engine as found in a barn in the Park, and with the Bursar, Douglas Wilson, after restoration by pupils of Theale Green School. It proudly joined in the parade in London in honour of the Queen Mother's 90th birthday in 1990.

128 *Top.* The Lodge provides a welcome change from bedsitter cuisine.

129 *Right.* The chefs putting the finishing touches to a meal.

130 Her Majesty The Queen Mother signing the Visitors Book, with Lord Vaizey, Principal of St Catharine's, on 4 March 1984, when the 40th anniversary of Amy Buller's miracle was celebrated.

As the elegance of the Lodge seemed to demand 'best behaviour', a foolproof recreation area was needed. The vast cellars were cleared of the accumulations of years, with the discovery, beneath a pile of coals, of the Chinese screen now on a landing, and some restorable pieces of furniture, as well as Lord FitzAlan's mushroom compost. Bricks dating back to the origins of the house were found and preserved in the entry to the cellar passage. Foolproof the area was thought to be until a student barrister, leaving a party at one in the morning, 'slipped and touched a pipe above his head to steady himself' (his explanation), breaking the pipe and unleashing thousands of gallons of hot water into the cellars. Lord Vaizey, called to the scene when all amateur efforts had failed, took it well. The spectacle of distinguished judges knee-deep in water in a cellar at dead of night was not an everyday one, and he liked style: the enormity of the incident suggested style rather than hooliganism—which he would not tolerate—and he ordered hot toddy all round as people dried themselves by the dying embers of the fire in the Tapestry Hall at four in the morning.

The social life of the Lodge was changed when the snug little bar down a side-passage was superseded by the former Equerries' Room, which became a common -room where coffee and tea could be served, as well as a bar. This avoided the trundling of trolleys through the house to the Tapestry Hall, which has remained a comfortable quiet lounge where people can read newspapers and journals, or where, in summer, they can go through the garden door to have lunch, or group sessions, in the garden.

Both Queen Elizabeth The Queen Mother and Princess Margaret visited the Lodge to see the work in progress, and the whole effort was crowned in March 1984 when the Queen Mother joined in a celebration of the 40th anniversary of Amy Buller's miracle—that first visit to Buckingham Palace when the project was still only a dream. After a service of thanksgiving at the Royal Chapel, there was a party at the Lodge, when people involved in all aspects of the life of St Catharine's were present; the Queen Mother cut a large anniversary cake, and planted a tree. It was a happy day of great rejoicing, not only for the 40 years, and for the thousands of people who have benefited from coming to the Lodge, but because it was by then becoming clear that financial disaster had been averted. We had turned the corner and could look ahead with a certain degree of confidence.

So we felt in March 1984. But the enormous task took its toll, and John Vaizey, who some years earlier had undergone major heart surgery, succumbed in a second heart operation in July.

***

The Lodge lived through a year's interregnum, under the supervision of Erwin Klinge as Chairman of the Executive Committee. In December 1984 the Foundation was deeply honoured when Princess Margaret agreed to become Visitor, in succession to Lord Denning who retired after many years' service as Chairman of the Trustees and then Visitor. 'If I am Visitor, I shall visit,' said the Princess, and she has been as good as her word. In August 1985 Tim Slack, former Director of the Foreign and Commonwealth Office Conference Centre at Wiston House, became Principal, bringing with him a welcome emphasis on Commonwealth links. Lord Charteris of Amisfield, Provost of Eton, who had nurtured the Foundation through eight eventful years as Chairman of the Trustees with incomparable wisdom, patience and skill, handed over to Lord Moore of Wolvercote at the end of 1986. In 1991 Her Majesty The Queen, by whose grace and favour St Catharine's is granted the use of Cumberland Lodge, honoured the Foundation with a formal visit.

131 The Visitor visits. HRH The Princess Margaret, Countess of Snowdon, signs the Visitors Book.

132 Visit of Her Majesty Queen Elizabeth, 1991. On the left is Lord Moore of Wolvercote, Chairman of the Trustees, and on the right Tim Slack, Principal.

Lord Moore has given his enthusiastic support through a decade of structural repair and internal improvement, while the essential work of the Foundation has continued. In 1995 Dr. John Cook succeeded Tim Slack as Principal, bringing insights from his work as Director of the Inner Cities Young People's Project. Dr. Geoffrey Williams, who came in 1988 as Director of Studies, has played a vital rôle, not least in promoting the work of St Catharine's Conferences with published reports reaching a wider public. In the work of renovation, St Catharine's found a wise, and very necessary, friend in the Deputy Ranger, Roland Wiseman (succeeded in 1995 by Marcus O'Lone). The Crown Estates Commissioners carried out a scheme of external repainting and maintenance, and also came to the rescue when dry rot was discovered in the west wing. Smoke and fire detection equipment was installed, and more fire escapes fitted: the folk-memory of the disaster of 1869 is still very much alive. The result of all this work is that the buildings have been completely refurbished, retaining their historic identity while providing modern equipment and comfort. This has been achieved by the drive and imagination of the Bursar, Douglas Wilson, who has seen the whole process through since 1982.

In the Lodge itself extra rooms have been created in ingenious ways. An old and sinister tank chamber on the top floor, constructed as an internal fire-fighting measure after the Great Fire and now redundant, has been miraculously converted into a large pleasant room. A house-keeper's work-room at the top of George III's central Gothic tower has become a charming bedroom with the best view in the house. Cleverly devised changes of this kind have produced 'en suite' rooms throughout the Lodge and the Mews, without loss of total accommodation. The Master of the King's Household, with his diffident request for an indoor water-closet in

1825, would surely have been gratified. In the Mews building extra space has been granted to the Foundation, and a fine well-equipped set of conference rooms has been produced; Princess Margaret, as Visitor, inaugurated these in 1990. Renovation has also taken place on the floor above, where a century ago the stable-lads lived, and where now there are 17 bedrooms of great decorative charm, opened by Lord Moore in 1996. Plaques in the Mews building commemorate these events.

Meanwhile the work of St Catharine's has gone on: well over 3,000 students a year stay at the Lodge, and professors still find that their freshers, or their new postgraduates, 'gell' over a weekend at the Lodge in a way that might never happen at all without it. They meet each other, and also a wide spectrum of people from public life who generously and freely give their time to come and talk with them. Matters of ethical concern are still discussed, though in keeping with contemporary pragmatism these tend to be specific issues (genetic engineering, nuclear energy) rather than the principles underlying conduct (authority, responsibility) as in the earlier days. Today in higher education, with merging institutions often miles apart, with bedsitters and self-catering accommodation displacing old-style halls, and with increased numbers, there is more need than ever for students and their teachers to be able to meet one another, to seek to integrate their fragmented lives and equip themselves to understand the forces operating in the world. There is much work for St Catharine's still to do.

Epilogue

Cumberland Lodge has now for half a century provided an ideal setting where young people can meet and gain fresh insights into their studies, their work, and the world around them. The old house, cherished home to some of the most spirited people of their generation, has been admirably adjusted to the purposes of The King George and Queen Elizabeth Foundation of St Catharine's, changing with the demands of modern life, but always retaining awareness of its historic past.

Like most earlier occupants, St Catharine's has adapted the house to suit its purposes. The puritan soldier John Byfield established in his new republic an elegant and sober dwelling, which, when the tide turned, was eagerly acquired by King Charles II as a royal hunting-lodge and a residence for the Ranger. Here King William III and his friend parted company, and the Earl of Portland found solace in planning his gardens. Sarah Churchill, in exile abroad, longed for her 'clean sweet house' which she had altered to make it 'a thousand times more agreeable than Blenheim'. Here Prince William Augustus, Duke of Cumberland, took refuge from the bitterness of ingratitude, converted the house into a princely dwelling, and discovered a new joy in creating an ideal landscape. For Prince and Princess Christian it became, after partial rebuilding, a much-loved family home, with children playing cricket, an open door of hospitality, and a pioneering spirit which changed the face of nursing in this country and beyond. Lord FitzAlan was to bring, along with his Tudor and Jacobean furnishings, a reminder of an earlier age when his forebears were not at liberty to express their beliefs, to form a background to his own life and loyalty to Church, Crown and Country.

It was King George VI and Queen Elizabeth who brought about the greatest revolution in the life of the Lodge by their bold and far-seeing decision, in 1947, to allow it to be the means of the fulfilment of Amy Buller's vision, born of Christian insights into the nature of a good society. It became a place apart where young people could meet and examine their beliefs and assumptions, and where all points of view could be discussed in the pursuit of understanding and truth. The house itself, through its history, its setting and its charm, has always been a potent factor in enabling this vision to be realised.

Appendix One

Transcript of the Contract by which Windsor Great Park was sold to Colonel John Desborough's Regiment in 1650

Contracts for the late King Queene & Princes Lands
Liber Primus
incipiens 4th Marty 1649*
Die Mercury 3tio Aprilis 1650

Berks & Surry

Agreed with the contractors for the purchase of all that parcell of impaled ground comonly called the great Parke situate lying and being in the parish of New Windsor and County of Berks and of Old Windsor Egham and Sunninghill in the Countyes of Berks and Surry or one of them Conteyning in the whole by estimacon Three Thousand Six Hundred and Seventy acres and thirty nine perches be they more or lesse and all that Mannour House Messuage or Lodge with the appurtenances now in the tenure or occupacon of Thomas Shemondes gent lying and being in the Mannour Walke and all that small decayed tenement called the Hill Lodge with the appurtenances situate also in the walke aforesd, and one other messuage or Lodge with the appurtenances in the tenure or occupacon of Edward Tirringham gent. situate and being in the Midle Walke within the parke aforesd, one other messuage or Lodge with the appurtenances in the tenure or occupacon of Francis Young Esqr situate lying and being in the lower walke within the park aforesaid, and one other messuage or Lodge with the appurtenances situate in the Paddock Walke within the park aforesd now in the tenure of Michael Oldisworth Esqr And also all that small tenement with the appurtenances situate in the midle walke aforesd at a certeyne gate there comonly called Sandpitt Gate. At the rate of fourteene yeeres purchase for the present yeerely value of the premisses being One Thousand Three Hundred Seventy one poundes in possession. And for the wood and underwood and Tymber trees and undertrees upon premisses over and above the number of Two Thousand Six Hundred sixty foure trees menconed in the pticlar to be marked out for the Navy Att the rate of the grosse sume of one Thousand Nyne hundred and Tenn poundes as valued in the pticlar, and for the deere of severall sortes within the said park att the rate of the grosse sume of Nyne hundred fifty one poundes as valued in the particlar. And lastly I agree that in case any of the trees for the present marked out for the Navy shall hereafter be thought fitt to be wayned and left to the disposall of the State, I shall give for such and soe many of them as shall be soe wayned and left such value as upon a Resarvey to be certified to the Register in that behalf the same shall be prized att. The purchase to be paid and satisfied in originall debentures charged upon the Creditt of the acte of Parliament in that behalf And noe Review to be expected for lessening the value of the premisses of Pay agreed on the behalfe of Colonill Disboroughs Regiment by whome I am intrusted as Attorney. By me.

Ted Scotton

* By the Julian Calendar then in use, the new year started on 25 March.
PRO E 313/173

Appendix Two

The Duke of Marlborough died on 16 June 1722 at Windsor Lodge. In her Green Book the Duchess gives her own account.

The afternoon before Her Father died, when I had no hopes of recovery, I was mightily surprised & troubled at what I did not expect, That the Dutchess of Mountagu, & my Lady Godolphin were without ... I am sure it is impossible for any tongue to express what I felt at that time, but I believe any body that ever lov'd another so tenderly as I did the Duke of Marlborough may have some feeling of what it was to have one's children come in, in those last hours who I knew did not come to comfort me, but like enemies that would report to others whatever I did, in a wrong way. However, at the time I thought my soul was tearing from my body, and that I could not say many things (which otherwise I would have done) before them, yet I would not refuse them to come in, for fear I should repent of it: Upon which I desir'd Mrs. Kingdon to go to them, & tell them that I did not know what disorder it might give their father to go to Him now; but I desired they would judge themselves, & do as they lik'd, but I beg'd of them that they would not stay long in the room, because I could not come in, while they were there, being in so much affliction. Mrs. Kingdon delivered this message, and she told me that the Dutchess of Mountagu answer'd That she did not understand Her, but that if she meant that they were not to see their Mother, they were very well used to that.

They staid a great while (as I thought) and not being able to be out of the room longer from Him, I went in though they were there, & kneel'd down by Him: They rose up when I came in, & made Curtsys, but did not speak to me, and after some time I call'd for prayers: when they were over I ask'd the Duke of Marlborough if He heard them well, & he answer'd yes, and he had joined in them.

After that He took several things, and when it was almost dark, these Ladies being all the time present, I said I believed he would be easier in His bed, the Couch being too narrow, And ask'd him if he lik'd to go to bed. He said Yes, so we carried Him upon the Couch into His own Room. When His blisters & inflammation upon his back were dress'd and He was in bed, To my Great Surprise the Dutchess of Mountagu & Lady Godolphin came in and some time after that, the Dutchess of Newcastle, and staid there a great while after the candles were brought in: the room not being very large was pretty full with Drs Surgeons, Apothecaries and Servants so I went my self to my Lord Sunderland and desir'd Him to go away, & sent Lady Anne Egerton, Di: & Her two Brothers out of the room. This, nor what I had said by Mrs. Kingdon did not make the others stir, upon which I desir'd Grace to go to the Dutchess of Mountagu, & tell Her that for many days I had been mightily harrass'd and I must lye down: and I desir'd Her to go into an other room with the other two, She answer'd Will our being here hinder Her from lying down? then I sent Grace to Her again, to ask her if she had such an affliction & was in my Condition, Whether she would like to have me with Her? She said, No. But did not go out till I sent to Her a third time, & then they all three went out of the room, and the Dss of Newcastle went quite away, but the Others staid in the Drawing room & Hall till four in the morning. When they went to London they & their Creatures reported to every body that I had turn'd them out of my House, & that I had order'd that no body should give them any thing to eat or to Drink; That I had told the Dutchess of Newcastle that I was glad it was over, for now I should never see Her again; and that as soon as I had put the two Sisters out, I took Mrs. Kingdon in, & that they heard us talk a great deal and laugh, as they sat in the next room; that the Doctors & Surgeons all knew every thing that had pass'd and therefore there was no keeping it a Secret, & that after such a Behaviour I had had to their Father, they would never any more take notice of me. Upon all these vile reports I could not help making an enquiry of all the servants in the House what ground there was for those things; but before I begin to give an account of that, I must say one thing that I forgot, That the sisters said, that when they came to the door they ask'd how their Father did & some servant answered that He was very well, to which (they say) they Replied that we desire to see Him whether He be well or ill. Now comes the examination. It was found upon enquiry, that Mr. Ffyshe was the first person they saw, & that help'd them out of the Coach, They ask'd him how their father did, He answer'd what the Drs had said last, He did not remember whether it was a little better or worse, Little Di said that she run to meet them & went in with them to the dining room, where she ask'd them if they would have any wine and bread, They said no, they would have nothing. But after they came out the first time from their Father, the Buttler John Griffiths said they sent to Him for bread and wine, and He gave it them as they were walking upon the stone walk before the House. After that Dorothy Foulkes the Cook went to them as they were sitting in the Hall, & Dr. Friend by them. she first ask'd the Dutchess of Montagu if she would have anything, and press'd Her mightily to have some broth, for she said she had some that was extream good, she answer'd No, but in a mighty civil way (as the cook reports it). But when she made the same request to my Lady Godolphin twice over she answer'd in another manner No, & that she would have nothing. One of the women that belongs to me went to the Duchess of Montagu, and ask'd her if she would have any drops. Hodges the Steward was sick in bed of the stone, & did not see them; so that besides these servants there were very few proper to speak to them. And as to another part of the Report which I forgot to mention That my Lord Sunderland was out of Countenance to go from them to supper without asking them, which He durst not do; Jane Pattinson's Evidence contradicts that, For she said the supper had been a great while upon the Table before the Physitians came out of Her Lords room, and she seeing my Lord Sunderland going up stairs she told Him that supper had been a good while upon the Table, and upon that He turn'd back & went into the dining room, and he was alone when she told Him, but eat nothing till the end of the supper. For my own Part I did not know when the Supper was, nor it could not be imagin'd, by any Human Creature that I could give any direction in those sort of things. But it was natural to think that the children would call for what they would have, and rather have look'd after the strangers that attended their Father than to have expected honour should have been done to them at such a time.

Mrs. Kingdon has again confirm'd what I said to Her, what she said to them, & the Dutchess of Mountagu's answer upon what they said of Her being in the room with me, not being capable of knowing who had been there in that extremity. Though I thought she never had been in the room, or spoke to me after The children went out, and she answer'd, That she was there but not above two minutes sitting in the window, just at the door about two a clock in the morning, & That as she was sitting I came down to the Table to fetch a Cordial, and seeing Her I beg'd of Her that if she would do anything for me as long as she livd that she would go out & go to bed, the first she did that moment, but she said she could not go to bed but she came into me after the Ladies were gone, and after the terrible stroke was given.

BL Ad.Ms.61451, f.99v-102

Appendix Three

A description of Windsor Lodge in Duke William's time

The two first Rooms of this Lodge are neatly hung with plain Paper, ornamented with Prints, among which are Views of the Improvements made by his Royal Highness in the Park.

In the Dining Room over the Chimney-piece, is his Royal Highness's Collection of Breeding Mares; and there is here a curious Table of petrified Water.

In the Passage is the Crossing of the *Rhine*, Marshall *Saxe*, three curious Fancy-pieces, by *Hoare*, a fine Drawing of *St. Pauls*, *Cleopatra*, *Rubens's* Family, &c.

In a Room called the *Black Hall*, is the Genealogy of the *Brunswick* Family, a Piece of Featherwork Flowers, four views of *Gibraltar*, *Windsor Castle* in Straw, and his late Majesty in Needle-work.

The White Hall is adorned with six curious carved Stags Heads.

In the Dressing Room are two *Pagodas* under Glasses, several curious Pieces of his Highness's Turning, and six different views of Cranbourn Lodge and Park.

In the Bed-Chamber is the Portrait of *James*, late Earl of *Waldegrave*, four Views of the Lodge, and the Battle of *Culloden*. The Bed is of green Damask and Gold.

The Card Room is hung with green Damask, and the Apartments above Stairs are all Bed-chambers hung with neat Paper, with Beds to match them.

Windsor and its Environs (Newbery and Cannon, London 1768), p.86.

Appendix Four

W.G. Grace and Cumberland Lodge[1]

The interesting cricketing associations of the Lodge became evident when the late Mr. Ronald Palmer presented to St Catharine's two photograph albums kept by his father, Thomas Palmer, valet to Prince Christian. They included photographs of W.G. Grace at a match at the Lodge, subsequently shown to have taken place on 10 June 1911 between Prince Albert's Veteran XI and Charterhouse.[2]

It was Prince Christian Victor, rather than Prince Albert, who distinguished himself as a cricketer and became friendly with 'the doctor'. Grace later recalled playing with Prince Christian Victor on 'very many occasions', describing him as 'a fine bat and good safe field and wicket keeper'.[3] Grace's biographer, Eric Midwinter, noted that his regard for him as a cricketer was such that, in a review of one of his books, a writer in the *Manchester Guardian* commented sarcastically that '[Grace] dismisses the famous Lancashire professional [Richard Barlow] with a shorter notice than he bestows upon that illustrious cricketer Prince Christian Victor of Schleswig-Holstein'.[4] Grace's judgment[5] that the Prince 'is the only member of the Royal Family who has yet shown anything approaching first-class cricket form' remains valid to this day.

133 Entry for the match from the Charterhouse Cricket Register.

134 Prince Albert's Veteran XI, Cumberland Lodge, 10 June 1911. From left to right. *Back row*: F. Dames-Longworth, H.W.R. Bencraft, P.J. de Paravicini, Capt. E.G. Wynyard, A.C.M. Croome, C.C. Clarke. *Middle row*: A.J. Webbe, W.G. Grace, H.H. Prince Albert, A.G. Steel. *Front row*: W.H. Brain, E. Smith, J.R. Mason. Photograph from the Collection of Roger Mann.

The Prince organised 'cricketing weeks' at the Lodge and, writing of his son in W.G. Grace's memorial biography, Prince Christian recalled him having 'brought to our ground men bearing names famous in the history of the game'.[6] In 1891 part of the planned celebrations to mark the silver wedding anniversary of his parents and the marriage of his sister, Princess Marie Louise, was a cricket match between the Lodge team and the Household Brigade, unfortunately called off because of rain. In the team on that occasion were several who were to feature in the 1911 match.[7]

The death of Prince Christian Victor was obviously a great blow to his family in Windsor, and royal interest in cricket at the Lodge seems not to have revived for a decade. Writing on the 1911 match, a writer in a local newspaper commented that 'in the days prior to the death during the South African War of Prince Christian Victor there had been frequent games at Cumberland Lodge in which well-known cricketers had figured, but of late the fixtures decided there have been only of a local character'.[8]

Why Prince Albert chose, in June 1911, to put together a veteran team to play Charterhouse, his old school, is not entirely clear, although it might have been connected with his retirement the previous year from the German army. However, he had managed to maintain his cricketing interests, having been captain of the Great Park Club from 1905 until war stopped play in 1914.

Interest in the 1911 match was such that Edward, the young Prince of Wales, attended, hurrying over from Windsor Castle where that morning he had been invested as Knight of the Garter. During the course of the afternoon he posed for a photograph with W.G. Grace, since featured in a number of publications.[9]

The team photograph[10] (Figure 134) seems, on the evidence of those padded up, to have been taken during the afternoon tea break. Only three had not played first class cricket. In batting order the team comprised Dr. W.G. Grace; A.G. Steel (Lancashire 1877-93; Cambridge University 1878-81 and England 1880-88; captain of England 1886 and 1888); E. Smith (Oxford University 1889-91; Yorkshire 1888-1907); J.R. (Jack) Mason (Kent 1893-1914; England 1897-98); A.J. Webbe (Oxford University 1875-1878; Middlesex 1875-1900); A.C.M. Croome (Oxford 1887-89; Gloucestershire 1885-92); W.H. Brain (Oxford University 1891-93; Gloucester 1893); H.H. Prince Albert of Schleswig-Holstein; P.J. de Paravicini (Middlesex 1881-92; Cambridge University 1882-85); F. Dames-Longworth; and C.C. Clarke. Croome had been a close cricketing friend of Prince Christian Victor at Wellington and Oxford. Webbe had served in the same regiment as the Prince. Of those who had played first class cricket, Mason was the youngest, who Croome recorded was 'brought in when Stoddart had to cry off' (presumably A.E. Stoddart of Middlesex, 1885-1900, who captained England in eight tests, 1887-98).[11] Croome's account of the match suggests that he, rather than Grace or the Prince, was the *de facto* captain.

W.G. Grace did not put up a memorable performance, A.C.M. Croome recalling that

to everyone's extreme annoyance he failed to score. He went in first with 'Nab' Steel, and in the Carthusian fast bowler's first over received one to cut. He made the stroke beautifully with all the old snap of the wrists and a good deal of shoulder punch behind it, but a boy, standing where no fielder normally stands, got one hand down to the ball just before it hit the ground to race to the boundary and held it.'[12]

However, Prince Albert's team took the match, Steel being the top scorer with 74, whilst Jack Mason, the former Kent player, made 73. Paravicini was not out 35, the Prince making 5. The detailed score, as recorded in the cricketing record of Charterhouse,[13] was:

Charterhouse

G.A. Wright, c Paravicini, b Smith	10
C.G. Stevens, c Smith, b Mason	95
G.E. Bond, b Smith	0
J.S.F. Morrison (capt), c Webbe, b Smith	18
R. Boosey, c Webbe, b Smith	6
H.G. Sanderson, run out	26
R.G. Morrison, c Smith, b Croome	0
H. Wesley-Smith, not out	48
K. King, c Clarke, b Mason	23
L. Gjers, c Smith, b Mason	3
F.S. Letten, c Smith, b Mason	0
Extras	10
Total :	239

Prince Albert's Veteran XI

W.G. Grace, c Sanderson, b King	0
A.G. Steel, c J.S. Morrison, b King	74
E. Smith, c Wright, b Stevens	30
J.R. Mason, c R.G. Morrison, b Stevens	73
A.J. Webbe, c J.S. Morrison, b King	0
A.C.M. Croome, c Wright, b Stevens	18
W.H. Brain, c Sanderson, b King	28
H.H. Prince Albert of Schleswig-Holstein (capt), b Stevens	5
P.J. de Paravicini, not out	3
F. Dames-Longworth, c Sanderson, b Wright	13
C.C. Clarke, c Stevens, b Wright	3
Extras:	4
Total:	251

The identity of most players in the team photograph can be decided with some confidence. The two not in whites are thought to be H.W.R. Bencraft (Hampshire 1876-96) and Captain E.G. Wynyard (Hampshire, 1878-1908 and England, 1896-1905/6), who might possibly have been umpiring.

It was, suggested A.C.M. Croome, the last match of more than local interest in which W.G. Grace took part. In 1898 Grace had played in his last Test and in his last game for Gloucestershire, although as late as 1908 he had played for the Gentlemen against Surrey. He was 63 when he opened for Prince Albert's Veteran XI, and just four years from his death in 1915.

The ground on which this match was played lay just beyond the fence of Cumberland Lodge in the direction of Royal Lodge, which had been used by the Windsor Great Park Cricket Club since about 1861. In 1924 they moved to a new pitch on Smith's Lawn and the Lodge pitch seems then to have been abandoned.[14]

Geoffrey J. Williams

Appendix Five

Extract from _The Times_ of 21 December 1912
Rebuilding of Cumberland Lodge

The work of rebuilding Cumberland Lodge, Windsor Great Park, the residence of Prince and Princess Christian, which has been in progress for the past ten months, has been completed. The contract for rebuilding was secured by Messrs W.E. Blake (Limited), London and Plymouth, and amounted to nearly £20,000.

During the excavations a number of subterranean passages were found, leading in the direction of Big Meadow Lake, also the remains of an old kitchen and bakehouse. New basements have been constructed, and the interior of the house is entirely new and made fireproof by heavy steel frames cased in concrete. The old external walls were shored up and retained, being tied to the new internal structure. Great difficulty was experienced in underpinning the old walls and retaining the picturesque old turrets. The roof is partly slate and partly ashphalt, and commodious servants' bedrooms have taken the place of the old attics. The new hall contains an old staircase, and the walls are panelled with oak and lit by a new stone window. A new secondary staircase has also been erected, formed of concrete encased with wood.

A new system of heating and electric lighting has been put in by Messrs. Wellman Brothers, of Windsor, and the elevation of the building towards Bishopsgate has been raised one storey. The architect was Mr. John Murry (Crown architect), and the building work has been carried out under the direction of Mr. W. Tidy, Hampstead, Clerk of the Works.

[A longer account appeared in the _Windsor & Eton Express_, 21 December 1912.]

Appendix Six

Extract from the Trust Deed of the King George VI and Queen Elizabeth Foundation of St Catharine's

The Trust fund and the income shall be applied for or towards such of the following purposes (so far as legally charitable) in such manner as the Trustees shall from time to time direct that is to say To encourage the investigation and discussion of the nature of Man and Society; the exposition of the Christian interpretation of Life in relation to the various secular alternatives; and to stimulate research on these and similar matters and on the inter-relation of the various academic disciplines (including Christian Theology) and their relevance to practical affairs: and to this end

(a) to provide a College or Colleges based on the Christian faith and philosophy of life, where Courses of Teaching and Study, Reading Parties and Conferences may be held;

(b) to serve the needs of students, particularly in London University and the Modern Universities, and to encourage an interchange of thought between British students and students from overseas and, in particular, from the British Commonwealth and Empire.

Notes

Shortened titles are given in full in the Bibliography; where no title is given, the note refers to the last-mentioned work of the author in question. To reduce the number of figures appearing in the test, successive references are sometimes grouped together in the same note.

DATES: Though in the text these are given in accordance with the modern calendar, in the notes the Old Style date (new year beginning 25 March) is also given to help identification.

Abbreviations used:

BL .... British Library
CP .... Cumberland Papers
CRES .... Crown Estate Papers
CSPD .... Calendar of State Papers, Domestic Series
CTB .... Calendar of Treasury Books
CTP .... Calendar of Treasury Papers
DNB .... Dictionary of National Biography
HMC .... Royal Commission on Historical Manuscripts
PRO .... Public Record Office
Pw A .... Portland/Welbeck Archive
RA .... Royal Archives
RL .... Royal Library
UL .... University of London
WORK .... Papers of the Ministry of Public Buildings & Works

Chapter One: Republican Origins

1. PRO Parliamentary Survey, Berks., no.36, 27 February 1649/50.
2. Whitelocke, *Memorials*, 26 March 1649.
3. Firth, *Cromwell's Army*, p.206; Berry and Lee, *A Cromwellian Major General*, p.89; PRO E 121 Bundle 1, No.2 Berks.
4. PRO E 313/173 (contract); E 304/1/B11 (indenture); *see also* E 320/B11.
5. Whitelocke, R.H., *Memoirs*, p.427.
6. PRO Survey: Early Entry Book 7, p.227, 22 January 1661/2.
7. à Wood, *Athenae Oxoniensis*, vol.2, p.324.
8. Bate, *And so make a City here*, p.107. As Byfield became vicar of Isleworth in 1615, and Shakespeare died in 1616, his supposed visit must presumably have been in that period.
9. Byfield, N., *Commentary on 1 Peter Ch.2.*
10. Brennan, G., *House of Percy*, p.213; Victoria County History: *Middlesex*, III, Isleworth.

11. à Wood, *Life and Times*, p.36.
12. Young, *The British Army*, p.336, quoting from Cromwell's Letter to the Suffolk Committees, 26 August 1643.
13. CSPD Charles II 1660-1, vol.1, no.73, May 1660 (PRO SP29/1/73); 1662, vol.53, no.74, 25 April 1662.
14. Pepys, *Diary*, vol.10, Companion, p.136.
15. CSPD Charles II 1660-1, vol.16, no.136 (PRO SP29/16/136).
16. Chambers, *The English House*, pp.94, 95; cf. Chevening in Kent, Thorpe Hall in Northants. *See also* Summerson, *Architecture in Great Britain 1530–1830*, pp.92-94.
17. *See* Chapter 2, note 13.
18. PRO Parliamentary Survey, Berks., no.36.
19. *See* Girouard, *The English Country House*, pp.106-8, for information about banqueting houses.
20. PRO Prob. 11/269 f23R24L.

Chapter Two: The King Returns

1. Venn, *Alumni Cantabrigiensis*. F.A. Inderwick, ed., *Calendar of Inner Temple Records*.
2. For purchase of Bagshot Park, *see* CSPD vol. IX, 1655-6, p.150; 1660-1, p.286; Hughes, *Windsor Forest*, p.333.
3. Douglas, D.C., ed., *English Historical Documents*, vol.8, p.57.
4. PRO SP29/1/73.
5. CSPD Charles II 1660-1, vol.5, no.97 (PRO SP29/5/97).
6. PRO SP 29/16/136; CSPD Charles II 1660, p.286, September 1660.
7. CSPD Charles II 1660-1, vol.22, no.184, November 1660 (PRO SP29/22/184).
8. CTB, 1660-7, vol.1, p.158, 9 September 1661.
9. PRO Early Entry Book 7, p.227, 22 January 1661/2.
10. CSPD Charles II, 1661-2, vol.29, no.59, 29 January 1661/2.
11. CSPD Charles II, 1661-2, vol.52, 14 March 1661/2.
12. CSPD Charles II, 1662, vol.53, no.74, 25 April 1662.
13. PRO Hearth Tax Records E179, January 1662/3, 243/24 and 243/25, p.603.
14. *Visitations of Berkshire*, vol.2, p.45.
15. CTB Charles II, 1669-72, vol.3, p.663; p.775; p.812; p.100.

Chapter Three: The Ranger's Lodge

1. Evelyn, *Diary*, vol.2, p.56, 28 August 1670.
2. PRO CSPD 20 September 1671; Early Entry Book 34; CTB 1676-9, 21 April 1676, vol.5, pt 1, p.192.
3. Ashmole, *History*, p. 208. Hughes, *Windsor Forest*, p.284.
4. Evelyn, vol.2, p.217.
5. CSPD 1671, 9 June 1671, p.308.
6. Burnet, *History*, vol.1, p.481; p.465.
7. DNB; Granger, *Biographical History*, vol.4, p.186.
8. Clarendon, *Life*, p.338. Pepys, vol.8, p.416.
9. Clarendon, *History of the Reign of Charles II*, vol.1, p.450.
10. Pepys, vol.7, p.525; vol.8, p.447.
11. *Ibid.*, vol.7, p.337.

12. Burnet, vol.1, p.465.
13. North, *Examiner*, p.186.
14. HMC House of Lords, 1675-80, p.247.
15. Menzies, p.17; but Roberts, *History of the Royal Parks and Gardens of Windsor*, Section B9, ch.9, suggests an earlier date.
16. Roberts, *History*, Historical Survey 2, ch.2.
17. Pepys, vol.8, p.418.
18. *Ibid.*, vol.9, p.557.
19. CTB 1693-6, vol.10, p.88; p.1037.
20. May's tomb in the Rutland Chapel gives the year as 1696, using the old calendar.

Chapter Four: The King's Friend

1. Luttrell, *Brief Historical Relation*, vol.4, p.193, 9 March 1696/7.
2. Temple, *Works*, vol.1, p.401.
3. Grew, *Bentinck and William III*, p.33. Schazmann, *The Bentincks*, pp.52ff.
4. Green, *Sarah*, p. 266.
5. Gregg, *Queen Anne*, p.74, quoting from Strickland, *Lives of the Queens of England*, vol.7, p.159.
6. Schazmann, p.73.
7. Formerly the home of the infamous Judge Jeffreys, who died in the Tower in 1689; now the British headquarters of World Evangelization for Christ International.
8. Green, p.62, quoting from Blen E 48; p.72.
9. Macky, *Memoirs*, p.60.
10. Grew, p.248, quoting a letter from van Loon to Hugens.
11. Portland Collection Pw A 1737, May-June 1697.
12. Japiske, *Correspondentie*, vol.3, p.444, 7 September 1697.
13. Pw A 1737, 5 June 1697. 'Il est impossible de vous aimer plus parfaitement que je fais.'
14. Grew, p.320, quoting from the *Mémoires* of the Duc de Saint-Simon.
15. Defoe, *Tour*, vol.1, p.183. *See* Roberts, *History*, Historical Survey 2, ch.2, for Charles II's interest in these gardens.
16. Pw A 708, Le Nôtre to Portland, 21 June 1698; and 709, 11 July 1698.
17. Pyne, *Royal Residences*, p.151.
18. Grew, p.389, quoting letter from Lady Giffard to Jane Temple, 14 September 1698.
19. RA Queen Victoria's Journal: 17 September 1838.
20. HMC Downshire, vol.1, pt.2, p.749.
21. Defoe, vol.1, p.193.
22. Macky, *Journey*, vol.1, p.61; *Memoirs*, p.58.
23. BL Blenheim, Ad. Ms. 61471, p.52.
24. *Ham House* (V & A, HMSO, 1976) p.64, and *Ham House* (National Trust, 1995), p.7; Hope, StJ., *Windsor Castle*, p.329.
25. Pw A 1804, 26 April 1699.
26. Marlborough, S., *Private Correspondence*, p.306, Godolphin to Marlborough, February 1709
27. Luttrell, vol.4, p.513.
28. Grew, p.366.
29. Quoted by Green, p.382.

Chapter Five: The Redoubtable Sarah

1. Churchill, W.S., *Marlborough*, vol.2, p.268; vol.1, p.561.
2. Marlborough, S., *Letters of a Grandmother*, p.147.
3. Gregg, p.110; p.101, quoting from Blen G17.
4. Snyder, *Correspondence*, vol.1, p.58; p.63; p.66, 19 May 1702.
5. Schazmann, p.123. In his will Portland left his English estates to his eldest son Henry, who was later made Duke of Portland, and his Dutch estates to William, the first son of his second marriage, who became Count Bentinck.
6. PRO King's Warrant Book XXI, p.440.
7. Luttrell, vol.6, p.58.
8. Churchill, W.S., vol.1, p.479, quoting van Goslinga's *Mémoires*, p.44.
9. Burnet, vol. 5, p.71 (OUP 1833 ed. vol.2, p.348).
10. Churchill, W.S., vol.2, p.187.
11. Snyder, vol.1, p.156.
12. Churchill, W.S., vol.2, p.586.
13. Snyder, vol.1, p,189; p.196.
14. BL Althorp D15.
15. For information about this account I am indebted to Mr. Hugh Roberts. *See also* Roberts, *History*, B9, ch.9 and note 7.
16. Downes, *Hawksmoor*, p.272: Letter from Sarah to Lord Chief Justice Parker, from Windsor Lodge.
17. HMC Downshire, vol.1, pt.2, p.828, 25 April 1704.
18. Snyder, vol.1, p.326; p.332; p.176; p.340.
19. Green, *Gardener*, p.55, 19 May 1702.
20. PRO Treasury Minutes Book 13, p.222-5; CTB 17, pt.1, p.64, p.66, 28 July 1702.
21. Snyder, vol.1, p.364.
22. Swift, *Stella*, Letter XXX, 8-25 September 1711. Swift met 'Stella' when he was secretary to Sir William Temple, whose natural daughter she was. Lord Portland met Temple when he was ambassador at The Hague, and later married his niece.
23. Fiennes, *Journeys*, p.244.
24. CTB, vol.24, p.309, 17 May 1710.
25. Green, p.80, quoting from Treasury Papers, 2 October 1716.
26. Coxe, *Memoirs*, vol.1, p.226.
27. Marlborough, S., *Private Correspondence*, vol.1, p.35, 8 July 1706.
28. Cowles, *The Great Marlborough*, p.407, quoting Vanbrugh, *Correspondence*, vol.4, p.170.
29. Snyder, vol.1, p.298; vol.2, p.743.
30. Burnet, vol.5, p.335 (OUP 1833 ed. vol.2, p.487).
31. BL Blenheim, Ad. Ms. 61456, 17 February [1708].
32. Green, *Sarah*, p.318, quoting from Blen G-1-7, 26 July 1708.
33. Snyder, vol.2, p.1075, August 1708.
34. Burnet, vol.5, p.454 and Lord Darmouth's note; vol.6, p.33-4 and Lord Dartmouth's note (OUP 1833 ed. vol.2, p.547; p.564).
35. Marlborough, S., vol.2, p.47, December 1710.
36. Swift, Letter XIII, 4 January 1710/11.
37. Marlborough, S., *Madresfield Letters*, p.36; p.77; p.89; p.93.

38. Churchill, W.S., vol.4, p.627.
39. Marlborough, S., p.145.
40. BL Blenheim, Ad. Ms. 61451, f.46.
41. Harris, *Life of Sarah*, pp.206, 221; Roberts, *History*, B9, ch.9, note 19.
42. Green, p.275, quoting from Blen F-l-32.
43. Marlborough, S., p.127; p.135.
44. BL Althorp D15.
45. BL Blenheim, Ad. Ms. 61456, f.185, 15 October [1722].
46. Green, p.243 quoting from Blen E 34.
47. BL Blenheim, Ad. Ms. 61471, p.52; Althorp D15; D13.
48. BL Althorp D15.
49. Marlborough, S., *Private Correspondence*, vol.2, p.198 (1737).
50. Walpole, *Letters*, vol.1, p.xcvii; *see* Harris, p.280.
51. Marlborough, S., *Letters of a Grandmother*, p.96. Henrietta's youngest child, Mary, was generally thought to be Congreve's. *See* Harris, p.258.
52. BL Blenheim, Ad. Ms. 61451, f.147.
53. Walpole, vol.1, p.cv.
54. BL Althorp D14, 30 August 1742.
55. Marlborough, S., *Private Correspondence*, vol.2, p.170; p.209.
56. *See* Harris, pp.332 and 339.
57. BL Blenheim, Ad. Ms. 61471, F-1-40, letter to Lord Townshend, 25 July 1728.
58. BL Blenheim, Ad. Ms. 61471, G-1-11, 13 August 1711.
59. Walters, *Royal Griffin*, p.171.
60. Marlborough, S., vol.2, p.464 (1726).
61. Colville, *Duchess Sarah*, p.325; p.349, quoting letter from Sarah to Mr. Scrope, 11 September 1744.
62. BL Althorp D14, 18 August 1744.
63. Marlborough, S., *Letters of a Grandmother*, p.108, 11 November 1733.
64. Walpole, vol.1, p.105.
65. CTP, 1742-3, pp.842 and 844, 22 May 1745.
66. History of Parliament, *House of Commons 1715–1754*, vol.2, p.432.
67. Walpole, vol.2, p.129.

Chapter Six: Butcher Cumberland—or Sweet William?

1. George II is remembered today for two things: he was the last reigning British monarch to lead his army in battle, and he stood for the Hallelujah Chorus.
2. Walpole, *Letters*, vol.1, p.cii.
3. Walpole, *Memoirs of the Reign of George II*, vol.3, p.307.
4. Walpole, *Letters*, vol.2, p.29.
5. *Ibid.*, vol.2, p.118.
6. Quoted by Harwood, *Windsor*, p.179.
7. *Letters of Thomas Gray*, ed. Paget & Whitley (Oxford, 1935): Thomas Gray to Thomas Wharton, 11 September 1746. I owe this reference to General Rex Whitworth.
8. Hore, *Royal Buckhounds*, p.337; RA CP 70/14-16.
9. RA CP 72.

10. Menzies, pp.25 and 43. Elliott, *Windsor Great Park*, p.19. The inscription was composed by Lord Holland. (*see The Holland House Diaries, 1831-40* (1977), p.35, 20 August 1831.)

11. RA CP 73-5 *passim.*

12. Flitcroft's early plan: RL 17931A.

13. Pote, *Antiquities*, p.21; *Délices*, p.73.

14. Hore, pp.345 and 338.

15. *Ibid.*, p.354.

16. RA CP 78/78.

17. Farington, *Diary*, vol.1, p.233. For general information about Thomas Sandby I am indebted to an unpublished monograph by Jane Roberts, 'The Sandby Brothers at Windsor'. *See* also Roberts, *Views of Windsor.*

18. *History of the King's Works*, Vol. V, p.88.

19. Walpole, vol.3, p.70; Harwood, p.181.

20. Offen, J., *Thoroughbred Style* (1987).

21. BL Althorp E11, Poyntz accounts, March and December 1767.

22. Walpole, vol.2, p.364.

23. *The Present State of Great Britain & Ireland* (Miege & Bolton), 1748, p.142; *The Gentleman & Citizen's Almanack*, 1763, p.49. RL CP Vol.1. Inventory of His Late Royal Highness the Duke of Cumberland at Windsor Great Lodge (1765).

24. RL CP O/S box. Explanatory Memorandum relating to His Royal Highness the Duke of Cumberland's Library at Windsor Great Lodge. I am indebted to Mr. Stephen Patterson for information about this document.

25. Wesley, *Journal*, p.180, 29 November 1771. (*see* Harwood, p.181)

26. Walpole, *Memoirs of the Reign of George II*, vol.1, pp.71-2; Chevenix-Trench, *George II*, p.247; Sinclair-Stevenson, *Blood Royal*, p.72.

27. Walpole, *Memoirs of the Reign of George II*, vol.1, p.79.

28. *Ibid.*, vol.3, p.87.

29. Hore, p.341.

30. Walpole, vol.3, pp.61-4.

31. Pyne, vol.3, p.18.

32. Walpole, *Letters*, vol.4, p.460.

33. *Ibid.*, vol.4, p.111.

34. Schomberg House was built for the Duke of Schomberg, a true European: born in Heidelberg of a German father and an English mother (daughter of Lord Dudley), he served in the armies of the Dutch States, Sweden, France (where he was made *maréchal*), Portugal and Brandenburg before joining William of Orange in his invasion of England in 1688; he was created Duke of Schomberg in the coronation honours, and in 1690 was killed at the Battle of the Boyne in Ireland and buried in Dublin (DNB).

35. Jesse, *Memoirs*, vol.1, p.314.

36. *Gentleman's Magazine*, December 1765, pp.544-5.

Chapter Seven: The Habitation of Princes

1. Walpole, *Memoirs of the Reign of George III*, vol.3, p.76.

2. Eden, *Auckland Correspondence*, vol.2, p.280. (cf. Jesse, vol.2, p.6n.)

3.   Walpole, vol.4, p.109.

4.   Walpole, *Last Journals*, vol.1, p.xviii; vol.1, p.114.

5.   Walpole, *Journal of the Reign of George the Third*, vol.1, p.31.

6.   Walpole, *Last Journals*, vol.1, p.59n.

7.   Walpole, *Letters to Sir Horace Mann*, vol.2, p.176.

8.   Walpole, *Last Journals*, vol.1, p.xx.

9.   Farington, vol.1, p.221 n.; Huish, *Memoirs*, vol.1, p.294. Lady Elizabeth Luttrell came to a bad end. Her huge gambling debts caused her to be thrown into gaol. 'There she gave a hairdresser £50 to marry her. Her debts thus becoming his, she was discharged. She went abroad, where she descended lower and lower, till, being convicted of picking pockets at Augsburg, she was condemned to clean the streets, chained to a wheelbarrow. In that miserable situation she terminated her existence by poison.' *See* Aspinall, *Correspondence of George Prince of Wales*, vol.1, p.224n.

10. Aspinall, *Correspondence of George Prince of Wales*, vol.8, p.393. It was even rumoured that he offered to give the Lodge up to the Prince. *See* Roberts, B9, ch.9.

11. PRO CRES 2/46.

12. In this passage from *The Windsor Guide* (1783) the visitor has entered the house at the new north end.

13. Aspinall, vol.2, p.178n.

14. PRO CRES 2/58.

15. Menzies, p.27.

16. *Gentleman's Magazine*, vol.60, July-December 1790, p.866.

Chapter Eight: A House in Abeyance

1.   Aspinall, vol.1, p.104.

2.   Aspinall, *Later Correspondence of George III*, vol.1, p.498.

3.   Morshead, *George IV and Royal Lodge*, p.7, quoting from *The Journal of Nathaniel Kent* in the Royal Library.

4.   *See* Roberts, *History*, B9, ch.9, for her clarification of the problem of the unfinished chapel.

5.   *Ibid.*

6.   For information about the Cumberland Great Vine I am indebted to Mr. T.H. Findlay and Mr. Leslie Stringer; and *see* Roberts, B9, ch.9, note 112.

7.   PRO WORK 4-19. Office of Works Minutes 20 July 1804.

8.   In 1806, Wyatt went to work on Ashridge in Hertfordshire, which can still be seen in all its Gothic glory. It was completed by his nephew Jeffry, as Wyatt Senior died in a road accident in 1813.

9.   Aspinall, *Correspondence of George Prince of Wales*, vol.5, p.91.

10. *Gentleman's Magazine*, vol.75, January-June 1805, p.67.

11. Aspinall, vol.5, p.161n.

12. *Windsor Guide* (1807), p.158.

13. Summerson, *Architecture in Britain*, p.293.

14. PRO WORK 19-45/11, 6 February 1815. For details of work undertaken by Nash *see* WORK 19-45/11, 1814-18; WORK 4-20, 1815; WORK 4-22, 1816-17.

15. Romilly, *Memoirs*, vol.3, p.249. PRO WORK 19-45/11, 2 June 1815.

16. When the King was asked by Jeffry Wyatt for approval of his change of name, he is said to have replied, 'Ville or mutton, call y'self what you like'. *See* Morshead, *Windsor Castle*, p.47. He was later knighted for his work on Windsor Castle.

17. *The Times*, August 14, 1985, p.11, 'On This Day, August 14, 1820'.

18. Creevey, *Creevey Papers*, vol.2, p.88.

19. Huish, *Memoirs*, vol.2, p.360.

20. Morshead, *George IV and Royal Lodge*, p.27.

21. *Greville Memoirs*, ed. Fulford, p.49, August 30, 1830. *See* Roberts, History, B9, ch.9 and note 84.

22. PRO WORK 19-45/11, 21 February and 20 August [1825]; 18 September 1815; 4 October 1818. *History of the King's Works*, vol.VI, p.396.

23. *Windsor & Eton Express*, 17 July 1830.

24. Roberts, B9, ch.9, notes 86 and 87.

25. *Windsor & Eton Express*, 13 October 1832; 18 December 1830.

26. PRO WORK 19-45/11, November 1831.

27. PRO CRES 4-10/101.

28. 1841 Census.

29. Paul, *The Scots Peerage*, vol.8, p.511; 1851 Census.

30. PRO WORK 19-45/11.

31. *The Annual Register* of 1869, p.130, describes the 'front building' (before the Great Fire) as consisting of 'a grand entrance-hall, a large banquet-hall, a drawing-room, a library, a reading-room, a billiard-room, and a range of apartments above'.

32. Campbell, S., 'The Genesis of Queen Victoria's New Kitchen Garden', *Garden History*, Autumn 1984.

Chapter Nine: An Unsung Princess

1. RA Queen Victoria's Journal: 10, 12, 15 June 1846.

2. Fulford, *Dearest Mama*, p.311. Quotations from Roger Fulford's books are reprinted by kind permission of Unwin Hyman Ltd.

3. *Letters of Queen Victoria* (2nd series), vol.1, p.85. *See also* Wake, *Princess Louise*, p.60.

4. Fulford, *Your Dear Letter*, pp.56-7; p.69; pp.75-6: correspondence with Crown Princess Victoria of Prussia (Vicky).

5. Stanley, *Later Letters*, pp.52-3

6. RA QVJ: 5 July 1866.

7. Fulford, p.78.

8. *Windsor & Eton Express*, 20 November 1869.

9. RA QVJ: 14 November 1869.

10. RA PP Windsor 722, 723, 725-7, 752; 806; PRO CRES 35/182.

11. RA PP Windsor 811/41.

12. RA QVJ: 6 July 1872.

13. *Windsor & Eton Express*, 21 September 1872; 12 October 1872.

14. Pamphlet *The Royal Stained Glass Works, Old Windsor, Berks.* (Windsor Local History Publications Group, 1997). I owe this reference to Kathleen Whelan.

15. RA Add. C20/11; J. Seymour to his wife Agnes, 28 November 1874.

16. RA PP Windsor 906, 907: Biddulph to Gordon, 5 September 1874; 1019: Biddulph to Gore, 21 April 1876.

17. Warren, *Christian Victor*, p.21.

18. Cooper, *Town and Country*, pp.59-60.

19. *Ibid.*, pp.56 and 58.

20. Spencer-Warren, 'The Prince and Princess Christian' in *The Strand Magazine*, July-December 1895, pp.367-375.

21. Ribblesdale, *The Queen's Hounds*, p.206.

22. Lutyens, *Lytton*, p.24.

23. *Windsor & Eton Express*, 19 December 1924; 15 June 1923.

24. Florence Bratmann tells how, as a small girl staying with her cousin at the College, she 'spent many summer days, generally once a week, with Prince Christian—self-called "College Head Gardener". He would ride over on a pony, put his coloured chalks in my pinafore pockets and we would go round marking trees to be cut down or saved. We made the "Vista" out of a jungle of huge trees, cut down the following year, and he then planted the "Grove" as he called it. He would himself plant very special shrubs. From a postscript to a talk 'Royal Holloway College 1908-14' by W.E. Delp, given to the Professors' Wives Club on 21 January 1969. I am indebted to Janet Hales of Royal Holloway College for this anecdote.

25. Cooper, p.53; Rose, *King George V*, p.39.

26. Warren, p.217. In Freetown the Prince came across a hospital called after his mother, The Princess Christian Cottage Hospital, where African women were trained as nurses.

27. I am indebted to the headmaster of Charterhouse for information from the *Charterhouse Register*, 1872-1900. As well as Prince Albert's family connection, there was an old alliance with Hesse, through royal marriages and shared interests with Hanover; Hessian troops, in return for subsidies, helped out the English army in several conflicts during the Hanoverian period.

28. The footman Cooper tells how the Emperor brought with him 'a case containing four silver forks; each had one tine sharpened to enable him to cut his food, on account of his withered arm; this arm also prevented him from mounting a horse from the proper side' (Cooper, p.61).

29. Quoted from Warren, pp.168-9.

30. Warren, pp.351ff. Lutyens, p.168.

31. The Empress Frederick died six months after her mother.

32. For all the following concerning repairs and alterations, *see* PRO CRES 35/220-225, 230.

33. PRO CRES 35/221.

34. PRO CRES 35/230, 22/11/1913, memorandum from A.J. Forrest in Office of Works.

35. RA Windsor, Geo V o.589: Letters exchanged between Miss E. Loch (Princess Christian's lady-in-waiting) 1/11/1912, and Lord Stamfordham 10/11/1912.

36. PRO CRES 35/223, 14/1/1912.

37. Fulford, p.288n; Palmer, *Crowned Cousins*, p.211; Rose, King George V, pp.173ff. Information from an unpublished history of Sunningdale Golf Club, pp.12-14, is reported by courtesy of the Club.

38. Prince Albert had a natural daughter, Valerie Marie zu Schleswig-Holstein, who was born in 1900 in Hungary, married in 1940 the ninth Duke of Arenberg, and died in France

in 1953 (*Burke's Royal Families of the World*, vol.1, Appendix A). I owe this reference to Dr. Geoffrey Williams of Cumberland Lodge.

39.   During the 300 years since the Duke of Schomberg's house, No. 77 Pall Mall, was built in the late 17th century, Nos. 77 and 78 have been made into one, separated, and renamed De Vesci House, while their neighbours Nos. 80 and 82 have taken on the name Schomberg House. In 1900 the Office of Works acquired Nos. 77 and 78 and reconverted them into one, and in 1902 as a Crown grace-and-favour residence the enlarged house was granted to Princess Christian; in 1906 it was renamed Schomberg House, 'causing ineradicable confusion'. I owe this information to Mr. Michael Hill of the Oxford and Cambridge University Club, which now occupies Nos. 71-77. *See also* Chapter 6, note 33. I owe the information about nursing to Kathleen Whelan, former matron of HRH Princess Christian's Hospital, Windsor.

40.   *Windsor, Eton & Slough Express*, 19 December 1924.

Chapter Ten: Lord FitzAlan of Derwent

1.   DNB; *Who Was Who 1941-50*; Bence-Jones, *The Catholic Families*.
2.   Hallam, *Silent Valley; Water under the Bridge*.
3.   This is the recollection of Lord FitzAlan's grand-daughter, the Hon. Mrs. Ward, and may explain the similarity between the panelling in these two different houses.
4.   Crown Estate Office records, Windsor Great Park. Some of the panelling remaining when Derwent Hall was repossessed was used by the Water Board to grace the entrance hall and boardroom of the Yorkshire Bridge filter plant near Ladybower, and some was sold to Derby Corporation.
5.   Victoria County History, *Worcestershire*, p.231.
6.   A pamphlet by Dr. Geoffrey Williams giving a full description of these coats of arms is available from St Catharine's, Cumberland Lodge, Windsor Great Park.
7.   UL St Catharine's Archive C11/1-2, Sale catalogue of furniture of Cumberland Lodge belonging to the executors of the late Lord FitzAlan of Derwent.
8.   Correspondence in Crown Estate Office records.
9.   Lees-Milne, *Ancestral Voices*, p.48.
10.   For Major Hardinge's role, *see* Hardinge, *Loyal to Three Kings*.
11.   It was one of the rare occasions when the great front door was used; otherwise people used the side-door. This custom must date from when the house was extended by Duke William, and its main entrance came to be at the north end.
12.   I am much indebted to the Hon. Mrs. Alathea Ward for material relating to her grandfather, Lord FitzAlan; and to Mrs. Ann and the late Mr. Ron Brown (who was at one time 'the odd man') and other Park residents for their memories of the domestic arrangements at this time.

Chapter Eleven: The Miracle

1.   Much of the material in this chapter is derived from Walter James's *Short Account*; from the St Catharine's Archive and files; from a conversation I had with Amy Buller in 1959, and from many conversations with trustees of St Catharine's and people who worked at or visited the Lodge.
2.   Moberly, *Crisis*, pp.219-20.

3. Buller, *Darkness*, Author's Preface.

4. UL St Catharine's Archive, B3/82: undated leaflet.

5. I owe this information about Bishop Woods to his son, the Rt. Rev. Robin Woods, a former trustee of St Catharine's.

6. Simon, *Sitting in Judgement*, p.82

7. UL St Catharine's Archive, tape of Elizabeth Elphinstone in conversation with Walter James.

8. *Ibid.*, M1/160, AB to EKT; M1/161, EKT to AB.

9. *Ibid.*, B1/39.

10. The tapestries are thought to be from Vanderbank's workshop in Soho, *c.*1700-25. I owe this information to Jonathan Marsden, Deputy Surveyor of the Queen's Works of Art.

11. Moberly, Preface.

12. *Ibid.*, p.26.

13. I owe this anecdote to Sara Bird.

14. UL St Catharine's Archive, McLachlan, N., 'The Cumberland Lodge Experience' in *The Melbourne Gazette*, vol.4, no.1, June 1953, p.31.

15. UL St Catharine's Archive, WJ tape of C. Curling. *See* Martin Buber, *I and Thou.*

16. Gombrich, Ernst, *A Lifelong Interest* (Thames & Hudson, 1993), p.129. I owe this reference to Mr. Tim Day.

17. Judge, *A Generation of Schooling.* pp.38-41.

Appendix Four: W.G. Grace and Cumberland Lodge

1. An earlier version of this paper appeared in *Windlesora*, Journal of the Windsor Local History Publications Group, No.13, 1994.

2. I am grateful to readers of *The Cricketer* who responded to my request for information.

3. In Warren, *Christian Victor*, p.460. This book has a chapter devoted to 'The Prince as a Cricketer'. The Prince's cricketing achievements are also outlined by W.A. Bettesworth in *Cricket: A Weekly Record of the Game*, 6 August 1894, pp.329-330.

4. Midwinter, *W.G. Grace*, p.163.

5. Grace, *Cricket*, p.367.

6. In Hawke et al., *Memorial Biography*, p.319. The Prince goes on: 'One was C.J. Thornton who, by the way, made one of his biggest hits at Cumberland Lodge: we still show visitors where the ball struck the stable wall, some hundred and forty yards from the wicket. It was either through him or my elder son that I made W.G.'s acquaintance at Lord's'.

7. Warren, *op cit.*, p.169.

8. 'Prince of Wales at a cricket match at Cumberland Lodge', *Windsor, Eton & Slough Express*, 15 June 1911.

9. e.g., Ziegler, *King Edward VIII*, p.46.

10. I am particularly indebted to Roger Mann for the team photograph and his help in identifying the players.

11. In Hawke et al., *op cit.*, p.321.

12. *Ibid.*

13. I am grateful to Mrs. A.C. Wheeler, Librarian of Charterhouse, for this extract.

14. Anon, *Windsor Great Park Cricket Club.*

Bibliography

Ainsworth, W.H., *Windsor Castle* (Chivers, 1974)

Alice, Princess, *For my Grandchildren* (Evans, 1966)

Angelo, H., *Reminiscences* (Colborn, 1828)

Anon (West, C.), *Windsor Great Park Cricket Club. 100 Years of Cricket, 1861-1961* (n.d., 1961?)

Aronson, T., *Princess Alice, Countess of Athlone* (Cassell, 1981)

Ashmole, E., *The History and Antiquities of Berkshire* (1719)

Aspinall, A. (ed.), *The Later Correspondence of George III* (C.U.P., 1962-70)

Aspinall, A. (ed.), *The Correspondence of George Prince of Wales, 1770-1812* (Cassell, 1963-71)

Aspinall, A. (ed.), *The Letters of King George IV, 1812-1830* (CUP, 1938)

Aylmer, G., *The State's Servants* (Routledge & Paul, 1973)

Bate, G.E., *And so Make a City here* (Thomason, 1948)

Bence-Jones, M., *The Catholic Families* (Constable, 1992)

Berry, J. and Lee, S.G., *A Cromwellian Major General* (Clarendon Press, 1938)

Brett, A.C.A., *Charles II and his Court* (Methuen, 1910)

Bryan, J. and Murphy, J.V., *The Windsor Story* (Granada, 1979)

Bryant, A., *King Charles II* (Collins, 1955)

Buber, M., *I and Thou*, trans. Gregor-Smith (T. & T. Clark, 1937)

Buller, A., *Darkness over Germany* (Longmans, Green & Co, 1943)

Burnet, G. (ed. Routh), *History of My Own Time* (OUP, 1833 and Olms Reprint, 1969)

Byfield, N., *A Commentary or Sermons upon the Second Chapter of the First Epistle of St Peter* (1623); Bodleian Library

Cathcart, H., *Royal Lodge Windsor* (Allen, 1966)

Chambers, J., *The English House* (Methuen, 1985)

Chenevix-Trench, C., *George II* (Allen Lane, 1973)

Churchill, W.S., *Marlborough, His Life and Times* (Harrap, 1934)

Colville, O. (Mrs. A.), *The Duchess Sarah* (Longmans, Green & Co., 1904)

Colvin, H.M., *Biographical Dictionary of English Architects, 1660-1840* (Murray, 1954)

Colvin, H.M. (ed.), *The History of the King's Works* (1963)

Cooper, C.W., *Town and Country* (Lovat-Dickinson, 1937)

Cowles, V., *The Great Marlborough and his Duchess* (Weidenfeld and Nicolson, 1983)

Coxe, W. (ed. Wade), *Memoirs of John Duke of Marlborough* (Bohn, 1848)

Creevey, T., *The Creevey Papers* (Murray, 1903)

Davies, R., *Journal* (Camden Society, 1857)

Defoe, D., *A Tour through the whole Island of Great Britain* (Folio Society, 1983)

Dictionary of National Biography

Donaldson, F., *Edward VIII* (Weidenfeld and Nicolson, 1974)

Downes, K., *Hawksmoor*, Studies in Architecture Vol.2 (Zwemmer, 1959)

Eden, Earl of Auckland (ed. Bishop of Bath and Wells), *Journal and Correspondence* (Bentley, 1861)

Elliott, R.J., *The Story of Windsor Great Park* (Crown Estate Commissioners, 1976)

Evelyn, J. (ed. Bray), *Diary and Correspondence* (Bohn, 1859)

Farington, J. (ed. Greig), *The Farington Diary* (Hutchinson, 1922-28)

Fiennes, C. (ed. Morris), *The Illustrated Journeys of Celia Fiennes* (Macdonald: Webb & Bower, 1984)

Firth, C.H., *Cromwell's Army* (Methuen, 1921)

Firth, C.H., *Regimental History of Cromwell's Army* (1940)

Fraser, A., *King Charles II* (Weidenfeld and Nicolson, 1979)

Fraser, A., *The Gunpowder Plot: Terror and Faith in 1606* (Weidenfeld and Nicolson, 1996)

Fulford, R., *The Prince Consort* (Macmillan, 1949)

Fulford, R., *Your Dear Letter, Private Correspondence of Queen Victoria and the Crown Princess of Prussia, 1865-1871* (Evans, 1971)

Fulford, R., *Darling Child*, 1871-1878 (Evans, 1976)

Fulford, R., *Dearest Mama*, 1878-1885 (Evans, 1981)

Gardiner, S.R., *History of the Great Civil War* (Longmans, 1893)

Gentleman's Magazine, The, 1765, 1790, 1805

Girouard, M., *Life in the English Country House* (Penguin Books, 1980)

Gombrich, E., *A Lifelong Interest* (Thames & Hudson, 1993)

Grace, W.G., *Cricket* (Simpkin Marshall, 1891)

Granger, J., *A Biographical History of England* (1775)

Green, D., *Gardener to Queen Anne* (O.U.P., 1956)

Green, D., *Queen Anne* (Collins, 1970)

Green, D., *Sarah, Duchess of Marlborough* (Collins, 1967)

Gregg, E., *Queen Anne* (Routledge & Kegan Paul, 1980)

Greville, C.C.F., *Greville Memoirs*, ed. R. Fulford (Batsford, 1963)

Grew, M.E., *William Bentinck and William III* (Murray, 1924)

Guide to Windsor and its Environs, editions of 1738, 1774

Hallam, V.J., *Silent Valley* (Sheaf, 1983)

Hallam, V.J., *Water under the Bridge*, (Evans, 1979)

Hamilton, E., *William's Mary* (Hamilton, 1972)

Hardinge, H., *Loyal to Three Kings* (Kimber, 1967)

Harris, F., *A Passion for Government: The Life of Sarah, Duchess of Marlborough* (Clarendon, Oxford, 1991)

Harwood, T.E., *Windsor Old and New* (privately published, 1929)

Harwood, T.E., BL Add. Mss. 41764 and 41768

Hawke, Lord, Lord Harris, and Sir Home Gordon (eds.), *Memorial Biography of Dr. W.G. Grace* (1919)

Haynes, A., *The Gunpowder Plot* (Alan Sutton, 1994)

Hedley, O., *Round and About Windsor* (Oxley, 1950)

Hervey, J. (ed. Sedgwick), *Memoirs of the Reign of George II* (Kimber, 1952)

Hibbert, C., *The Court at Windsor* (Longman, 1964)

Hibbert, C., *George IV, Prince of Wales* (Longman, 1972)

Hibbert, C., *George IV, Regent and King* (Allen Lane, 1973)

History of Parliament Trust, *The House of Commons 1660-1690*, ed. Henning (HMSO 1983)

History of Parliament Trust, *The House of Commons 1715-1754*, ed. Sedgwick (HMS0, 1970)

Hore, J.P., *The History of the Royal Buckhounds* ('The Compiler Newmarket', 1895)

Hughes, G.M., *A History of Windsor Forest* (Ballantyne & Co., 1890)

Huish, R., *Memoirs of George IV* (Kelly, 1831)

Hyde, E., Earl of Clarendon, *Calendar of Clarendon Papers* (1872)

Hyde, E., *The Life of Edward Earl of Clarendon* (Oxford, 1759)

Hyde, E., *The Secret History of the Court and Reign of Charles II* (1792)

Inglis, B., *Abdication* (Hodder & Stoughton, 1966)

James, W., *A Short Account of Amy Buller and the Founding of St Catharine's, Cumberland Lodge* (St Catharine's, 1979)

Japikse, N., *Correspondentie van Willem III en van H.W. Bentinck* (Rÿks Geschiedkundige Publicatien, 1927)

Jesse, J.H., *Memoirs of the Life and Reign of George III* (Tinsley, 1867)

Judge, H., *A Generation of Schooling* (O.U.P., 1984)

Kenyon, J.P., *The Popish Plot* (Penguin Books, 1974)

Lees-Milne, J., *Ancestral Voices* (Faber, 1984)

Lees-Milne, J., *Prophesying Peace* (Chatto & Windus, 1977)

Lewis, T., *Double Century: the story of the M.C.C. and cricket* (Hodder and Stoughton, 1987)

Linstrum, D., *Sir Jeffry Wyatville* (Clarendon Press, 1972)

Longford, E., *Victoria R.I.* (Weidenfeld and Nicolson, 1964)

Ludlow, E. (ed. Firth), *Memoirs* (Clarendon Press, 1894)

Luttrell, N., *A Brief Historical Relation of State Affairs from 1678 to 1714* (Oxford, 1857)

Lutyens, M. (ed.), *Lady Lytton's Court Diary* (Hart-Davis, 1961)

Lysons, D. & S., *Magna Britannica* (Cadell & Davies, 1806)

Macky, J., *A Journey through England* (1732)

Macky, J., *Memoirs of John Macky, Esq.* (Roxburgh edition, 1733)

Marie Louise, Princess, *Letters from the Gold Coast* (Methuen, 1926)

Marie Louise, Princess, *My Memories of Six Reigns* (Evans, 1956)

Marlborough, S., *An Account of the Conduct of the Dowager Duchess of Marlborough* (1742)

Marlborough, S., *Letters of the Duchess of Marlborough* (from manuscripts at Madresfield Court) (Murray, 1875)

Marlborough, S. (ed. Thomson), *Letters of a Grandmother* (Cape, 1943)

Marlborough, S., *Private Correspondence of Sarah, Duchess of Marlborough* (Colburn, 1838)

Marlborough, S., *A True Copy of the Last Will and Testament* (Cooper, 1744)

Menzies, W., *A History of Windsor Great Park* (Longman, 1864)

Midwinter, E., *W.G. Grace, His Life and Times* (George Allen & Unwin, 1981)

Millar, O.N., *Pictures in the collection of H.M. The Queen* (Phaidon, 1963-9)

Moberly, W.H., *The Crisis in the University* (SCM, 1949)

Morshead, O., *George IV and Royal Lodge* (Regency Society of Brighton and Hove, 1965)

Morshead, O., *Windsor Castle* (Phaidon, 1951)

Nevill, B. St. John (ed.), *Life at the Court of Queen Victoria* (Webb & Bower, 1984)

Newcourt, R., *Repertorium* (Bateman, 1708-10)

Nicholas, D., *Mr. Secretary Nicholas, 1593-1669* (Bodley Head, 1955)

North, R., *Examen* (1740)

Norton, L., *The Sun King and his Loves* (Folio Society, 1982)

Nuttall, P.A. (ed.), *Fuller's Worthies of England* (Tegg, 1840)

Oppé, A.P. *The Drawings of Paul and Thomas Sandby in the Collection of H.M. The King at Windsor Castle* (Phaidon, 1947)

Palmer, A., *Crowned Cousins* (Weidenfeld and Nicolson, 1985)

Peacock E., *The Army Lists of the Roundheads and Cavaliers* (Chatto & Windus, 1874)

Pepys, S. (ed. Latham & Matthews), *The Diary of Samuel Pepys* (Bell & Hyman, 1970-83)

Pocock, T., *Sailor King: The Life of King William IV* (Sinclair-Stevenson, 1991)

Pote, J., *The History and Antiquities of Windsor Castle* (1749)

Pote, J., *Les Délices de Windsor* (1755)

Pyne, W.H., *The History of the Royal Residences* (Dry, 1819)

Ribblesdale, *The Queen's Hounds and Stag-Hunting Recollections* (Longman, 1897)

Ritchie, L., *Windsor Castle and its Environs* (1840)

Roberts, J., *Royal Artists* (Grafton Books, 1987)

Roberts, J., *The History of the Royal Parks and Gardens of Windsor* (Yale University Press, 1997)

Roberts, J., *Views of Windsor: Watercolours by Thomas & Paul Sandby* (Merrell Holberton, 1995)

Romilly, S., *Memoirs of the Life of Sir Samuel Romilly* (1840)

Rose, K., *King George V* (Weidenfeld and Nicholson, 1983)

Rowse, A.L., *Windsor Castle in the History of the Nation* (Weidenfeld and Nicolson, 1974)

Royal Commission on Historical Manuscripts: *Downshire* (HMSO, 1924); *House of Lords Calendar of Manuscripts, 1678-88,* Appendix II to 11th Report of RCHM (HMSO, 1887); *Melbourne Hall* (HMSO, 1888)

Rylands, W.H. (ed.), *Visitations of Berkshire* (Harleian Society Publications, 1907)

Schazmann, Paul-Emile, *The Bentincks* (Weidenfeld & Nicolson, 1976)

Scott-James, Anne and Lancaster, Osbert, *The Pleasure Garden* (Penguin Books, 1979)

Sidney, *Diary of the Times of Charles II* (London, 1843)

Simon, U., *Sitting in Judgement 1913-1963* (SPCK, 1978)

Sinclair-Stevenson, C.T., *Blood Royal* (Cape, 1979)

Snyder, H., *The Marlborough-Godolphin Correspondence* (Oxford, 1975)

South, R., *Royal Castle, Rebel Town* (Barracuda Books, 1981)

South, R., *Royal Lake* (Barracuda Books, 1983)

Speck, W.A., *The Butcher* (Blackwell, 1981)

Spencer-Warren, M., 'The Prince and Princess Christian' in *Strand Magazine*, July-December 1895

Stanley, A. (ed. Dean of Windsor & H. Bolitho), *Later Letters of Lady Augusta Stanley, 1864-1876* (Cape, 1929)

Summerson, J., *Architecture in Britain 1530-1830* (Penguin Books, 1953)

Summerson, J., *John Nash* (Allen & Unwin, 1949)

Swift, Jonathan, *Journal to Stella*. ed. G.A. Aitken (1902)

Temple, W., *Works* (1740)

Thomson, G.M., *The First Churchills* (Secker & Warburg, 1979)

Tighe, R.R. and Davis, J.E., *Annals of Windsor* (1858)

Tomasson, K. and Buist, F., *Battles of the '45* (Book Club Associates, 1978)

Trevelyan, G.M., *England under the Stuarts* (Methuen, 1904)

Turnor, R., *James Wyatt* (Art & Technics, 1950)

Victoria County History, *Berkshire*

Victoria County History, *Middlesex*

Victoria County History, *Worcestershire*

Victoria, Queen (ed. Buckle), *Letters of Queen Victoria (2nd series) 1862-1869* (Murray, 1926)

Wake, J., *Princess Louise, Queen Victoria's Unconventional Daughter* (Collins, 1988)

Walker, J., *Suffering of the Clergy* (1714)

Walpole, H., *Journal of the Reign of George the Third* (Bentley, 1859)

Walpole, H., *The letters of Horace Walpole* (Bentley, 1840)

Walpole, H. (ed. Steuart), *The Last Journals of Horace Walpole* (Lane, 1910)

Walpole, H., *Letters to Sir Horace Mann* (Bentley, 1843)

Walpole, H., *Memoirs of the Reign of George II* (Colburn, 1847)

Walpole, H., *Memoirs of the Reign of George III* (Colburn, 1894)

Walters, J., *The Royal Griffin* (Jarrolds, 1972)

Warner, M., *Queen Victoria's Sketchbook* (Crown Publishers, 1979)

Warren, T.H., *Christian Victor: the Story of a Young Soldier* (Murray, 1903)

Wesley, J. (ed. Jay), *The Journal of John Wesley* (O.U.P., 1987)

Whitelocke, B., *Memorials of the English Affairs* (1682)

Whitelocke, R.H., *Memoirs of Bulstrode Whitelocke* (Routledge, Warne & Routledge, 1860)

Whitworth, Rex, *William Augustus, Duke of Cumberland* (Leo Cooper, 1992)

Williams, G.J., *The Heraldry of the Wintour Family at Cumberland Lodge and its association with the Gunpowder Plot* (St Catharine's, 1996)

Windsor, The Duke of, *A King's Story* (Cassell, 1951)

Windsor (ed. Knight), *A Compendious Gazette* (1794)

Windsor (ed. Knight), *The Windsor Guide* (1783, 1804, 1807, 1811, 1875)

Windsor (ed. Knight), *Windsor and its Environs* (1768)

Wood, A. à (ed. Bliss), *Athenae Oxoniensis* (Rivington 1813-20)

Wood, A. à (ed. Clark, abridged), *The Life and Times of Anthony à Wood* (World's Classics, 1961)

Young, P., *The British Army* (Kimber, 1967)

Young, P., *The English Civil War Armies* (Osprey, 1973)

Young, P., *Edgehill 1642* (Roundwood Press, 1967)

Ziegler, P., *King Edward VIII* (Collins, 1990)

Index

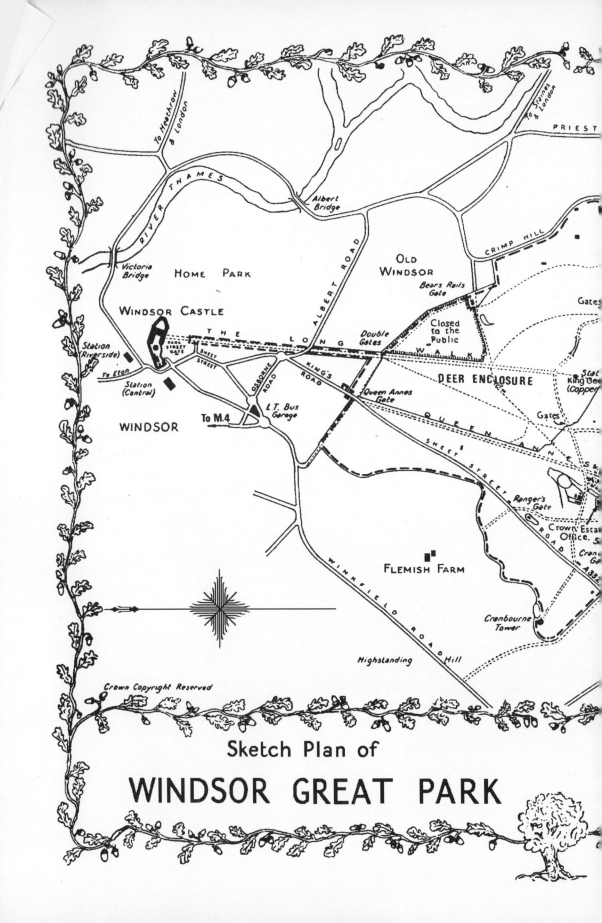

Sketch Plan of

WINDSOR GREAT PARK